Damnyankee in a Southern Kitchen

A Revival Feast

By Helen Worth

Westover Publishing Company

Richmond, Virginia
A Media General Publication

Copyright 1973 by Helen Worth.

All rights reserved.
This book, or parts thereof, must not be reproduced
in any form without written permission from
Westover Publishing Company.
Printed in the United States of America.

Table of Contents

	Foreword	vii
1.	A Sea of Soups	1
2.	A Succulence of Meats	22
3.	A Strut of Poultry	65
4.	A Wave of Seafood • A Grouse of Game	89
5.	A Round of Squares	108
6.	A Cream of Sauces	121
7.	An Eden of Vegetables	129
8.	A Tang of Salads • A Piquance of Relishes	152
9.	A Dapple of Cornmeal • A Hill of Hominy	165
10.	A Peel of Breads • A Flow of Batters	184
11.	A Seduction of Desserts	200
12.	An Extravagance of Pastry	216
13.	A Brio of Beverages	235
	Appendix: A Primer of Provisions	252
	Bibliography: A Glut of Knowledge	260
	Index	265

Dedication

To A.B.
Who knows the meaning of
a multitude of words
and especially
the few that mean so much.

Acknowledgments

I must ask your forbearance, if in these pages, you do not find every Southern recipe you seek. Actually, the enormous wealth of them from an area that dined richly, profusely, and well, would require an encyclopedia. Those that are here include classics, and many that may be strange to Damn Yankees, as well as to Southerners from differing regions.

In testing and tasting the recipes, I have been aided and abetted by all the help I could muster, notably members of the Goshae and Burtt family, who set me straight on Southern ways.

My gratitude also goes to Joyce Gilbert's untiring fingers, whether dealing with typewriter keys or with pots and pans. I thank Sophia Press, who sometimes allowed me the grammatical freedom I justify as poetic license. And I am grateful to my editor, Tom Humber, who nobly fought his way through my wild chaos of commas, and gave the manuscript immeasurable practical and literary help.

Finally, my thanks go to all of you, for taking the time to read through this book before you begin tantalizing all those gathered at your table.

When I heard the glowing and accomplished actress, Eugenia Rawls, read this praise-of-cooking poem in one of her superb one-woman shows, I asked permission to print it. Permission was graciously granted by this charming Southern lady.

A Certain Light

There is a certain light in afternoon
Falling between the orchard and the creek.
Slanting through ivied locust trees
And touching on the kitchen window sill,
That brings a sense of other afternoons
And other women standing here,
Hands lightly floured with supper preparations,
Some biscuits rolled and cut, grits stirred,
A gravy made from ham,
Small lettuce and tomatoes from the garden;
And such a sense of timelessness surrounds me,
And such a peace from simple tasks
Performed in an accustomed way
That I, continuing the pattern,

Turn to my child, fasten an apron
Round the slim young waist, and say,
"This is the way you measure—
This the recipe."

—Eugenia Rawls

Foreword

Southern cooking, then as now, is serious cooking. It features stores of wonderful food, served in profusion, and the recipes are truly international in scope. A superb illustration of the largesse, appears in an old cook book that gave readers the word on proper holiday dining, adjusting the menu for families rich, for families of limited means, and for families poor.

Breakfast on the gala day was to include Sliced Oranges; Small Hominy and Milk; Broiled Tenderloin Steak; Potatoes à la Creole; Omelette à la Creole; Rice Cakes; and Café au Lait.

At noon came dinner. It involved putting knife, fork, and spoon to a first course of Gumbo Filé, accompanied by Radishes, Cress, and Pickled Onions. Next, "for all except the poor," came Cou' B (court bouillon) and Mashed Potatoes.

Diners carried on with Roast Turkey and Oyster Stuffing, and Old-fashioned Chicken Pie—which poor families were invited to omit.
The entree accompaniments included Baked Yams, sliced and buttered; Stewed Tomatoes; Lettuce Salad with French Dressing; Orange Fritters; and Cranberry Sauce.

Then the desserts piled the table: Plum Pudding; Mince or Apple Pie; Pineapple Sherbet, which the poor had the privilege of excluding; Sponge, Jelly, *and* Pound Cakes; an Assortment of Nuts and Raisins; Apples, Oranges, Bananas, and Grapes ("Choose just one or two fruits," the poor were advised); Creole Bonbons; Cheese and Crackers and Raspberry Marmalade.

Finish! Café Noir.

Presumably eyes were not bigger than stomachs, because supper composed itself of leftovers: cold turkey and cranberry sauce; cheese and jelly; small cakes; and tea.

Contrast this with a recent Southern anniversary celebration, encompassing a different, but no less delectable, kind of heartiness: Baked Ham; Smoked Neck Bones cooked with Whole Green Beans and New Potatoes; Pigs' Tail simmered with Onion, Whole Dried Limas, and hot red pepper; Sauerkraut and Spareribs; Cornbread Muffins; and Sweet Potato Pie.

This extraordinary bounty from elegant to down-home is typical of knowledgeable cooks from past to present. They always have prized what the land and waters provide. They have fit recipes from their homes across the sea into regional wherewithal. And they have every reason to smile politely at what either a beloved, or a Damn Yankee, considers a groaning board.

It was hard for me to write "The End," because always lurking in my Test file was another unknown with the intriguing challenge: How will it taste? But this book was not intended as an encyclopedia and in these pages you will find a multitude of treasured examples of Southern hospitality, and pick and choose from largesse that will enrich your repertoire—and your living.

A SEA OF SOUPS

In writing of what went on in days of yore, it is good to be able to state categorically—as noted in *La Cuisine Creole*—that soup was the first course served at all ordinary dinners.

Whether or not what came out of the pot was beautiful, the tureen from which it was ladled was a thing of joy. Authorities on antiques state that a soup tureen was the most massive and decorative single object to adorn long-ago tables.

To encourage variety in repetition of this standard first course, the anonymous author of *La Cuisine Creole* intelligently listed the vegetables most often used in soups, followed by suggested combinations.

Just like soups of today, beef or chicken stock provided the base. But the complications! "Take the hind Shin of Beef," the recipe for Beef Soup in the *Williamsburg Art of Cookery* commands, and continues, "cut all the Fleſh off the Leg-bone."

Cheſtnut Soup, in the same book, requires that a "Half Hundred" nuts be roasted for 30 minutes, and stewed for an hour in Veal or Beef Broth. If lucky, the cook had the broth on hand, because now a pigeon—the first of three—flew into the pot. But there was a concession—it was possible to substitute a partridge for one of the pigeons. "Put in ſome toaſted Bread cut in Dice, and ſerve it up," the Cheſtnut Soup recipe ends, indicating that, for dinners ordinary or not, no one ever forgot the croutons.

It may, or may not, be a pity if tureens do not clasp pigeons or partridges, but it is a blessing that today, no cook attempts to cure "The Beginning of Conſumptions" by Snail Broth alone.

The chief difference between Southern and Damn Yankee soups, even today, lies in the enrichment of the simmering stocks with bacon, salt pork, or ham hocks, and the fact that the fat is never skimmed. As one born on Southern soil remarked, "What went into the pot went into your mouth."

Pork, as the Italians, Spanish, and Chinese well know, is a powerful enricher of stock. It may be omitted, and in line with our current knowledge of nutrition, it seems more intelligent to serve soup from which the fat has been removed.

According to some historians, the soup kitchen may have been born in feudal England when the steward was called upon to feed the multitudes who lived in the great castles. Tureens there swam with meat and vegetable broth, and hunks of bread—sops—were dipped in. By that fascinating transformation language undergoes, the liquid came to be called *soupe*.

By any name and by any spelling, soup is an economical menu extender. Serve the concentrated essence—bouillon—which comes from the French *bouillir*, "to boil," or *consomme*, a clarified bouillon that translates to consummate—the peak of perfection—and warm either an ordinary table or one set for folk who sit above the salt.

To Store Stock, pour strained, fat-free stock into ice cube trays, remove frozen cubes, and store in plastic bags in freezer.

Beef and Broth
Soupe et Bouilli

This Creole name for a soup-entree splits the difference between English and French. Damn Yankees call the dish boiled beef, serve the sliced beef with horseradish sauce to mask the fact that the meat has given all its flavor to the stock. Creole cooks choose mustard sauces.

Brisket*, the cut on the inside of the shank valued for its wealth of fat, is the typical beef cut. It attracts different names in different areas of the United States, so your market may call it deckle, boneless brisket, beef breast, brisket pot roast, or "barbecue beef brisket."

The canners produce a very credible beef stock labelled "broth" or "bouillon." But in the cold of winter, there can be real satisfaction in starting from scratch.

Prepare Soupe et Bouilli on a house-bound day, to serve on the next. The refrigerator will make removal of the fat easy and carving the meat a cinch. Arrange the slices on a separate platter surrounded by additional vegetables, cooked until just done. Choose any, or all: carrot, celery, turnip. Pass the mustard sauce separately and have additional prepared mustard on hand.

- 6 pounds beef brisket
- 1 pound pork or ham, cut up, optional
- 1 tablespoon salt
- ¼ cup dry wine, white or red, optional
- 1 large unpeeled onion, cut coarsely
- 3 stalks celery and leaves, cut coarsely
- 2 medium unpeeled carrots, cut coarsely
- 3 medium unpeeled turnips, cut coarsely, optional
- 1 clove crushed garlic, optional
- 6 whole cloves
- 6 sprigs parsley
- 1 teaspoon dried thyme
- 1 teaspoon dried marjoram
- 1 teaspoon peppercorns

Place beef, fat side up, on rack in large pot. Add remaining ingredients and enough water to almost cover meat. Cover pot, bring liquid to boil rapidly, reduce heat and simmer until tender, about 4 hours, turning meat halfway through cooking, and skimming if necessary. Strain, and discard vegetables.

*The asterisks in these pages indicate that the recipe and/or further information is detailed elsewhere in the book. Check the Index.

Refrigerate; when cold, remove fat, and serve meat sliced.
To Serve Southern Style: Put a French roll (call it a sop) in each soup plate, and ladle the clear, fat-free broth over it.

MUSTARD SAUCE

- **1 tablespoon butter, melted**
- **3 tablespoons flour**
- **1 cup beef broth, strained**
- **1 teaspoon Dijon-style mustard**

Prepare a roux* with butter and flour and cook until reddish brown. Gradually stir in broth and cook, stirring until mixture comes to a boil. Add mustard to taste, and heat sliced meat in sauce. Makes 6-plus servings.

Chicken Stock
White Consomme of Fowl

This savory sounding title for white stock (broth) makes the base for a myriad of Dixie dishes. And no canner can equal a pot of it prepared by loving hands at home.

Most flavorful made with a stewing chicken, a small amount of adequate stock can accrue from the giblets, neck, and heart of a young chicken. The freezer makes an excellent bank for these dividends. Save them until you have enough for a respectable quantity of stock. Unless your family loves the bony parts—back and wings—add these to the stock pot, too. Although young chicken parts will be done in about 45 minutes, more flavor is extracted when simmering goes on longer.

In Sterne's eighteenth century novel *Tristram Shandy,* Mr. Shandy offers the following recipe advice: "Take a Knuckle of Veal, You may buy it or ƒteal . . ." To be sure your stock will gelatinize, go and do likewise, adding the veal knuckle with the vegetables.

- **1 5–6 pound stewing chicken, cut up**
- **1 pound pork or ham, cut up, optional**
- **1 tablespoon salt**

¼ cup dry wine, white or red, optional
1 large unpeeled onion, cut coarsely
1 large unpeeled carrot, cut coarsely
4 stalks celery and leaves, cut coarsely
2 small unpeeled turnips, cut coarsely, optional
6 sprigs parsley
1 teaspoon peppercorns
2 whole cloves
1 ¼-inch piece of mace or ¼ teaspoon powdered mace, optional

If time allows, to extract maximum flavor from chicken and pork, soak about an hour in cold water with the salt. Place remaining ingredients in bottom of large pot. Put gizzard, heart, neck on vegetables. Add pork and meaty pieces of chicken, bone side down, and top with breast.

Add soaking water, plus additional cold water, if necessary, to almost cover ingredients. Cover pot, bring liquid to boil rapidly, reduce heat and simmer until chicken is tender, about 3 hours. Test frequently toward end of cooking and remove chicken parts as they finish cooking.

Place chicken in bowl and pour strained stock over. As with Soupe et Bouilli*, the dish improves with overnight refrigeration, and the fat is easy to remove. Makes about 2 quarts stock. Remove fat and use chicken and stock as required.

Chicken Cooked For Made Dishes
Casseroles, Salads, etc.

To retain flavor in the chicken, proceed as above, but instead of soaking it, bring cold water to boil and pour into pot in which vegetables and chicken have been arranged, adding enough to half cover ingredients.

Cream of Chicken Soup

Although New York's Hotel Plaza cannot be considered a bastion of the deep South, it serves this delectable dish—a staple in every Southern cook book—on Sundays and holidays. Unfortunately, to avoid separation, it must be served as soon as it is egg-laced and it cannot be reheated. If this poses a timing problem, there's no reason not to serve it cold as the first course of an elegant summer dinner party.

2 cups chicken stock
1 cup cooked chicken, diced
¾ cup cooked rice
1 cup cream
2 eggs (or 4 egg yolks)
2 tablespoons minced parsley

In saucepot, heat stock, chicken, rice, and ½ cup cream. Beat eggs slightly with remaining cream and beat in some of the hot soup. Repeat until eggs warm and pour into main mixture. Cook over low heat, stirring constantly, until thickened, but do not allow it to boil. Season to taste, garnish with parsley, and sprinkle with paprika, if desired. Makes 4 servings.

Chicken Soup With English Peas

With all that lovely chicken stock on hand, serve the following, preferably with Plain Flour Dumplings*.

1 cup frozen peas
4 cups chicken stock

Do not thaw peas. Place in saucepan with stock and bring to boil. Season to taste and add dumplings. Makes 3–4 servings.

Clear Watercress Soup

This far simpler version of Gumbo Z'Herbes* is delicately appealing.

1 bunch watercress
1 small cucumber, cut coarsely
1 teaspoon instant minced onion
3 cups chicken stock
Grated rind of 1 lemon
¼ teaspoon dry mustard, approximately

Add watercress, cucumber, and onion to stock and simmer until soft, about 10 minutes. Purée or whir in blender. Add lemon rind and mustard, and season to taste. Serve hot, garnished with a watercress sprig. Yields about 5 cups soup; 4 servings, and may be frozen.

Mulligatawny

Mulligatawny, spelled mullagatawny way back when, is a corruption of two Tamil words—pepper and water. Expect it to be delicious, because Tamil cooks reputedly serve up the best of East Indian fare. It can be as spice-hot as your taste demands.

A big soup, it is adequate as a luncheon entree, a Sunday supper, or on any day that has been preceded by a business lunch.

Cooks who adhere to tradition cook their chicken in veal stock. A veal knuckle may be added to the stock pot, if desired. Obviously, the dish will be more flavorful if the chicken pieces have been cooked *in* stock, rather than used to make the stock, and if a stewing chicken is used.

- 2 tablespoons butter
- 1 small onion, diced
- 6 ribs (about ¾ cups) celery, diced
- 1 carrot, peeled and diced
- 2 medium apples (preferably greenings), diced
- ¼ cup flour
- 2 teaspoons curry powder, approximately
- 2 quarts (8 cups) chicken stock
- 1 chicken, cut into parts and cooked in stock

Melt butter in saucepan. Add vegetables and simmer covered 5 minutes. Add apple and simmer covered 10 minutes. Stir in flour and curry powder and when smooth, stir chicken stock in gradually. Bring to boil, stirring constantly and add chicken. Simmer, covered, until chicken is hot and season to taste. Makes 6 servings.

Note:
Add ¼ cup cooked rice with chicken and/or follow the South's lead and pass 1 cup cooked rice separately.

SEAFOOD SOUPS

Southern waters swarm with all manner of fish and shellfish, and cooks sensibly take advantage of the largesse. They usually call these seafood soups "stews." Louisiana adds crab and shrimp to gumbos. South Carolina specializes in simple shrimp and milk chowders; Maryland fancies bisques.

Overwhelming are the number of recipes for the final swim of these denizens of the deep, and in many cases, overpowering is the word for the many operations that precede a plate of soup on a Southern table.

The base is sometimes made with chicken or beef stock, sometimes with chicken *and* veal, or beef *and* veal stock, and all are usually enriched with ham, bacon, salt pork, or even just lard. Court Bouillon*, a vegetable stock, is favored by cooks of French heritage.

Further variations of seafood soups include paling them with milk or cream, and thickening them with flour, okra, or filé powder*. The multitude of variations to be found in Southern cook books, from way back when to today, prove that cooks went their own ways, and were not tied to recipes.

Herewith, a handful of seafood soups and stews, to be prepared swift or slow, to be used as is, or trifled with, depending upon *your* ways, wants, and provisions.

Court Bouillon
Vegetable Stock

No self-respecting Southern cook would dream of dumping seafood into water. The New Orleans corruption of the title is *Cou' B.*

Poaching in stock offers two advantages—it adds flavor to the seafood, and the resulting liquid can be reduced to make a sauce. The following is enough for about 1½ pounds seafood.

- 1 teaspoon salt
- 2 tablespoons dry wine—white or red—lemon juice, or vinegar
- ¼ teaspoon peppercorns
- 1 small unpeeled onion, quartered
- 1 small unpeeled carrot, cut coarsely
- 3 sprigs parsley
- 1 stalk celery and leaves
- 1 small clove garlic, crushed, optional
- 1 teaspoon dried herbs, or a combination (see below): tarragon, basil, summer savory
- 2 cups water

Combine ingredients in large pot, cover and boil until vegetables are tender, about 20 minutes. Reduce heat and when liquid stops bubbling add seafood. Cover pot and cook below simmering until seafood is done.

Fish Fumet
Remove cooked seafood and boil stock and vegetables uncovered, until reduced to 1 cup. Use as base for a sauce.

Herbs: Although fresh herbs are infinitely preferable, they depend upon season and how your garden grows. Use any that you prefer, realizing that tarragon complements seafood perfectly, and that the French favor thyme and bay leaf.

Fish Velvet

The blender makes this sumptuous, beautifully named soup an easy-to-do elegance. Pilot crackers, formerly called sailor's or ship, biscuits, were used for thickening, once upon a time. Any unsalted cracker or oysterettes will do, and flour may be substituted.

Nutmeg may be added. About ¼ cup lean cooked ham can go into the blender with the fish and any leftover "velvet" can be turned into a soufflé.

   1 pound white-fleshed fish fillets
   2 cups Court Bouillon* or clam juice
   ½ cup chopped celery and leaves (about 4 stalks)
   1 large pilot cracker
   1 unpeeled lemon, sliced
   1 cup milk; or half milk, half cream
   2 tablespoons dry white wine, optional
   ½ teaspoon sugar
   Dash cayenne pepper

Whir raw fish and 1 cup court bouillon in blender with celery and cracker until smooth. Pour into saucepan and add lemon and remaining court bouillon. Cover and simmer gently until fish is cooked, about 20 minutes. Add milk and wine and bring to boil. Remove lemon. Season to taste with sugar and cayenne pepper and garnish with paprika and/or parsley. Serve hot or cold. Makes 3–4 servings. May be frozen.

Seafood Bisques

Choose your favorite seafood, forget about the agonized procedures demanded by haute cuisine recipes, and let the blender whir you a bisque that is sumptuous indeed.

   1 small peeled onion, chopped coarsely
   2 stalks celery, chopped coarsely
   1 medium peeled carrot, chopped coarsely
   2 sprigs parsley
   2 cups water
   Seafood (see below)
   ½ cup dry white wine
   ¼ cup brandy
   2 cups cream
   1 tablespoon butter
   ¹⁄₁₆ teaspoon cayenne pepper
   Nutmeg, optional

Boil onion, celery, carrot, and parsley in water until vegetables are tender, about 30 minutes, and add and poach raw seafood. Drain when done, reserving stock. Whir seafood and vegetables in blender with enough stock to liquefy. When smooth, place in saucepan with wine and brandy, and gradually stir in cream, then butter. Heat gently, and season to taste. Serve hot or cold, garnish with nutmeg. Makes 6-plus servings.

Raw Seafood: For above amount, poach approximtely a pound delicate-flavored, white-fleshed fish fillets, or ¾ pound shrimp, cut coarsely. They will poach in about 15 minutes, and a pint of shucked stewing-size oysters will poach in about 5 minutes.

Cooked: Add a half pound picked hard crab, or an equivalent amount of frozen crab with wine.

Petite Bouillabaisse

If, despite the wrangling over the word, bouillabaisse *does* translate to low boil, this ruddy, quickly put together version of shellfish surely qualifies. Serve it in soup bowls with crackers, as a lunch or supper entree.

- ¼ cup catsup
- 2 tablespoons butter, melted
- ¼ cup cream
- 2 tablespoons grated cheese, preferably Parmesan
- 1 teaspoon Worcestershire sauce, approximately
- Dash cayenne pepper
- 12 small (about ½ pint stewing-size) oysters
- ½ cup lump crab meat

In saucepan, stir catsup into butter. Reduce heat, and stir in cream, the cheese, Worcestershire sauce, and seasonings. When hot, add oysters and enough of their liquor to thin to bisque consistency. Cover pan and cook gently until oysters begin to plump, about 3 minutes. Stir crab in, cover and cook over low heat until oyster edges ruffle and mixture is hot, about 3 minutes more, being careful not to overcook shellfish. Season to taste—it should be spicy. Makes 2 servings.

GUMBO

What makes gumbo a gumbo is this African word for okra. From the welter of ancient and modern recipes for this soup—and often soup-entree—the fact that emerges loud and clear is that gumbos were suited to larder supplies.

Rice, "cooked grain for grain," is a gumbo inseparable, and Southerners prepare and serve it separately, either spooning some into each soup plate or passing a help-yourself bowl.

Directions for adding filé powder* are varied and finicking—ranging from: Spoon it on top just before serving to avoid gumminess—to: Stir in just before serving until the gumbo becomes mucilaginous. To do it as cooks were bid in the eighteenth century, prepare it in an "earthen Pipkin, or very nice iron pot." The advice translates to: Use a heavy pot—and is as pertinent today.

According to Louisiana's famous writer and *fin bec*—Scoop Kennedy —the Acadiens of southwest Louisiana celebrate all festive occasions by carrying ingredients for a gumbo to a common pot.

GUMBO INGREDIENTS

In addition to the numerous recipes for gumbo in these pages, the following suggestions will allow you to go your own way, mixing and matching to please you and yours.

Fats   Choose from lard, butter, a combination, or for smoky flavor bacon drippings.

Flavoring Vegetables   In only one Southern cook book did a gumbo recipe not call for onion. I must assume that the author considered it standard operating procedure.

Okra—canned, frozen, fresh.

Tomatoes, bell peppers, leek.

Herbs and Spices Make it spicy-hot with cayenne pepper—especially for Creoles, and add the typical French herb triumvirate: parsley, thyme, bay leaf.

Filé Powder* may be substituted for okra.

Meat Stewing chicken (a "grown" chicken, in the South), a young chicken or already-cooked chicken, find their way into gumbo. So do ham, brisket of beef or veal, and any seafood.

Liquid Choose any—from water to stock, and don't waste your oyster liquor.

Chicken Gumbo Soup

- 1 small green pepper, diced
- 1 small clove garlic, minced
- 2 cups sliced okra*
- 1 small onion, diced
- 3 tablespoons butter or other fat
- 2½ cups (1-pound, 4-ounce can) tomatoes
- 4 cups chicken stock
- 1 cup cooked chicken, diced
- $\frac{1}{16}$ teaspoon cayenne pepper, optional
- 1 tablespoon filé powder, optional

In soup pot simmer green pepper, garlic, okra, and onion in butter until lightly browned, about 20 minutes. Add tomatoes and cook briskly until most of liquid evaporates; about 20 minutes. Add stock, and chicken, season to taste, cover pan and heat. Serve sprinkled with filé powder*, if desired. Makes 4–6 servings.

Shrimp Gumbo

Season to taste can mean enough cayenne pepper for a fiery brew.

- 1 pound raw shelled shrimp
- 3 cups strained Court Bouillon*
- 1 tablespoon butter
- 1 tablespoon flour
- 1 onion, diced

1 green pepper, diced, optional
1 cup clam juice
¼ teaspoon sugar
1 tablespoon filé powder*, optional

Add shrimp to boiling court bouillon, and poach, covered, until done. (If time is not a factor, the heat can be turned off.) In large saucepan, prepare roux* with butter and flour. When brown, add onion and green pepper, and cook, stirring occasionally, until roux browns, about 20 minutes. Add shrimp, strained court bouillon, and clam juice. Cover pot, bring to boil, add sugar, season to taste, and serve sprinkled with filé powder. Pass boiled rice separately. Makes 4 servings.

Variation—Add to the court bouillon 2 cups canned tomatoes.

Shrimp Gumbo Soup With Okra
For speed, add 1 cup sliced okra, unthawed frozen, or canned (plus liquid in can), with the cooked shrimp. If using fresh okra, cook it in the court bouillon until tender.

Drum Point Corn Chowder

A bride in 1858 titled this "Fresh Garden Corn Chowder." If you are not picking corn kernels from the grocer's shelf or freezer, grate the kernels from 4 cooked, medium-size ears.

1½ cups chicken stock
1½ cups milk
2 cups corn kernels
2 tablespoons softened butter
½ teaspoon instant minced onion
2 egg yolks
½ teaspoon sugar
Dash cayenne pepper

Place half the liquid, corn, butter, and onion in blender container, and whir smooth. Heat remaining liquid in saucepan. Add puréed mixture and bring to boil. Egg-lace*; and when thickened, add sugar and pepper and season to taste. Serve garnished with minced parsley and paprika. Makes 4 servings.

Green Pea Family Soup

To a Damn Yankee, peas mean small, green rounds, enclosed in pod, can, or freezer package. Southerners call them Green English peas, to differentiate them from blackeye or marrowfat peas. An anonymous, long-ago Creole author chose the above title for her excellent receipt and remarks that if you add a half-pound of butter and a spoon of sugar, you will have prepared Queen Victoria's favorite green pea soup.

Too bad the lady had no access to the speedy easy things of life, reflected in this brought-up-to-date version. Whether for family or for royalty, dumplings or croutons *and* Fried Bread* were the accompaniments demanded.

- 1½ pounds cooked ham, diced
- 1 package (10-ounce) frozen peas
- 1 can (10½-ounce) condensed pea soup, undiluted
- 1 can (10½-ounce) condensed beef broth, undiluted
- 1 cup water
- ½ teaspoon dried thyme
- Cayenne pepper, to taste

Combine ingredients and bring to boil. Correct seasoning and serve hot with dumplings or croutons and pass fried bread. Makes 6-plus servings.

Peanut Soup

How wonderful not to have to plant, pick, roast, or shell the nuts before making this star-of-Virginia soup. How even better to put can opener and blender to work and achieve such good taste and so much nutrition, economically and in a matter of minutes!

- ½ cup Virginia peanuts*
- 2 cans (10½-ounces each) beef broth, undiluted
- 1 cup milk
- Dash cayenne pepper

Whir nuts and 1 can broth in blender until smooth. Pour into saucepan, add remaining ingredients, cover and bring liquid to boil. Reduce heat, and simmer 15 minutes to blend flavors and season to taste. Yields about 4 cups soup, good hot or cold.

PUMPKIN SOUPS

Chilled soups, research indicates, "were introduced to England by the French aristocrats and soon found their way to Southern tables."

Cold pumpkin soup is a Southern specialty that may have traveled there by way of Spain. Mashed winter squash or yams may be substituted.

The Teche Pumpkin Soup

- 2 cups (1 pound can) pumpkin
- ⅔ cup brown sugar
- 1¾ cup milk
- ½ teaspoon nutmeg
- ½ teaspoon cloves
- 1 teaspoon cinnamon
- ½ teaspoon allspice
- ¼ cup brandy, optional

Combine all ingredients except brandy. Cover and bring to boil over low heat, stirring occasionally. Chill and stir in brandy. Garnish with cinnamon or serve in wine glasses with cinnamon stick muddler. Makes 4 servings.

Cream of Pumpkin Soup

- ½ cup diced onion
- 2 tablespoons butter
- 3 cups chicken stock
- 2 cups canned pumpkin
- ½ cup cream

In medium-size saucepan, sauté onion in butter for about 2 minutes, but do not let it brown. Stir in 1 cup stock and simmer until onion is tender. Cool and whir in blender with pumpkin. When smooth, stir in remaining stock and ½ cup cream. Season to taste and serve chilled, garnished with whipped cream, if desired. Makes 6 servings.

Tomato Soup with Vegetables Very Fine

The recipe is my adaptation of one from an 1800s Creole cook book and the title is courtesy of the anonymous author, who describes it as, "An elegant family soup, particularly nice in summer when the vegetables are fresh." The vegetables the author had in mind were onion, carrot, turnip, and celery.

Frozen mixed garden vegetables and modern transportation make it a year 'round staple for fortunate us. Although straining the soup may seem unnecessary, it produces a clear, brilliant red broth.

> 4 cups tomato juice
> 1 teaspoon instant minced onion
> 1 small bay leaf
> ¼ teaspoon powdered ginger
> ¹⁄₁₆ teaspoon powdered cloves
> 1 teaspoon dried basil
> 1 cup mixed frozen vegetables

Bring all except frozen vegetables to boil in covered pan and simmer 5 minutes. Strain, add vegetables, cover, and cook until steaming hot. Season to taste. Makes 4 servings.

Variations

With Rice: Add ¾ cup cooked rice with the vegetables.

With Ham: Add ¼ cup cooked ham, chopped fine, with the vegetables.

Savory Tomato Soup
Substitute 2 cups beef stock for 2 cups of the tomato juice and substitute marjoram, thyme, and mace for the spices and herbs called for. Consider this version a kind of madrilene.

Blackeye Pea Soup

Southern cooks take advantage of economical dried vegetables—pigeon peas, split peas, small white beans, etc.—for soups and also providently flavor pots with leftover bones and/or gravy. Despite many recipe directions to the contrary, blackeye peas do not require soaking.

1½ cups blackeye peas
1 cup diced ham
1 large onion, diced
⅛ teaspoon hot red pepper
½ teaspoon salt
7 cups water
¼ cup dry wine, white or red, optional

Combine ingredients in large saucepot, bring to boil rapidly, lower heat, and simmer about 3 hours or until blackeye peas are tender. Makes 6-plus servings.

Note:
A package (10-ounce) frozen blackeye peas may be substituted. Then use only 4 cups water, adding more as needed and cook only until peas are mealy-soft, about an hour.

SOUP ACCOMPANIMENTS

Fried bread from England, and croutons, a French specialty, were and are the crunch served up with soup in the South. Vermecelli, and macaroone, spelled just that way, also lurked in soups, and Dumplings delighted, too. Here are a few accompaniments that are all to the good.

Pasta in Soup

"Delicate stomachs" seem to be an age-old affliction. Our ways of dealing with the problem are not as delicious as those suggested way back when. Dyspeptic types in days of yore were pampered with veal, chicken, or beef soup containing pasta. The pasta mentioned most frequently was vermicelli (the thinnest of the tubular variety), and it

was boiled in the stock, providing real largesse—because it absorbs so much of the broth.

Sometimes delicate stomachs were treated to soups with the "special nourishment of the final addition of a can of tomatoes and a bit of butter, added in time to heat through." Good for good or bad stomachs —simply add ¼ pound of pasta, a 1-pound can of tomatoes, and 2 tablespoons butter to 6 servings soup. In the interest of economy, boil the pasta separately in water.

Plain Flour Dumplings

1 egg
1 tablespoon cold water
¼ teaspoon salt
5 tablespoons flour, approximately

Beat egg and water together lightly. Gradually beat in enough flour so mixture is lump free and holds together. Drop teaspoonfuls into boiling soup (test a bit to be sure) and boil approximately 5 minutes. Makes about 10 dumplings; enough for 2–3 cups soup. Dumplings may be frozen before or after cooking.

Egg Balls

Egg yolks to use up, and the blender, make this multipurpose specialty simplicity itself. Originally served in a curry sauce, they grace a bowl of soup and also make splendid cold hors d'oeuvre. Then, for allure, dust with paprika.

4 hard-cooked eggs
1 raw egg yolk
¼ teaspoon instant minced onion, optional
1 teaspoon flour
1 teaspoon minced parsley
Seasonings (see below)

Whir cooked eggs in blender, and when smooth, combine with remaining ingredients and your choice of seasonings. Using the large end of a melon-baller or a 1-teaspoon measuring spoon, drop into simmering soup or water. Simmer covered 5 minutes, turning half-way through cooking.

Seasonings: Season to taste with salt, paprika, cayenne pepper, chili- or curry-powder. Choose from the additional following dried herbs, using about 1½ teaspoons of one or a combination: sage, savory, or thyme. Add about 1 teaspoon celery or cumin seeds to an appropriate combination.

Queen Bee Dumplings

Queen Bee is Kentucky colloquial for a lady who henpecks her husband. If she turns out dumplings such as these, perhaps she is forgiven. They may be dropped into thickened gravy. Other herbs, spices, and/or grated cheese will vary the recipe.

- ¾ cup flour
- 2½ teaspoons baking powder
- ½ teaspoon salt
- 1 egg, beaten
- ⅓ cup milk
- ¼ cup minced parsley
- 1 teaspoon grated lemon rind, optional
- **Dash cayenne pepper**

Mix flour with baking powder and salt. Combine egg and milk with remaining ingredients. Add dry ingredients, stirring only until smooth. Drop from a large teaspoon, making sure dough rests on meat and/or vegetables. Cook uncovered 5 minutes to allow dumplings to puff, then cover pan tightly and cook gently until done, about 10 minutes more. Makes about 8 dumplings.

Cornmeal Dumplings
Dodgers

Huey Long, Louisiana's visionary politician, platformed on a "Share Our Wealth" policy. He also is credited with popularizing those indisputable culinary riches—cornmeal dodgers. They are almost *de rigeur* with Pot Likker Portmanteau*, and with them, make the dish a complete entree.

- 2 tablespoons drippings, preferably pork
- 1 cup cornmeal
- 1½ cups boiling water, approximately
- ½ teaspoon salt

Add fat to cornmeal and stir in enough water to make a dough stiff enough to hold shape. Pat into ½-inch thick and 2-inch long dumplings and place on cooked Pot Likker Portmanteau.* Cover pan, and cook gently 10 minutes. Turn and cook until firm, about 10 minutes more. Makes about 6 dumplings; 4 servings.

Note:
Add about 1 tablespoon onion, minced fine and an egg and fry the dumplings along with fish (whole or fillets).

Elizabeth's Pulled Dumplings

Elizabeth, another good-cook Goshae, is awarded the accolade for this Georgia way with dumplings. They taste very much like noodles, are an excellent way to use leftover scraps of pie dough, and, when dropped into stews such as Smothered Chicken*, eliminate the necessity for thickening the gravy. When company's coming, coarsely-cut hard-cooked eggs add a topping.

Roll pie dough paper thin and cut 1-inch strips. Pull strips into 1½-inch lengths, and drop into pot of boiling stew, one at a time. When top of stew is covered, stir, then add remaining strips. Cover, and cook gently until done, about 5 minutes.

Toasted Seeds

No provident cook, in the South or elsewhere, would willingly discard pumpkin or winter squash (acorn or Hubbard) seeds. Remove fibers (good relaxing finger exercise) and slip seeds onto a baking sheet. Let dry overnight. Toast in the oven until browned and crisp—any temperature up to 400° F. will do, stirring occasionally. It will take about 10 minutes in a hot oven. Pass to pop into soup or to serve as a snack.

Salted Seeds: After removing fibrous material, soak seeds in heavily-salted water about an hour. Drain, let dry overnight, and toast as above.

A SUCCULENCE OF MEATS

Before modern transportation, indigenous foods had to precede recipes, so Southern cooks were obliged to pay primary attention to pork. However, a country with so many English forebears yearned for beef. Its comparative scarcity meant advantage was taken of everything except the moo—and in extending ways.

Beef sometimes was combined with ham to bake in rich pastry, but possibly the most extending use was in an *ollo,* of Spanish derivation. It surrounds beef with pork, mutton, chicken, snap and lima beans, squash, tomatoes, apples or pears, to be further furbished with a handful of mint.

Burgoo, another Southern stew, gathers together beef, chicken, squirrel, and bacon. For good measure, corn and lima beans go into this melting pot, too, and it fills voters' plates at political rallies. Unless, of course, the office-seeker has been prodigal to the point of providing a whole barbecued beef.

An invitation to a relatively cool outdoor affair must have more than gladdened the hearts of long-ago Southern cooks forced to wrestle with stoves which Dickens, after his visit here, referred to as "red-hot monsters."

We produced—and still do—more stoves, and in more profuse variety than any other country. Oscar Wilde also objected to stoves as those "heat-radiating decorations often seen in the center of the room."

Initially, ladies who had learned to cope with the vagaries of fireplace cooking did not accept them with alacrity, either. Even Catherine Beecher, one of the first to grasp the essentials of efficient kitchen organization, raised practical objections. "The cooking materials and utensils, the sink and the eating room," she wrote, "are at such distances apart that half the time and strength is employed in walking back and forth to collect and return the articles used."

She was right, of course, because originally stoves were fueled with wood or coal, and there was no efficient channeling of heat.

Today, if, in addition to your perfectly behaved range, you also are pampered with a microwave oven, your need to conserve energy may not be as great, so you can glory in efficient organization for its own sake. But in cooking meat, do pay attention to words of wisdom from the 1800s, and do not salt it before cooking because, as the ladies were rightly advised, "it draws out juice."

PORK

Frontier-day pigs were as hardy as the pioneers, and along with them, ranged the forests, amicably foraging for food and fiercely standing off any wild creatures that came their way. The athletic regimen produced pigs that were sturdy and slim when they went into the pot; lean and stringy when they came out.

Hogs changed dramatically when a wily husbandman thought to feed them corn, thereby turning them from farm scavengers into lolling tenants. The shotes, waxing fat, furnished the needed richness for diets.

Now that we, too, loll much of the time, we demand lean pork. So, today, in the interest of tenderness, although hogs still are encouraged to be lazy, they are fed less fattening food; the Jack Sprats are kept for breeding; and packers and retailers trim excess fat closely. We profit by more meat per pound and fewer calories.

Pork is saluted as a nutritional enviable. A high quality protein, and one of the best sources of thiamine (vitamin B1), it also provides iron and niacin.

Hogs usually are marketed when less than a year old. The meat should be a delicate uniform rose or grayish-pink, with smooth velvety texture, and firm, white outer fat.

It would be nice, if, as in other countries, hogs were processed to eliminate the danger of trichinosis, because, as with any meat cooked only to the rare stage, less of the flavor-containing juices are evaporated. Presumably this is in the works. Until then, the U.S. Department of Agriculture rules that, depending upon the cut, fresh pork should be heated to an internal temperature of 170°–185° F. on a meat thermometer. The final determinant obviously is color. After cooking it should not be pink—so, to achieve succulence, snatch it from the heat as soon as it is just done.

Tim Turkeys

I claim no credit for this coy title from an old book. Cut a pocket in double loin pork chops and fill lightly with any desired stuffing. You will find several in the Poultry Chapter. Close opening with toothpicks. Arrange on a bed of sliced onion, and add enough chicken stock to reach a depth of ¼-inch. Cover pan, bring liquid to boil rapidly, lower heat and simmer until chops are tender, about 45 minutes. Season to taste, and thicken pan liquid, if desired, as for gravy. Allow 1 chop per serving.

Toasted Canadian Bacon

Toasted Ham* is what the South calls ham that has been patted with bread crumbs or cornmeal before baking. They also call what Canadians do not call Canadian bacon, back bacon. This large, boned, smoked muscle that lies along the top of the pork loin is almost fat-free, and offers the advantages of easy carving, good flavor, and very little waste. The advantages rightly make it costly. Although usually used only at breakfast or brunch, it provides a superb dinner roast, and when "toasted," the cornmeal forms a wonderful rich, crisp crust to hold in the meat juices.

For a perfect sandwich, let whole wheat bread clasp leftover slices of Canadian bacon and raw white turnip.

- 1 egg
- 1 tablespoon water
- 1 cup cornmeal
- 3–4 pound piece of Canadian bacon

In deep plate, beat egg and water just enough to blend. Spread cornmeal on wax paper. Dip bacon in meal, then egg mixture, then meal. Continue dipping, until egg is used and meat is completely coated. Let stand about 20 minutes to firm crust. Roast on rack in pan with low sides in preheated moderate 350° F. oven until done, allowing about 45 minutes per pound. Makes 4-plus servings.

Pressed Pork

In my first book, the *Down-on-the-Farm-Cookbook,* a recipe for Headcheese can have been meaningful only to families possessing an imposing hog's head. It called for one weighing about 25 pounds. A more commodious way to prepare the flavorful, shimmery hors d'oeuvre Southerners call Pressed Pork or Souse, is with fresh pigs' knuckles or pigs' feet. Serve it as the first course at dinner on a scorcher, or as a luncheon entree. Sharp mustard is the perfect accompaniment.

The large proportion of bone insures jellying. After cooking, discard the fat and add the meat to the strained fat-free liquid. In France, the aspic is seasoned with nutmeg and served from a terrine.

For a dinner party, prepare Pressed Pork in a loaf, turn out, center on a platter, and surround it with lettuce cups into which you have tucked sharp pickles, pimento strips, green olives, and pickled onions.

3–4 fresh pigs' knuckles
Pepper Stock*
½ cup parsley sprigs, cut coarsely
2 tablespoons instant minced onion
¼ cup dry white wine, optional

Cook knuckles in enough Pepper Stock* to almost cover. When meat is tender, pour strained stock over, and refrigerate. When cold, remove fat, cut meat into small pieces and reduce stock to 2½ cups. Add meat and remaining ingredients and season to taste—it should be piquant.

Turn mixture into mold measuring about 9 x 5 x 3 inches. Stock must cover top of meat. Cover with waxed paper and place a heavy weight on top. Refrigerate until firm. Makes 6–8 servings.

Deviled Bones
Barbecued Spare Ribs

Although that stalwart feeder, the pig, may seem more Falstaffian than devilish, there is every reason to spice up his bland, rich bones. And considering one medieval legend, the recipe title is eminently apropos. It seems the devil attempted, in a series of encounters, to shake St. Anthony's faith and frighten him into submission. Satan failed and for punishment, was changed into a pig, which followed around at the saint's heels.

Spareribs are more succulent if cooked covered, about an hour, before splitting, but have butcher cut through bony part for ease in separating after cooking.

For 4 servings as entree, buy a 2-pound rack (about 14 ribs) and bake whole. For hors d'oeuvre, have ribs separated and cut in 1-inch pieces. Brush with quick-browning aid, and place in baking pan with low sides, bone side down. Cover and bake in preheated, slow 300° F. oven 30 minutes. Uncover, turn bone side up and brush with any spicy tomato or Barbecue Sauce*. Continue cooking until crisp and browned.

To Grill: Cook ribs until done, about 1 hour, and brush sauce on both sides before grilling. Grill bone side down first, and brush both sides when turning. Preferably turn only once.

For extra-crisp results, freeze cooked ribs and grill frozen.

Dorothy Atkin's Pork and Corn

Artist John Atkin married a transplanted flower of the South, who sat me down to this in their New York apartment. A four-star Southern entree, it is so simple to prepare it seems too good to be true. Serve with grits and butter, or with boiled or mashed potatoes—and don't forget the biscuits.

- 1 pound ground lean pork
- 1 onion, diced
- 2 cups corn kernels

Heat heavy skillet and add pork and onion. Fry over medium high heat, stirring until meat crumbles. Drain fat, reduce heat, cover skillet, and cook gently until onion softens and flavors blend, about 20 minutes. Add corn (unthawed, if frozen) and continue cooking, covered, until hot, about 10 minutes. Season to taste with salt and black pepper. Makes 4 servings.

Pickled Pigs' Feet and Hocks Knuckles

Pigs' knuckles (pork hocks to the South), available fresh or smoked, are interchangeable in recipes. Pigs' feet (trotters to the British), are available fresh only. They are interchangeable with pigs' knuckles in recipes and are meatier. The feet provide a feast for Henry Jones types: Save the bones for Henry Jones—'Cause he don't eat no meat.

Sharp mustard and pickles are perfect accompaniments and, when chilled, there is no better first course at dinner or lunch, or as a supper entree on a day of wilting heat.

Place ingredients for Pepper Stock* in large pot. Cover, bring liquid to boil rapidly, add knuckles or feet, lower heat and simmer until tender, about 1½ hours for fresh; 2 hours for smoked hock. Serve hot or cold.

GUMBO DES HERBES

This rite-of-spring Creole recipe is colloquially called Gumbo Z'Herbes or Gumbo Zhebes, and is served for good luck on Holy Thursday. I found it mentioned in only two books, with laconic directions that could hardly be called recipes. The odd combination of ingredients so intrigued me, that preparing it became a challenge. As I proceeded, flying blind, it suddenly occurred to me that what I was making basically, was kin to my grandmother's creamed spinach—but more lavish.

Seven (the lucky number) greens comprise the gumbo, so it demands a large family—or many guests. Those who sampled it as a soup and entree at a dinner party here considered themselves fortunate indeed. Before modern transportation, I can imagine the spring joy of picking the first new greens of the season after a winter of root vegetables. Ours market-pick, and although frozen spinach is not as alive in flavor, it makes everything easier.

Roquette (rocket plant), points to the recipe's French background. The Italian dictionary lists this piquant green as *ruca* or *ruchetta*. New York's Italian greengrocers call it *arugola* or *rugola* (and charge grandly for a small bunch). A member of the mustard family, American encyclopedias list it as "rocket."

The following is "my way." If not "authentic," let me know. The nutritional iron should give you enough strength for a *long* letter.

Amounts and proportions are not of paramount importance, but before you begin, be sure you have a large pot—and bless the blender.

Meat Choose one or a combination—veal or pork breast (brisket). Have the butcher chop the meat into 3 to 4 inch chunks with bone. Pigs' knuckles need to be split in half; pigs' feet quartered. A ham bone can go into the pot, as can ¼-pound piece of unsliced bacon, and game can be added. After cooking, the meat can be picked from the bones and fried with onion roux to make a whole meal, or served on the bone, as entree.

Greens Use instead of any of those listed below, mustard greens (available chopped, frozen); green cabbage (the flavor of this may take over), collards (fairly dominating flavor—available chopped, frozen); beet or turnip tops; any variety of lettuce.

Seasonings Hot red pepper is an imperative; thyme and bay leaf may be used.

Rice That stalwart accompaniment to all gumbos seems to me to absorb too much of the flavor of the soup, so pass it separately—and admire the gorgeous green and white color contrast.

Stock

> 2 pigs' knuckles (about 2 pounds)
> 2 pounds veal brisket
> 2 bunches (about 4 ounces) rocket
> 1 bunch scallions (green tops only)
> 1 bunch watercress (about ½ pound)
> 1 pound fresh spinach leaves (remove stems)
> 1 bunch parsley (about 3 ounces)
> ¼ pound chicory
> ½ pound escarole
> ¼ cup dry white wine, optional
> ¼ teaspoon hot red pepper

Place meat in bottom of large saucepot. Add vegetables, wine, pepper, and 4 cups water. Cover pot, bring liquid to boil rapidly, lower heat and simmer until pigs' knuckles are tender, about 1½ hours. Strain, reserving meat and liquid. Chop greens fine, whir in blender, or purée.

Roux

> 1 large onion, diced
> 2 tablespoons lard
> ¼ cup flour

Cook onion in lard until very soft, about 15 minutes. Stir flour in and cook, stirring, until browned. Gradually stir in reserved liquid. When smooth, stir in chopped greens. Season to taste and pass rice. Makes 6–8 cups soup. May be frozen.

Sauerkraut and Hocks

This is a Southern variation of *choucroute garnie* (garnished sauerkraut). Dumplings made with baking powder biscuit dough—use a 2-cup flour proportion for four servings—dropped into the pot by the tablespoonful the last 15 minutes of cooking, add a thought the French never had. You might prefer adding potatoes.

The hocks can be split, or pigs' feet (quartered, if desired) substituted. And, of course, the entire gamut from pork neck bones to ears can be used. If choosing pork shoulder, buy and have 2 pounds cut in chunks.

- 1 can (1 pound) tomatoes
- 1 pound sauerkraut, drained
- 2 medium onions, diced
- ¼ teaspoon sugar
- 4 pigs' hocks
- ¼ cup dry wine, white or red, optional

Place all ingredients except pork in heavy pot. Top with pork, cover pan, bring liquid to boil rapidly, reduce heat, and simmer gently until hocks are tender, about 2 hours. Makes 4 servings.

Side-Dish Sauerkraut

Substitute ¼ pound salt pork for hocks. Tomatoes may be omitted.

Pigs' Tail

Although I may be going out on a limb shaky as a pig's tail, I have an idea that the Southern word souse, for meat in its own aspic, comes from the German *sulz*.

Containing so much bone, naturally the cooking liquid jellies, and "souls" cook and eat pigs' tail either hot, or cold in its aspic. It can be simmered in Pepper Stock* or braised as for Ox Tail* and so can the ear, which I cannot admit to liking.

In a very good restaurant in Paris, I savored fried pigs' tail, which tasted very much like cracklings. Broiling is a less flavorful alternate.

Fried Pigs' Tail

Allow 1 cooked pigs' tail per serving. Remove skin (to serve separately to admirers) and fat, and cut in 2-inch sections. Roll sections in cornmeal or fine dry bread crumbs, and fry in lard until crisp and browned. Drain, and serve hot.

Tennessee Chicken

To Damn Yankees, this may sound like a cupboard-is-bare recipe, but Southern children consider it a treat. Named as above, it comes from a child of Georgia. Tennesseans probably call it Georgia Chicken.

Copiously-peppered milk gravy, as in Ham with Red-Eye Gravy*, to pour over hot biscuits, is its optional companion.

Allow 2 slices salt pork cut ¼-inch thick for each serving. Place in skillet, add water to cover, cover skillet, and bring to boil. Drain pork and pat dry. Wipe skillet dry, and fry pork slices covered, turning to brown both sides.

Or, remove slices from water, dry, batter-dip, and fry, uncovered in about an inch of lard.

Homemade Pork Sausage

On a do-it-yourself day, you might want to make your own pork sausage. You might even want to call it, as strangely enough *The Virginia Housewife* does—bologna. There is no need to force the meat into skins—simply shape patties. Pork shoulder is the usual cut, pork liver may be added, and salt pork may be substituted for bacon. For a fiery combination, substitute ¼ teaspoon hot red pepper for the cayenne.

When seasoning a pork mixture to taste, simply touch your tongue to it.

    ½ pound each: bacon, lean pork, veal
    1 onion
    ¼ cup fine dry bread crumbs
    1 teaspoon dried rosemary

1½ teaspoons dried thyme
1½ teaspoons dried sage
⅛ teaspoon cayenne pepper
1 teaspoon salt
Dry red wine, optional

Grind meat and onion, and combine with all ingredients except wine. Knead lightly, moistening if necessary with small amounts of dry red wine or water, until mixture holds together. Season to taste, and shape patties of any desired size. Yields ¾ pound, about 4 small patties and may be frozen.

HAM

Ham is the hind leg of a porker, and I have never really known whether or not country folk are pulling *my* leg when they announce that the right leg of a left-handed (footed?) pig is more tender.

To preserve *any* leg of this sumptuous cut, through the long hot summers, Southerners treated it to a salt rub-down (cure), and hung it high in the rafters, to smoke and dry for lengthy periods—and gain a reputation.

According to Virginians, Virginia or Smithfield hams are the best—a point Kentucky folk consider arguable. A "long-cut" Smithfield ham is even more exalted—the long shank includes part of the sirloin. Ham labeled "Virginia or other style," has been cured and smoked in another geographical area.

In this era of convenience, packers taking care of the arduous preliminaries, have provided us with hams all ready to eat—at a price. But the well-worth-it cost makes them a special occasion splurge. A Southern wedding table that did not include salty, full-flavored slivers of ham clasped between halved beaten biscuits would be considered sadly inadequate. (Today, beaten biscuits, an oh-what-a-job recipe, are available in packages—from tiny button, to normal—2-inch diameter—size.)

Dixie cooks are likely to boil ham rather than heat up the kitchen by baking. Research turned up a more-work-for-mother curiosity which directed that a ham be boned, stuffed with chow-chow, simmered in apple vinegar and brown sugar, and as crowning glory, topped with pickle slices. It probably was served by the same cooks who shaped beaten biscuit dough into chickens.

When cooking a half-ham, realize that the more expensive butt end yields more meat; larger slices. The shank end possibly proves that the meat next to the bone is sweetest. Unless country-cured ham* is labeled ready-to-eat, there's work ahead. And even when hams are labeled fully-cooked, realize that heating improves flavor and texture.

Country-Cured Ham

Soak overnight in cold water to cover. Next morning, wash, scrubbing well with stiff brush. Insert meat thermometer, place ham on rack and pour over enough cold water that has been brought to a boil to almost cover ham. Cover pan, bring liquid to boil rapidly, lower heat and simmer about 20 minutes per pound, or until thermometer registers 160° F., adding water as necessary.

Lacking a thermometer, judge doneness by the hock bone—it will be slightly loose. As a further test, insert an ice pick in thickest portion of the underside. The juice should be pinkish white. While hot, remove skin with scissors and sharp knife, and score fat. For ease in slicing, cool completely, and cut paper-thin.

For a flavorful variation, add to cooking liquid ½ cup vinegar and ½ cup molasses.

To Glaze: Brush with quick-browning aid (optional) and/or molasses and bake in preheated, hot 400° F. oven about 25 minutes.

Loose-Bone Ham

It is possible to approximate the flavor of a Virginia ham by overcooking a fully-cooked ham at a high temperature, a glorious happy-accident discovery of Chattanooga's Helen Exum. Practically all the fat melts away, and the juices concentrate in the ham, resulting in sweet, but characterful, flavor. Once you have prepared ham the following ways, you probably will be spoiled forever for the anemic results of low-temperature roasting.

In any case, score fat. Then it will melt readily and appearance will be improved. Toppings of whole cloves and the like seem to me to be fuss-fuss, with no flavor dividends, but "Toasting," as follows, is a days-of-yore advantage.

Of the many suggested ways to carve a whole ham, the simplest is the old Southern trick of slicing horizontal to the shank.

Fully-Cooked Whole Ham (about 15 pounds)

Roast in preheated, moderate 375° F. oven until meat around shank bone shrinks and bone loosens, about 3½ hours.

Fully-Cooked Half Ham (about 6 pounds)

Roast, cut side down (do not use a rack), in preheated, very hot 450° F. oven, about 2 hours. If browning is excessive, cover top with foil.

Toasted Ham

In this old-fashioned Southern "way," cornmeal may be substituted for bread crumbs.

1 approximately 6-pound fully-cooked ham butt
2 tablespoons fine dry bread crumbs
¼ cup brown sugar
½ teaspoon cloves
2 teaspoons dry mustard
1 teaspoon salt

Remove any skin on ham and score fat. Combine remaining ingredients and pat firmly on fat. Place ham in baking pan cut-side down (do not use a rack), and bake in preheated, moderate 350° F. oven about 20 minutes per pound, or until meat thermometer registers 130° F.

HAM SLICES

For economy and variety when buying a half ham, have butcher cut a few center slices off, to freeze them for another day. They can be cut up to an inch thick and a slice weighing about a pound makes 2 servings. Slash outer rim of fat every inch or so to avoid curling as it cooks.

Ham With Red-Eye Gravy

Although seemingly it is a gaffe to order a Mint Julep* in Kentucky, that Southern staple—Ham with Red-Eye Gravy, made with country-cured ham—is literally forced on one there. But unless one has been born to the specialty, a palate that enjoys an ocean of salt is required.

The following Kentucky recipe calls, of course, for a country-cured *Kentucky* ham. Different states have different ways with the dish. Some fry the slice in fat, lard, or bits cut from the ham. Some soak it in water to cover for about 3 hours to remove some of the salt. Some substitute cider for water; others call for coffee. Typical dinner accompaniments are sweet or mashed potatoes, succotash, okra, and banana cream pie.

The following pan-broiling method and a non-Virginia type ham slice should appeal to Damn Yankees. Either may be served with the following cream gravy.

Kentucky Country-Cured Ham With Red-Eye Gravy

Cut a ¼-inch center slice from an uncooked ham. Heat a heavy skillet until very hot; and brown ham on both sides. Add enough boiling water to cover, cover skillet, reduce heat, and simmer until ham is tender, about 30 minutes. Pour skillet juice over ham. Makes 1 serving.

Fully-Cooked Ham with Red-Eye Gravy

Fry a ham slice, weighing about a pound, uncovered over low heat until browned on both sides, about 20 minutes in all. Makes 2 servings.

Cream Gravy: Remove ham in either of the above recipes and add ½ cup milk to skillet. Cook, stirring to scrape up browned particles, and when hot, pour over ham. Flour-thicken pan liquid, if desired, or boil uncovered until it thickens. Makes 2 servings.

HOTPOTS

In the beginning—or at least as far back as research seems to reach—there was a Germanic word for shake, which, in Medieval French became *hocier*. The Middle Ages made it *hocher*. Eventually, the "r" was dropped and a "pot" picked up. This—*hotchpot*—was turned into the onomatopoetic hotchpotch, but finally beaten out by hodge-podge—a quiver of dissimilar ingredients. It is my linguistic whim to call the following composition—which is not shaken at all—hotpot.

Ham Hotpot

If you like, substitute double pork chops for ham, choosing loin for meatiness; shoulder, for economy.

- 1 **center slice ham, cut about 1 inch thick**
- 2 **medium potatoes, peeled and sliced thin**
- 1 **medium onion, sliced thin**
- 2 **tablespoons flour, approximately**
- ½ **cup milk, approximately**

Place ham in casserole or skillet, and top with alternate layers of potato and onion, ending with potatoes. Season each layer with salt and pepper and sprinkle lightly with flour. Pour in enough milk to be just visible. Cover and bake in preheated moderate 350° F. oven until potatoes are tender, about 45 minutes. Uncover the last 15 minutes, if desired, to brown top layer of potatoes. Makes 2 servings.

Yam Hotpot

Call it smothered Ham and Yams a la Mississippi and simplify the procedure with frozen candied sweet potatoes.

Place a ½-inch thick ham slice in buttered baking dish. Thaw a package (12-ounce) of frozen sweet potatoes enough to separate slices. Arrange in layers over ham, dotting with butter and sprinkling with brown sugar. Cover and bake in preheated moderate 350° F. oven 25 minutes. Uncover, sprinkle top with additional brown sugar, and continue baking until potatoes are tender, about 20 minutes longer. Makes 2 servings.

Cottage Dinner

Italy's *bollito misto* (boiled mixture), Ireland's corned beef and cabbage, and the South's pork butt and collards are sisters under the skin. All begin gloriously—and end economically, because after the feast, the liquid provides the base for simmering dried vegetables or the makings for a dried vegetable soup.

The pork can be fresh shoulder or boneless smoked ham butt—which Georgians call smoked tenderloin. In my old Ohio home, it was known as cottage ham, hence the Damn Yankee title for an international meal in a pot.

Change any of the vegetables at will. If collards are to your liking, substitute them for beans. They will cook in about an hour. To substitute dried vegetables for fresh, see Cassoulet of Blackeye Peas*.

    3–4 pounds meat: fresh pork shoulder or smoked ham butt
    6 medium potatoes, quartered
    4 medium turnips, quartered
    1 medium cabbage, cut in eighths
    1 pound green beans, ends removed

Place meat on rack in large pot. Almost cover with cold water brought to a boil. Cover pot, and simmer until meat is tender, about 2 hours, turning halfway through cooking. Remove meat to large platter to keep warm.

Bring cooking liquid to boil, add potatoes, and boil 15 minutes.

Add turnips and boil 5 minutes. Add cabbage and beans, and boil 10 minutes, or until all vegetables are tender. Surround the meat with the vegetables. Makes 6-plus servings.

HOPPIN' JOHN

Although Damn Yankees may never have prepared Hoppin' John (a pity), most are familiar with the fact that it is traditionally served for luck on New Year's day. In her Holiday Cook Book (Little, Brown), Helen Evans Brown writes that tradition instructs diners to perform a one-foot hop around the table before their first mouthful. A two-mile walk after indulging in this lusty casserole would seem more to the point.

According to the *New York Times,* the recipe originated with the spouse of a crippled slave. The time—the 1800s. The place—Charleston, South Carolina. And the title comes from himself—Hoppin' John.

Actually, it is a *cassoulet,* an invariable sustainer in countries short on meat, long on dried vegetables. According to "Gourmet Magazine," the recipe originally was prepared by Languedoc folk from the village of Issel in an earthenware *cassolle*. Hence, *cassole d'Issel*. Time, they aver, transformed the word to cassoulet. However, my guess is that the word cassoulet corrupts casserole—from the Greek *kauthion*—a diminutive of the word for cup.

A Southern cassoulet is put together with the regional plenty—blackeye peas, rice, and pork. However, Georgia cooks substitute potatoes for rice.

The nutritional value is high, and sliced tomatoes, usually suggested as accompaniment, add food value to the menu. Drench them with vinegar to cut the cassoulet's richness.

Hoppin' John can be prepared ahead and gets better with every reheating.

Georgia Hoppin' John

- 1 pound (about 2 cups) dried blackeye peas
- 1 large onion, diced
- ¼ teaspoon hot red pepper
- 5 cups water
- ¼ cup dry wine, white or red, optional
- 1½ pounds smoked boneless pork shoulder butt
- 4 medium potatoes, peeled and quartered

Pick over peas, discarding any that are soft. Place in large saucepan with all ingredients except pork and potatoes, and bring to boil. Add pork, cover pan, bring liquid to boil rapidly, lower heat, and simmer about 2 hours, or until peas are cooked, and pork is tender, adding more water, if needed to prevent scorching.

Add potatoes (and additional water if necessary), the last half hour of cooking. Refrigerate overnight, if desired, for easy removal of top layer of fat.

To serve, fill casserole with peas and potatoes, top with sliced meat, and heat. Makes 6 servings.

Carolina Hoppin' John

Substitute 1½ cups rice for potatoes in Georgia Hoppin' John, above. It takes experience to add the rice at the exact moment and, if necessary, the judicious amount of liquid for cooking it. To let discretion be the better part of valor, cook the rice separately and combine before serving.

Hoppin' John With Hog Head

Have a 2-pound smoked hog head split into 5 pieces as substitute for pork butt in either of the above. Or substitute fresh hog head.

BEEF

Southern recipes for beef wear names familiar in similarity to the countries from which they came. Beef collops relates to the German *klops* (split), the French *escalope,* the Italian *scaloppini* (chisel). Virginia housewives referred to a stew as a *fricando* from the French *fricandeau.* The "olaves" of Elizabethan England, became Beef Olives, and, in one of the oldest Southern cook books I was privileged to examine, Spain's *Ropa Vieja* was listed with title and spelling intact.

In a tangle of cooking terminology, however, in Creole country, broiled steaks were called "Roasted Beefsteaks," and cooks were advised to be sure to have a clear fire of coals and to catch the blood as the steak was turned. The "caught" blood made the gravy. Possibly ladies in other regions were not clever enough to catch the blood for they were directed to serve a gravy of tomato sauce or catsup.

Beef was roasted in a stove, and for these new contraptions, firm, clear directions were imperative. The recipe titled, "To Roast Beef in a Stove," comes from *La Cuisine Creole,* and begins, "A fine roasting piece of beef may, if properly managed, be baked in a stove so as to resemble beef roasted before a large, open fire." The trick was accomplished by assiduous basting with water.

Beef went into steamed puddings and pies, while, as in England, spiced top rounds made a Christmas-table *piece de resistance*. Leftover beef was treated with the usual frugal respect—North Carolina hashed it with leftover mashed potatoes, to shape into cakes for frying. Mississippi combined bits of cooked beef with stewed tomatoes to top with leftover baking powder biscuits before heating.

Beef shoulder was a standby to offer guests from distant plantations. Because their journey was so long and arduous, they were expected to visit for several days. Undoubtedly those who overstayed their welcome were made aware of their lapse of politesse by repeated servings of cold shoulder.

Fillet With Wine Merchant Sauce
Chateaubriand with Marchand De Vin Sauce

Compared to the French, the English words for this specialty that was carried to New Orleans seem stodgily anticlimactic. By any title, the recipe is well worth what some cooks might construe as trouble and others as an opportunity to grace their tables with one of the great classic dishes of the world. Even if you omit the wine sauce, turn the fillet in what is actually Maitre d'hotel Butter, adding to it—as good New Orleans cooks do—chopped shallots, either raw, or simmered briefly in the butter. Slices from the following provide 2 to 3 servings and the recipe may be increased to serve a circle of honored guests.

Fillet

> 1 double fillet steak, weighing about 1 pound
> Marrow from a 4-inch beef bone, cracked
> Quick-browning aid, optional

Have butcher cut a piece of steak from heavy end of fillet, at least 3 inches thick. Dice marrow fine (easy to do when frozen). Cut a pocket in steak, brush with quick-browning aid, and stuff with part of marrow. Brush outside of fillet with quick-browning aid and sprinkle lightly with marrow. Place on broiler and, using medium flame, broil until browned. Turn, sprinkle with additional marrow, and broil to desired doneness.

Butter Sauce

- 1½ tablespoons butter, melted
- 1 teaspoon lemon juice
- 2 tablespoons parsley, chopped fine

Combine ingredients and pour on platter. Place steak on platter and carve ½-inch thick slices. Spoon some butter sauce over slices.

Wine Merchant Sauce

- ½ cup dry red wine
- ¾ tablespoon marrow
- ¾ tablespoon flour
- ½ cup beef stock

Boil wine uncovered until reduced to ¼ cup. Add marrow and stock, and flour thicken as for Gravy*. Season to taste, and pass in gravy boat.

POT ROASTS

Proust devoted many loving words to *Boeuf à la Mode,* a dish as at home on elegant buffets as on farm tables. Southerners of French extraction *daube* or *dobe* the meat, although their ancestors correctly called this classic *Boeuf à la Mode en Gelée* and it came to table encased in a dark jelly, thick with mushrooms. The *Williamsburg Art of Cookery* refers to a pot roast straightforwardly as a Buttock of Beef, but suggests that it be served "Glacée, For Cold Suppers."

In any language or country, the bottom round produces the best looking slices. The beef may, as many recipes suggest, be gashed to stuff with suet, chopped onions, and spices, or larded with thin strips of salt pork that have been rolled in herbs and spices. But the superb meat available today, needs only barding. Let the butcher oblige, and, if he doesn't know the term, just tell him to tie thin strips of fat—beef or salt pork—on top of the meat.

It certainly is fit to eat cold, as the "accomplished gentlewoman" was advised in the *Williamsburg Art of Cookery*. But, unless bones are added, the sauce will not jell. Maryland cooks added lean veal and pig's feet with the beef, but a veal knuckle may be used instead. If desired, after cooking, the veal may be removed from the bone, minced, and added to the strained stock.

Boeuf a la Mode

- **5 pounds beef, preferably bottom round**
- **Quick-browning aid, optional**
- **1 unpeeled onion, cut in chunks**
- **½ teaspoon peppercorns**
- **6 whole cloves**
- **1 large unpeeled clove garlic, crushed**
- **1 teaspoon whole allspice**
- **1 veal knuckle**
- **¼ cup cognac**
- **2 cups dry red wine, approximately**

Have butcher tie and bard bottom round of beef. Brush with quick-browning aid. Arrange onion and spices on bottom of heavy pot. Add veal knuckle and top with beef, fat side up. Add cognac, and just enough wine to reach a depth of 4 inches.

Cover pot, bring liquid to boil rapidly, reduce flame, and simmer gently until beef is tender, about 3 hours, turning halfway through cooking. Strain liquid and pour over beef and veal knuckle to refrigerate overnight. Next day, remove barding fat, slice beef, and arrange slices in attractive casserole. Thicken liquid, if desired, as for gravy, season to taste, and pour over sliced beef. Serve hot or chilled in the jellied gravy. Makes 10-plus servings. May be frozen.

Note:
A pair of calves' feet, or 4 pigs' feet may be substituted for veal knuckle.

Belle Chasse Pot Roast

    2 tablespoons lard
    3 tablespoons flour
    ¾ cup beef stock, approximately
    ¼ cup red wine, optional
    1 onion, diced
    1 teaspoon thyme
    ½ teaspoon marjoram
    Dash hot red pepper flakes
    3–4 pound bottom round of beef, barded
    Quick-browning aid, optional

Prepare a brown roux* with lard and flour. Stir in beef stock and wine, and when smooth, add vegetables and seasonings. Brush meat with quick-browning aid and place on vegetables, fat side up. Continue as for Boeuf a la Mode*, above. Makes 6-plus servings.

POKOMOKE CIDER POT ROAST

The spice-enlivened cider in this exceptional Maryland recipe gives the beef slight sweetness and slight acidity, making it similar to Germany's *sauerbraten* but more delicate in flavor.

    1 clove garlic, minced
    1 teaspoon salt
    ½ teaspoon peppercorns
    1 teaspoon whole allspice
    2 onions, diced
    1 1-inch stick cinnamon
    1 tablespoon chopped parsley
    3 pounds bottom round of beef
    Quick-browning aid, optional
    2 cups cider

Crush garlic with salt in mortar and pestle. Add peppercorns and allspice and crush. Place onions, cinnamon stick, parsley and spice mixture in heavy pot. Brush beef with quick-browning aid and place in pot, fat side up. Add cider, cover and bring liquid to boil rapidly. Lower heat and simmer until tender, about 4 hours, turning halfway through cooking. Continue as for Boeuf a la Mode. Makes 6-plus servings.

VALCOUR AIME BEEF WITH MUSHROOMS
Boeuf Au Sec

Similar to pot roast in preparation, the virtue of this recipe is the fact that the end result is an already-thickened, and richly delectable gravy. For attractive service and ease, prepare a pie shell with slices of Cheese Pudding* baked in a square pan. Simply line bottom and sides of casserole and fill with beef and gravy.

- 2 tablespoons lard
- 1 teaspoon paprika
- 1 large onion, sliced thin
- 1 pound top round steak, cut in 1-inch cubes
- Quick-browning aid, optional
- ½ cup flour, approximately
- 1 cup dry red wine
- ¾ pound fresh mushrooms, sliced or 1 can (⅛ pound) freeze-dried mushrooms

Melt lard in pan, preferably heavy. Add paprika and cook onion until softened, about 10 minutes. Toss meat with quick-browning aid, then with flour. Add to onion, preferably in single layer. Add wine, cover pan, bring liquid to boil rapidly, lower heat and simmer until tender, about 1 hour. Remove cover, add mushrooms, increase heat, and cook until liquid is very thick and meat almost dry. Makes 4 servings.

BEEF BRISKETS

All my years I heard only one market command concerning brisket: Buy it boneless, and be sure it is not first-cut.

It never occurred to me to ask why, until Ann, my Southern assistant brought brisket from her Harlem market for testing this recipe—a thick piece of meat with bone. Questioning a butcher revealed that boneless brisket is boned shoulder, and the reason for avoiding the first cut is that it is excessively fat.

The Southern-style, cut with bone, comes from the center of the brisket, and is perfect for small families.

BRISKET IN BARBECUE SAUCE

Dice 1 onion and add to Barbecue Sauce*. Pour over a piece of brisket with bone, cut 2 inches thick and weighing about 2½ pounds. Bake covered, in preheated, moderate 350° F. oven until tender, about 2 hours. Makes 2-3 servings.

BRISKET RAGOUT

Of course Louisiana calls a stew a ragout, and cooks brisket in a madrilene combination of beef stock and spicy tomato sauce. As with any stew, it tastes better as time goes by.

- 2 pounds beef brisket, cut into 1-inch chunks
- Quick-browning aid, optional
- 1 onion, diced
- 1 clove garlic, diced
- ½ pound mushrooms, sliced
- ½ cup beef stock
- ½ cup Barbecue Sauce*

Remove as much fat as possible from meat and brush with quick-browning aid. Place onion, garlic, and mushrooms in heavy pot. Top with meat and add stock and Sauce. Cover pot, bring liquid to boil rapidly, reduce heat and simmer until beef is tender, about 2½ hours. Or bake covered, in preheated, slow 300° F. oven about 3 hours. Skim off as much fat as possible, thicken pan liquid, if desired, as for gravy, and season to taste. Makes 4 servings. Note: ½ cup freeze-dried mushrooms may be substituted. Add them after fat has been removed from gravy.

BARNWELL BARBECUED BRISKET

Unless, like the South, you are richly possessed of freshly-hewed hickory wood, you can not achieve the real thing. But you can emulate by putting the correct cut of meat on your grill.

Cook until done a whole, boned brisket, weighing about 6 pounds, as for Brisket in Barbecue Sauce*. Brush with additional Barbecue Sauce and place on outdoor grill. Brown, brush again, and turn. Brush top, and grill until second side browns. Serve with additional Barbecue Sauce. Makes about 12 servings.

POMPEY'S HEAD

Pompey was one of ancient Rome's great generals. How his "head" traveled to the South is a mystery, but it is prepared in various ways. One Georgia author mentions a Pompey's Head made of stuffed fillet of veal, and the recipe varies considerably from state to state. The following, from Georgia, intrigued me, but it was a long time before I willingly put that quantity of beef to the test. I wish I had been quicker, because Pompey's Head is a glory, hot or cold, and can highlight a buffet table.

An egg may be added for each pound of meat and sausage may be substituted for salt pork. For a Creole caprice, after searing, add to baking pan 2 cups drained canned tomatoes, 1 diced onion, and 1 diced green pepper.

Meat Mixture

>   3 pounds lean beef, ground
>   ¼ pound salt pork, chopped fine
>   2 tablespoons quick-browning aid, optional
>   3 onions, chopped fine
>   1 tablespoon dried sage
>   ¼ teaspoon hot red pepper
>   ½ cup water

Crust

>   **Flour**
>   6 tablespoons butter, melted

Knead ingredients for meat mixture lightly until they leave bowl clean, and season to taste. Shape into a ball and brush with additional quick-browning aid. Roll ball in flour and make a 1-inch circular hole halfway through center. Bake in greased, shallow pan in preheated, extremely hot 500° F. oven 10 minutes. Drizzle with melted butter, adding a bit to hole, and reduce heat to slow 300° F. After 10 minutes, dredge with flour again and continue baking until browned and crusty, at least an additional hour, basting with melted butter about every 15 minutes. Make gravy, if desired, using pan drippings. Makes at least 10 slices.

BEEF DUMPLINGS

The soft Southern words Beef Dumplings certainly sound more enticing than meat balls. And the seasoning in these smacks of Southern savor. The soaked bread extender is typical with all waste-not-want-not cooks, and it takes good bread to make good dumplings.

Change the seasonings to suit your palate, omit pork, if desired; and, if company's coming, add sliced mushrooms to the stock.

Meat Mixture

- ½ cup stale bread, crumbled
- ¼ cup milk, approximately
- 1 tablespoon minced parsley
- ½ teaspoon dried thyme
- ¼ teaspoon mace
- Dash cayenne pepper
- ½ pound ground beef
- ¼ pound lean pork, ground
- 1 egg
- Quick-browning aid, optional
- 2 cups beef stock
- ¼ cup flour

In large bowl soak bread and herbs in enough milk to cover, about 20 minutes. Combine with all except last three ingredients and knead lightly until mixture holds together.

Season and shape into balls about 2 inches in diameter. Roll in quick-browning aid.

In large pot, bring stock to boil, reduce to simmer, and add dumplings. Cover pot, reduce flame, and cook gently about 15 minutes, turning halfway through cooking. Remove with slotted spoon and thicken liquid with flour. Season to taste and add dumplings. For easy removal of fat, preferably refrigerate overnight. Makes 20 dumplings; 4 servings.

VEAL

Veal is treated with deserved deference in Italy and France, and lack of grazing space accounts for the fact that their veal is just that—infant beef—white as a pearl. Here, this pearl of great price, worth every penny, is called *plume de veau* and unfortunately, is available only in large cities with a cosmopolitan population.

Whether superb or not, veal is immature and, therefore, contains little flavor or fat. Southerners offer it rich companionship with pork, ham, butter, olive oil, and cream; pique it delicately with wine and lemon juice; and are wise to Mediterranean ways of endowing veal with charming accents—shallots, mushrooms, tomato. And any Southerner worth his salt would not hesitate to substitute venison in veal recipes.

Veal hash, topped with poached eggs, appears at breakfast. Veal is creamed or made into loaves and chopped hard-cooked eggs find their way into veal pies and patties. Another Southern star is boned veal shoulder stuffed with cornmeal dressing before roasting.

Pressed Veal
Daube Glacé de Veau

Shimmery cold entrees are welcome in Damn Yankee heat, too. How nice if the herbs are fresh from your garden. The daube is perfect for a company buffet. Save the pigs' feet and veal knuckle for a fine family dinner.

Of course, this can be served hot. Then, if you enjoy sculpting, cut potatoes and carrots like olives and add them to finish cooking at the same time as the meat and serve with butter-browned onions.

Veal Preparation

    3 pounds veal round, barded
    Quick-browning aid, optional
    4 pigs' feet
    2 veal knuckles
    2 onions, cut coarsely
    3 stalks celery with leaves, diced
    1 teaspoon dried rosemary
    1 teaspoon dried thyme
    4 sprigs parsley
    1 teaspoon crumbled bay leaf
    ½ teaspoon peppercorns
    ½ cup dry white wine, optional

Prepare as for Boeuf a la Mode*, but do not thicken liquid.

Garnishing Vegetables

    4 medium carrots
    1 large green pepper, diced
    1 tablespoon chopped parsley

Peel carrots, slice thin rounds and boil until just tender.

Serving the Daube

Oil an oblong mold and pour in enough stock from veal to coat bottom. Chill until set, dip garnishing vegetables in the stock, and arrange attractively on the jellied layer. Chill again until firm. Trim veal, if necessary, for appearance, and place on vegetables.

Combine remaining vegetables with remaining stock and pour over veal. Cover with plastic wrap, and place a weight on veal so liquid will cover it. Refrigerate until firm, 2 hours or overnight. Unmold, slice at table, and serve with mayonnaise into which chopped parsley and sliced scallions have been folded. Makes 8-plus servings. May be frozen.

Veal with Olives
Veal Olaves

Oiseaux sans Tetes (birds without heads) acquired a head in American terminology. Possibly in Henry the VIII revulsion, Elizabethan England sought dainty finger food—forks had not yet been devised— and came up with Veal Olaves.

Veal flank or shoulder sliced ¼-inch thick makes the most economical purchase; supermarket veal cut for scaloppini may be substituted. And the whole piece of veal may be stuffed and rolled.

Add olives to veal olaves (or birds), as this New Orleans version does, to dress it up for a party, or substitute cooked chestnuts for the olives.

One lemon yields about 2 tablespoons juice. One can (8-ounce) olives yields about 16.

Meat

    1 pound veal
    Quick-browning aid, optional
    ½ cup chicken or beef stock, approximately
    Flour, optional
    24 pitted ripe olives, cut in ¼-inch wedges

Have butcher cut a slice of veal ¼ inch thick, and pound it thin. Cut 4-inch squares and dice scraps to add to stuffing. Brush veal with quick-browning aid.

Stuffing

> ¼ pound cooked ham, diced fine
> 1 hard-cooked egg, chopped
> ¼ cup minced parsley
> 1½ teaspoons dried thyme
> Juice of 1 lemon
> ½ cup fine dry bread crumbs
> 2 tablespoons butter, melted
> 1½ tablespoons instant minced onion
> Dash cayenne pepper

Combine all ingredients, reserving half the parsley for garnish. Season to taste. Spread stuffing on veal, roll into packages, and tie with kitchen twine. Place in skillet in single layer, with enough stock to reach a depth of ½ inch. Cover, bring liquid to boil rapidly, and simmer until veal is tender, about 1 hour.

Remove veal, discard twine, and thicken pan liquid, if desired, as for gravy. Return veal to pan with olives and season to taste, adding lemon juice, if needed for piquancy. Garnish with reserved parsley. Makes 4 servings; about 8 birds.

LAMB

In the beginning, Southern ways with lamb were few—even as today—because food traditions begin with "things that mother used to make." And, when confronted with lamb (or more likely, mutton), mama put together some curious things.

Mutton shoulder was boiled in milk. "Fricandellons" of mutton—glorified hamburgers—gained some kind of glory by being served "dry on a serviette."

Carolina's mutton hash boasted anchovies, and a Maryland specialty was lamb, sweetbreads, and oysters, all baked in a pie. However, the laurel for ways with lamb, may belong to an old Virginia "Frica*f*y" which contained lamb, "Oy*f*ters, Balls, and Palates."

Lafayette Lamb Stew

Irish stew traveled to America via Ireland by way of France, and produced a grand tangle of recipe titles. The French treated lamb as they did veal, in a style called *blanquette*—from the word for white—containing white-colored vegetables in a white sauce. It included onions and potatoes. But when the meat was lamb, turnips were added and the recipe was called *navarin,* probably from *navet*—for turnip.

Another French lamb stew, *Haricot de Mouton,* which a French dictionary translates to Irish Stew, contained white kidney beans—*haricot,* which led to the Virginia title corruption *"To Harrico Mutton."*

The ladies were exhorted to pound chops from the rack, prepare gravy from the "inferior parts," season with any kind of catsup, and add cooked diced turnip and carrot, thereby, of course, achieving a *navarin,* rather than an *haricot.*

This way with it eliminates the need for a salad, a separate vegetable, and a starch. If lima beans are added, you won't need a cooked vegetable either. Add turnips and call it a *navarin* and realize that you will enjoy it along with your guests because of its days-ahead preparation.

Stock for Cooking Lamb

- 2 pounds lamb shoulder
- 3 medium unpeeled carrots, quartered
- 1 large unpeeled yellow onion, sliced
- 1 large clove garlic, crushed
- 4 sprigs parsley
- 2 stalks celery and leaves, diced coarsely
- ½ teaspoon peppercorns
- ½ teaspoon slivered lemon peel
- 3 whole cloves
- 1 teaspoon ginger
- ¼ cup dry wine, white or red, optional

Have butcher trim excess fat from lamb and chop meat and bone in 2-inch cubes. Arrange vegetables in bottom of large, heavy pan. Tie peppercorns, lemon peel, and cloves in cheesecloth. Place in pan and add ginger and wine. Top with lamb, preferably in a single layer.

Add enough boiling water to almost cover. Cover pan, bring liquid to boil rapidly, lower heat, and simmer until lamb is tender, about an hour. Strain stock, discard vegetables and spice bag, and pour over lamb.

Vegetables to Serve With Lamb

- 4 tablespoons butter
- 1 teaspoon sugar
- 1 pound peeled small white onions
- 1 can (1-pound 4-ounce) cannellini

1 package (10-ounce) Fordhook lima beans, optional
Flour
¼ pound raw spinach leaves, stemmed

Melt butter in saucepan, and add sugar and white onions. Cover and cook gently until tender, approximately 30 minutes. Add to lamb and refrigerate overnight. Skim and discard fat. Measure liquid and thicken, using ¼ cup flour for each cup. Add lamb and beans and heat.

On deep platter, make a bed of spinach leaves. Spoon lamb and vegetable mixture on, leaving a scalloped edge of spinach as frame. Pour sauce over, and sprinkle with paprika. Makes 4 servings. Keeps at least five days in refrigerator; may be frozen.

Crusted Lamb Chops
English Lamb Collops

Supposedly, bread crumbs to coat meat originated in the fourth century, when, as the result of a famine in Milan, St. Ambrose, the city's bishop, proposed that crumbs be used to extend veal. (It is Marie Antoinette-engaging to think of a glut of veal; a dearth of bread.) However, the French refer to breaded meat as à l'Anglaise. By whom, where, or whenever devised, a crumb crust also seals in juices and adds crunchy texture. Southern cooks saluted the advantages by breading loin lamb chops to serve with additional crunch—fried parsley.

After trimming, the chops resemble hearts and would make a coyly charming St. Valentine's Day dish. Add the trimmed tail meat to a lamb stew for less romantic dining.

4 loin lamb chops, cut 1-inch thick
Quick-browning aid, optional
2 egg yolks
½ teaspoon dry red wine
¼ teaspoon dried parsley
⅛ teaspoon dried thyme
⅛ teaspoon dried marjoram
⅛ teaspoon dried savory
¼ teaspoon salt

Dash cayenne pepper
¼ teaspoon grated lemon peel
3 tablespoons fine dry bread crumbs
2 tablespoons butter

Trim exterior fat from chops and cut off tail meat and outside rim of fat. Dip chops in quick-browning aid. Beat egg yolks with wine and 1 teaspoon water. Add herbs, seasonings, and lemon peel.

Coat chops by dipping in crumbs, then egg mixture, then crumbs. Continue dipping until egg mixture is used and allow coating to dry —it will take about 20 minutes. Heat butter in skillet and brown both sides of chops. Cover, reduce heat, and cook to desired doneness, allowing about 10 minutes in all for pink-centered chops. Makes 4 servings and may be frozen.

Belle Grove Lamb Scallops
Escalopes de Mouton

This is my chafing-dish adaptation of an old Creole recipe. Cook as many scallops at a time as will fill blazer without crowding. A skillet may be substituted and black olives, preferably Nice, may be substituted for truffles. (Unfortunately, canned black truffles have little, if any, flavor.)

If using fresh mushrooms (you will need about a dozen), toss briefly in the butter until just cooked, about 2 minutes, but realize that freeze-dried mushrooms are preferable, because chafing-dish preparation should be speedy. The scallops may be flamed with Cognac just before serving.

12 lamb scallops
Quick-browning aid, optional
1 cup freeze-dried mushroom slices
4 tablespoons butter, approximately
1 teaspoon white truffles, diced very fine, approximately
3 tablespoons medium dry Sherry, approximately

Have butcher bone a loin of lamb, remove outer layer of fat, and slice meat into ½-inch thick scallops—*noisettes*—to the French. Brush surfaces with quick-browning aid. Soak mushroom slices in enough water to rehydrate and drain thoroughly. Heat enough butter to cover bottom of blazer and, when it bubbles, add truffles, and fry scallops, turning to brown both sides.

Add mushrooms, and enough Sherry to reach a depth of ¼ inch in blazer, and cook until lamb is done, about 5 minutes in all for medium. Remove to warmed plate, reduce pan liquid until syrupy, season to taste, and spoon over lamb. Makes 4 servings.

SUNDRIES

A sneer is the expression Yankees usually reserve for sundries—a word that Webster defines as: "Miscellaneous articles, details, or items of inconsiderable size or amount." But Northerners and Southerners, especially of French or Oriental background, admire these sophisticated details.

The French word—*bouillir* (to boil), was metamorphosed into the recipe title Bouilli*, indicating beef boiled to make soup and following beef butchering, canny New Orleans cooks prepare a gallantly-seasoned bouilli of the sundries—the kidney, heart, and lungs. In Mississippi it is known as Dobe, while in other areas the spicy melange is more forth-rightly called Cow Gumbo.

Tripe (the lining of the cow's stomach), and chitterlings (the casing of the pigs' intestine) also are favorite Southern sundries.

There is nothing complicated about cooking any of the sundries. Those that are tough are prepared by braising or poaching; the tender by dry heat methods—roasting, frying, or broiling. Herbs, spices, and vegetables provide the variations.

Pepper Stock

Hot red pepper for character and authority, the acid of vinegar to tenderize and cut richness, are unvarying Southern ingredients for water-cooking tough food. Garlic, bay leaf, and cloves—all optional additionals—add savor, and if you, too, like things hot, don't go easy on the pepper. The following proportion is for about a pound of boneless meat, such as tripe. Increase at will for larger amounts and preferably refrigerate overnight for full development of flavor and easy removal of fat.

1 large unpeeled onion, cut coarsely
¼ teaspoon hot red pepper
⅛ teaspoon instant garlic
1 bay leaf
¼ cup sharp vinegar
2 whole cloves
1 teaspoon salt
1 quart cold water

Place all ingredients in pot, cover, bring liquid to boil rapidly, and add meat. Simmer until meat is tender, about 3 hours.

Chitterlings
Chitt'lins

We are led to believe that "soul food" was hands-off feasting for Southern swells. Not so. Although high-on-the-hog cuts *may* have been restricted to their tables, everyone feasted low on the hog. As well they might, because all parts of the pig are perfectly delicious.

Chitt'lins is the Southern colloquialism for the small intestine of the pig. When I asked what they were commonly served with, meaning sauce or the like, my authority answered firmly: "Potato salad, collards, and beer." Try hot pepper sauce and pickles, too—or serve them as one restaurant in Harlem reputedly does—in a burst of reverse snobbery—with Champagne. The day I prepared them under a watchful "soul" eye, they were companioned with hush-puppies.

"Clean," the usual recipe direction for preparing chitt'lins is a misnomer, so don't let the word put you off. They *are* clean, in the regular sense, and usually to be found in supermarket freezers in five- or ten-pound packages.

"Cleaning" refers to removing the clinging fat, of which there is an inordinate amount, and so doing requires an inordinate amount of time. Simply pull ("pick") off as much fat as possible—fingers are the best tool—and soak in cold water to thaw. Turn inside out to pick and cook. Simmer in Pepper Stock* until tender, about 2½ hours. If picking is not for you, pull a package of already cooked chitt'lins with sauce from the grocer's freezer and expect to pay dearly for the trouble you've saved.

South Carolinians call cooked chitt'lins, cut into short lengths, Tom Thumbs, and treat them to an egg-cornmeal coating. As a preliminary, the chitt'lins may be peppered violently, before crisp-browning in deep fat. As an alternate, coat them in the batter for Feather Fritters*.

TRIPE

Most Southerners of French or German ancestry admire tripe. It is the inner lining of a pig's or calf's stomach. Honeycomb tripe, from the second stomach, is more delicate than plain tripe. Often, pigs' feet or calves' feet went into the pot along with the tripe. Today, tripe can be purchased partially cooked, or canned. A pickled-tripe fancier *may* settle for the store-bought variety.

One pound tripe makes about 1½ cups.

Pickled Tripe

No one has ever saluted tripe for handsome appearance, but as any fashionable Southern belle will tell you, just as beauty comes before comfort, so, in food, flavor comes before beauty.

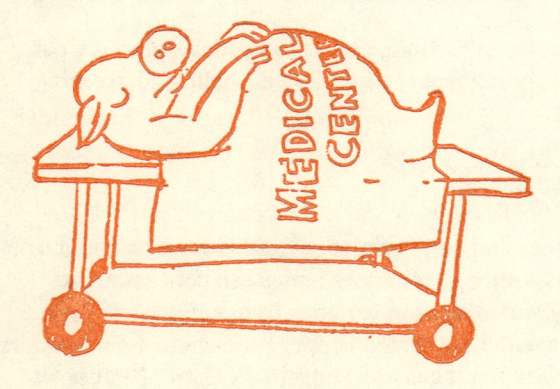

Masking tripe in a sauce solves the beauty problem, but pickled tripe stands alone. If its lack of aestheticism troubles you, serve on small plates, as a first course or as an hors d'oeuvre, and realize that it also can star on a smorgasbord.

    1 cup cooked tripe
    1 small onion, diced

    3 tablespoons sharp vinegar
    2 tablespoons water
    2 teaspoons sugar
    2 whole cloves
    1/16 teaspoon hot red pepper

Cook tripe in Pepper Stock* and cut into narrow ¾-inch long strips. Combine with remaining ingredients, season to taste, allow to marinate at least 2 hours, and serve at room temperature. Keeps at least a week in refrigerator, and may be frozen.

Tripe Fritters

Superb as hors d'oeuvre—or for pampering people at lunch—and either way, delicious served with French Market Sauce*.

Cook tripe in Pepper Stock*, drain, and cut 1½-inch squares. Drain, dip in batter for Feather Fritters*, and fry in deep fat, preferably lard.

Crumb-Fried Tripe

Breakfast, lunch, or supper tables can hold plates of this delectable.

Cook tripe in Pepper Stock*, drain, and cut 1½-inch squares. Coat with cornmeal, flour, or cracker crumbs. Fry in shallow fat, turning to brown both sides.

Quick Tripe Creole

Fresh garden tomatoes and bell peppers make this superb—and a seasonal dependent. Although tomatoes and green peppers are a market staple today, out-of-season varieties frequently are joyless. Preparing this sauce with dehydrated peppers and canned purée offers convenience and speed and takes less budget toll. Lard or salt pork substituted for ham and its fat add up to economy.

    1 pound cooked tripe
    2 tablespoons ham, diced fine
    2 tablespoons ham fat, diced fine
    2 teaspoons instant minced onion
    2 tablespoons dehydrated bell peppers

¾ cup tomato purée
   1 cup Pepper Stock*
   1 teaspoon salt
   ¹⁄₁₆ teaspoon cayenne pepper

Cut tripe cooked in Pepper Stock* in 1-inch pieces. Cook ham and fat in covered skillet over low heat until most of fat melts. Add remaining ingredients and simmer covered 25 minutes. If sauce is too thin, uncover skillet, increase heat, and reduce to desired consistency. Add tripe, season to taste and serve hot, over rice. Makes 4 servings.

Afton Villa Brains

As with liver, sophisticated Southerners dress this epicurean treat to their fancy. If you know your guests' tastes, serve it with French bread as a luncheon entree, add it to a buffet table, or make it an hors d'oeuvre. It has the happy advantage of day-before preparation.

Court Bouillon

   1 lemon, sliced about ¼-inch thick
   ¹⁄₁₆ teaspoon cayenne pepper
   2 bay leaves
   1 tablespoon instant minced onion
   2 cups water

Meat

   1 pair calves' brains (approximately 1 pound)

Day Before: Place court bouillon ingredients in saucepan, and boil covered to extract flavor about 20 minutes. Rinse brains with cold water, reduce court bouillon to a simmer and add brains. Cover pan and cook gently until brains are just done (they will feel firm when tapped lightly in thickest portion), about 15 minutes, turning if necessary for even cooking. Drain and refrigerate.

Next Day: Prepare dressing by combining ¼ cup chopped onion, ¼ cup minced parsley, 3 tablespoons olive oil, 3 tablespoons wine vinegar, and ⅛ teaspoon cayenne pepper. Season, adjusting oil and vinegar to taste, but keep it on the sharp side.

Before Serving: Cut chilled brains into thin slices and toss gently with dressing. Cover a round chop plate with stemmed spinach leaves. Mound brains in center and garnish with parsley sprigs and capers.

Arrange around brains any of the following: Black olives; pimento strips; green pepper strips; sour pickles; artichoke hearts; wedges of hard-cooked egg, tomato, fennel; marinated mushrooms. Makes 6-plus servings.

Accompaniments   Cruets of oil and wine vinegar; bread—French, Greek, Armenian, or Italian whole wheat.

HEART

Braising beef or calf heart (sometimes after stuffing), or poaching, are the usual Damn Yankee recommendations for preparing this often-overlooked entree. Southerners, however, adopting Spanish ways, roast, broil, or fry heart, producing a superb menu addition that, by virtue of its flavorful fat, is delicious as steak. Cod fat is the butcher's name for the fat surrounding beef heart. They respect its flavor as second best to the fat surrounding veal kidneys. Leaf lard, the most choice, comes from the fat surrounding pig heart.

Beefsteak Montfort

The word beefsteak in this recipe is the same fancy-footwork titling evidenced in Chicken Terrapin*. But with more reason. Because thin-cut slices have the texture of, and taste like, steak.

   1 beef heart, weighing about 4 pounds
   2 large onions, sliced thin

Marinade

   3 tablespoons quick-browning aid, optional
   3 tablespoons butter, melted
   6 tablespoons dry red wine
   ¼ teaspoon cloves

1 teaspoon crumbled bay leaf
1 teaspoon dried thyme
½ teaspoon black pepper

Unless butcher has done so, split heart from side to side without separating halves. Rinse off any large blood clots. Combine marinade ingredients and season to taste. Marinate heart about two hours or overnight, turning occasionally, and spooning marinade mixture into the split area. Drain heart and enclose some onion slices in the split area and toothpick remainder in a single layer to top of heart. Roast uncovered on rack in pan with shallow sides in moderate 350° F. oven, allowing about 25 minutes a pound for rare. Carve upper half of heart first (slice down as for poultry breast). Makes 10-plus servings and may be frozen.

Beefsteak Grits

Simmer marinade drained from heart until thickened. Add liquid from roasting pan and stir into hot cooked grits.

Plaquemine Parish Liver

I was an "I *hate* liver" type until I tested this à la Creole version. A hefty piece of liver, rather than thin slices; and baking, rather than frying make it special.

1½ tablespoons quick-browning aid, optional
2 tablespoons butter, preferably clarified, melted
3 tablespoons dry red wine
⅛ teaspoon cloves
½ teaspoon crumbled bay leaf
½ teaspoon dried thyme
Black pepper
1 pound calves' liver, cut in one thick piece
2 strips bacon

Combine all ingredients except liver and bacon in heavy baking pan. Turn liver in mixture to coat. Cut bacon strips to fit top of liver and coat them with mixture. Arrange bacon on liver, and bake in preheated, hot 400° F. oven, until done (preferably pink-centered), about 20 minutes. Slice, and coat both sides of slices with pan drippings. Makes 2-3 servings. May be frozen.

Burnt Ordinary Oxtail Stew

Damn Yankees usually do oxtail soup; the Southern version provides a rich, flavorful entree feast—especially for those who love to pick bones. Diced turnip, tomatoes, sliced leek, or powdered cloves are optional additions or variants to suit your cupboard and taste. And better prepare it yourself, rather than trying to find the old tavern called the Burnt Ordinary.

- 1 onion, sliced
- 1 carrot, diced
- 3 ribs celery and leaves, diced
- ⅛ teaspoon cayenne pepper
- 1 teaspoon allspice
- ¼ teaspoon mace
- 1 oxtail (about 2 pounds) cut in joints
- Flour
- 1 can (10½-ounce) beef broth
- ¼ teaspoon Worcestershire sauce

Place vegetables and spices in large pot, preferably heavy. Dredge oxtail with flour. Arrange on top of vegetables. Bring undiluted beef broth to boil and add to pot. Cover and simmer about 2 hours, or until meat is tender. Preferably, refrigerate overnight for easy removal of fat and to blend flavors. Add Worcestershire, season to taste, and thicken pan liquid, if desired, as for gravy. Makes 2–3 servings.

A STRUT OF POULTRY

Fried chicken and the South are as irrevocably wedded as ham and eggs. But it is only one of the savories in their superb roster of poultry recipes. Choose plump brown roasts with savory stuffings, velvety-tender "smothers," redolently-spiced Creole dishes, and cocottes with French airs, to add sparkle to dinner parties—or provide uncommon delectability on a family table.

CHICKENS IN THE POT

Old, tough, and flavorful are the words for a stewing chicken—sometimes called a fowl or old hen. In rural areas, these birds cavort in barnyards until time to be captured, and slowly simmered to tenderness. Folk who grew up on them, rightly or not, sneer at today's market hens for lack of flavor. And to be at all plump and well-fatted, city-bought fowl require a good butcher. They should weigh about 5 pounds—and take kitchen time.

Because country chickens did not sit around and gain weight, Southern recipes call for pork (usually streak o' lean), to simmer along with them—wisdom also found in the cuisines of France, Spain, and the Orient. Pork shoulder, neck bones, and the like, or ham, may replace the salt pork.

Damn Yankees will probably prefer to prepare stews made with old hens a day ahead, so any fat can be removed—a step at which Southern cooks would sniff. However, although it adds distinctive flavor, no pork or ham need be added at all.

Today, the small all-purpose bird (broiler-fryer) which can be prepared by any cooking method has all but supplanted the stewing chicken. These young chickens can weigh up to 3½ pounds. To prepare them for stock or for Made Dishes*, proceed as for Chicken Stock*, but cook only about an hour.

Crisp-Poached Chicken

Various Southern recipes intelligently direct frying chicken parts that have been cooked for stock. The procedure is a real treat for admirers of crisp brown skin, and the frying fat should be rich—lard, bacon fat, or clarified butter. Place the drained chicken parts in a heavy pan, skin side up first, and turn to brown both sides.

The following poaching-broiling procedure for a young chicken offers the same double advantages—velvety-textured meat and crisp brown skin, but omits the fat providing time- and calorie-saving. After cooking, the liquid can make a first-course soup, a base for dumplings, or be thickened for gravy to spoon over hot biscuits.

>   Chicken stock*
>   1 young chicken, cut for fricassee
>   Quick-browning aid, optional

In wide skillet, bring to boil enough stock to reach a depth of about 3 inches. Add chicken pieces in a single layer and cover pan. Bring liquid to boil rapidly, lower heat, and simmer until almost done, about 40 minutes.

Drain chicken, brush surfaces with quick-browning aid, and broil at medium high 450° F., skin side down first, allowing about 10 minutes in all, turning to brown both sides. Makes 3–4 servings.

CHICKEN IN MADE DISHES

Either start from scratch, as directed in Chicken Cooked for Made Dishes*, or cannily turn leftover chicken (or turkey)—even roasted—into the following treats with which thrifty Southern cooks grace their tables. The skinned poultry looks best when pulled into large chunks, rather than minced. Chicken Stock makes the base for the sauces.

Chicken Pot Pie

Southern cooks often omit the bottom crust of a chicken pie—a good idea when calories count. Remove skin, and pull the cooked chicken from the bones in large pieces. Lay lavishly in a pie pan and add any desired cooked vegetables. Pour on almost to cover, a gravy composed of half chicken stock and half cream. Top with pie dough (cut an opening so steam can escape) and bake in preheated, hot 425° F. oven, about 12 minutes or until crust browns.

To substitute baking powder biscuits for pie dough, place filled pan in oven, and when gravy bubbles, top with the biscuits. Bake as above until biscuits are done.

Chicken Terrapin

This terrapin way to sauce cooked chicken, is reminiscent of the Chinese recipe "Shrimp with Lobster Sauce." The first contains no terrapin (turtle); lobster is non-existent in the second. Consider both recipes a saucy switch to equally compatible foods and if you like, terrapin a calf's head, too.

- 2 **cups cooked chicken**
- 2 **tablespoons butter**
- 1 **tablespoon flour**
- ¾ **cup cream**
- 2 **eggs, hard-cooked**
- ¼ **teaspoon mace**
- **Pinch cayenne pepper**
- 2 **tablespoons Sherry, approximately**

Pull chicken from bones in chunks and discard skin. Prepare Thickened Sauce* with next three ingredients. Mash hard-cooked egg yolks and blend sauce in gradually. When smooth, add remaining ingredients. Season to taste—make it peppery and garnish with chopped egg whites. Makes 4 servings.

Chicken Pudding

This silken custard, perfect for a ladies' luncheon, should smooth even the sharpest gossip's tongue.

- 1½ cups top milk
- ½ cup chicken stock
- 3 tablespoons flour
- 3 eggs, beaten slightly
- 1½ cups cooked chicken, diced
- 1 teaspoon dried tarragon
- 2 tablespoons dried parsley

Prepare Thickened Sauce* with first three ingredients. Egg-lace* and add remaining ingredients. Season to taste, and fill a buttered casserole (or baking cups) ⅔ full. Set in a pan of hot water and bake in preheated, moderate, 325° F. oven about 30 minutes, or until tip of paring knife inserted halfway between center and outer edge comes out clean. Makes 4-plus servings.

Louisville Chicken Sandwich

You may call it Chicken Shortcake, and preferably use halves of boned, skinned chicken breasts that have been poached. Butter squares of baked cornbread, and top with cooked chicken. Cover with another square of cornbread and pour sauce over.

Sauce

- 2 tablespoons instant minced onion
- 2 tablespoons butter, melted
- ¾ cup (about 4 stalks) celery, minced
- 3 tablespoons flour
- ½ cup chicken broth
- ½ cup cream
- Chicken (see above)
- Cornbread (see above)

Cook onion in covered saucepan in butter 5 minutes. Add celery and cook uncovered until onion browns lightly, stirring as necessary. Make a light brown roux* with flour and add liquids as for sauce. Makes 4 servings.

Marbled Chicken

This noble cooling dish can be gussied up for a summer luncheon, or add allure to a buffet. Call it Chicken en Gelée, Chicken in Aspic, or, in the old way—Pressed Chicken ("pressed," because weighting insures that the aspic will engulf the poultry), or Chicken Cheese (because the curds are pressed in making cheese).

I have used Maryland's pretty name, and you can do as they do by adding diced cooked ham or tongue, too. The aspic also may be "marbled" with frozen mixed vegetables, thawed and drained.

The stock must be firm enough to gel—test a bit in the freezer—and add gelatin, if necessary.

Slices of cucumber, tomato, hard-cooked egg; olives; watercress sprigs; or avocado wedges make pretty aspic patterns and also may be used as platter garnish. Slice the mold with a sharp knife and serve with any variety of mayonnaise or salad dressing.

4–5 cups cooked chicken
   ½ cup parsley sprigs
   2 tablespoons instant minced onion
   1 tablespoon grated lemon peel
   2 cups Chicken Stock*
   1 tablespoon dry white wine, approximately

Put chicken and parsley through coarse grinder and add onion and lemon peel. Add stock and wine, and season to taste. Arrange vegetables in a pattern on bottom of 5 cup mold, preferably oblong, and continue as for serving the daube in Pressed Veal*. Makes 6-plus servings.

Chicken Breasts
Le Moyne Supremes de Volaille

In Russia, cooks stuff chicken breasts (supremes de volaille) with butter that spurts; in Maryland, they fill them with oyster stuffing and add an oyster sauce.

It is a good idea to double the stuffing recipe to bake in a separate casserole because the chicken breasts hold so little. Allow about 30 minutes for the top to brown and crisp.

CHICKEN BREASTS

   2 whole chicken breasts
   2 tablespoons butter, melted
   1 tablespoon quick-browning aid, optional

Skin and bone breasts and split them. Place between two sheets of waxed paper, skinned-side up, and pound thin. Melt butter, add quick-browning aid and brush both sides of chicken breasts, with mixture. Add remaining butter mixture to baking pan with low sides.

STUFFING

   2 cups stale white bread
   ½ pint (8 ounces) shucked stewing oysters
   ¼ cup celery, cut very fine

2 tablespoons butter, melted
1 teaspoon instant minced onion
2 tablespoons minced parsley
½ teaspoon paprika
⅛ teaspoon nutmeg
Dash cayenne pepper
2 tablespoons milk, approximately

Remove crusts, and pull bread into ¼-inch pieces. Cut oysters into ½-inch pieces (a scissors makes it easy). In covered pan simmer celery in butter until softened, about 5 minutes. Add onion, half the oysters with part of their liquor, and remaining ingredients. Toss, adding if necessary, enough more milk to moisten stuffing, and season to taste.

Fill each breast with about a tablespoon stuffing and fold into a package. Place in baking pan, folded side down and bake in preheated, hot, 400° F. oven until chicken is done, about 15 minutes, basting halfway through cooking, if chicken seems dry.

Oyster Sauce

2 tablespoons butter
3 tablespoons flour
¼ cup half-and-half
¼ cup dry white wine
½ pint (1 cup) stewing oysters cut small
¼ cup oyster liquor
½ teaspoon paprika

Prepare Thickened Sauce* with first four ingredients. Add remaining ingredients, and simmer covered until oysters are done, about 5 minutes. Season to taste and pour over chicken breasts. Makes 4 servings.

Chicken Colette

Somewhere I read that rabbit, prepared this way, was Colette's favorite dish. This is my adaptation of a chicken version I discovered in a New Orleans cook book. Rabbit would do as deliciously and the cream can range from light to heavy.

    1 young chicken, cut for fricassee
    Quick-browning aid, optional
    Creole Mustard*
    1 cup cream, approximately

Coat chicken parts with quick-browning aid and add enough Creole Mustard to marinate. Marinate about 4 hours or overnight, turning pieces occasionally. Place chicken parts in single layer in heavy skillet, skin side up, with liquid in which it was marinated, and add enough cream to reach a depth of ¼ inch.

Cover pan, bring liquid to boil rapidly, lower heat, and simmer 20 minutes. Uncover, and simmer 15 minutes. Turn chicken parts and continue to cook until chicken is done, about 10 minutes more—when sauce should be reduced almost to glaze consistency. Remove chicken to platter (and continue reducing sauce if necessary). Stir reduced sauce to smooth it, and scrape up any brown particles. Season to taste, and spoon over chicken. This rich elegance deserves a silver platter and watercress sprig garnish. Makes 4 servings.

Fried Chicken

Ah—the contradictions in Southern recipes for this specialty! Oh—the storms of protest if this Damn Yankee should insist that the following is the only correct way to prepare it! Interestingly, fried chicken is mentioned in writings as early as 1649, and came to America via the English colonists of Jamestown. With the expanding Virginia frontier, taverns sprung up, and the dish became a featured menu specialty.

This is Ann Burtt's Georgia method—the best, fastest, and easiest way to fry chicken that I have ever encountered.

    ½ cup flour
    ½ teaspoon salt
    ⅛ teaspoon pepper
    ⅛ teaspoon paprika
    1 young chicken, cut for fricassee
    Lard

Shake flour and seasonings in a bag until mixed. Add a few pieces of chicken at a time and shake until coated. In heavy pan, add enough lard to reach a depth of about 1 inch, and heat to medium high, 375° F. (Test temperature with a bit of chicken skin. It should attract small singing bubbles.)

Add chicken, skin side up, placing meaty pieces in fat first and do not crowd pan. Cover, and fry until brown, preferably turning only once. Meaty pieces will cook in about 15 minutes; breast pieces in about 10 minutes. Remove to absorbent paper and drain. Makes 3–4 servings.

Storing: For best flavor, eat it cold or store in freezer for reheating. Then without thawing, place under broiler, or on pan in a single layer and allow about 10 minutes in preheated, extremely hot 500° F. oven; about 20 minutes in preheated, moderate 350° F. oven.

Pillowed Chicken

Chicken parts bake speedily on a layer of any stuffing and then carving can be forgotten. The glass insert of a silver-footed holder adds elegance.

Spread a 1½-inch layer of Cornbread Stuffing From a Mix* lightly into 9 × 13 × 2 inch baking dish. Brush pieces of 2 young chickens with quick-browning aid (optional), and arrange on stuffing, close together in a single layer, skin side up.

Bake in preheated, hot 425° F. oven 20 minutes. If chicken seems dry, brush with melted butter. Continue baking until done, about 20 minutes more. Makes 8-plus servings, and may be frozen.

Chicken Creole

Freezer and oven can speed dinner to table deliciously for unexpected guests. The thickened sauce provides a sturdy support for the chicken, which will emerge crisp, juicy, and beautifully browned. The method works equally well for pork or veal chops, seafood, and even hamburgers.

> Creole Tomato Sauce*
> 1 young chicken, cut for fricassee
> Quick-browning aid, optional

Spread sauce in 9 × 13 × 2 baking dish. Brush chicken with quick-browning aid, and arrange on sauce in a single layer, skin side up. Bake in preheated, hot 400° F. oven until chicken is done, about 45 minutes. Makes 4 servings.

SMOTHERED CHICKEN

Smothering, the South's all-purpose term for braising, even encompasses vegetable stews. Among other meanings, the current *Webster* defines smothering as "a confused multitude of things." Another definition succinctly provides a comprehensive description of braising: "To cook in a covered pan or pot with little liquid over low heat." And, an ancient dictionary's definition wraps up the way to smother and/or stew: "Cover closely and exclude air." Interestingly, even today in Rouen, very young ducks are smothered, rather than butchered.

The trick to smothering chicken is to cook it until the meat almost falls off the bone. Of the many variations I have tested, all are virtually mistake-proof—and unfailingly delicious. Their delectability depends upon the flavor of the chicken, and obviously, more can be wrung from an aged hen, than from a young bird. As braising liquid, Chicken Stock* augments flavor.

New Orleans cooks naturally begin their "smother" with a roux, and fancy the additions of green onion tops, parsley, and mushrooms. Marylanders call a smother a fricassee. For a Brown Fricassee, the chicken is fried before smothering. When the preliminary frying step is omitted, it becomes a White Fricassee.

Mulcalong, a Charleston specialty, smothers chicken in veal stock seasoned with turmeric and lemon juice. The title probably is a corruption of Mulligatawny, a kind of curry.

Chancelorsville Chicken Gumbo

This is a variation of smothered chicken and a stewing chicken may be substituted for a young bird when time is not of the essence. If using frozen okra, add it without thawing about 20 minutes before chicken finishes cooking.

- ½ cup diced salt pork
- 1 large onion, diced
- 1 clove garlic, minced, optional
- ½ teaspoon dried thyme
- ¼ teaspoon crumbled bay leaf
- 1 tablespoon chopped parsley
- $\frac{1}{16}$ teaspoon cayenne pepper
- 2 tablespoons flour, approximately
- 2 cups fresh okra, sliced ¼-inch thick
- 1 can (1 pound) tomatoes in tomato purée
- 1 young chicken, cut for fricassee
- 1 teaspoon filé powder*, optional

Render salt pork, covered, over low flame in heavy flame-proof casserole. When enough fat has been rendered to cover bottom of pan, add onion, herbs, and cayenne. Cook covered over medium heat, until onions are lightly browned, about 10 minutes. Make a roux* with flour. Add okra, contents of can of tomatoes, and chicken parts, skin side up, preferably in a single layer. Cover pan, bring liquid to boil rapidly, lower heat, and simmer until chicken is done, about 40 minutes. Season to taste and sprinkle with filé powder. Makes 4 servings.

Deep-South Smothered Chicken

Except for the absence of a bouquet of spices, smothered chicken bears strong resemblance to an East Indian curry. When curry powder is added, in some areas, the dish is called Yorkshire Captain. So you could round out a menu with typical curry accompaniments such as lemon wedges, sliced cucumbers and tomatoes, salted peanuts, chutney.

Rice makes the typical accompaniment, and, for dessert, you might want to fill a platter with a profusion of those exotic fruits—persimmon, coconut, banana, mango, pomegranate.

- **1 young chicken, cut for fricassee**
- **1 tablespoon lard, approximately**
- **1 medium onion, diced**
- **2 teaspoons salt**
- **1 teaspoon pepper**
- **½ cup flour**
- **Quick-browning aid, optional**

In pan, preferably heavy, that will hold chicken in a single layer, heat to the smoking point enough lard to reach a depth of about ⅛ inch. Brown onion lightly uncovered. Combine salt, pepper, and flour. Moisten chicken parts in quick-browning aid (then omit browning step) or water, and roll in flour mixture until coated. Brown chicken and onion and add enough chicken stock or cold water to half-cover chicken. Cover pan, bring liquid to boil rapidly, lower heat and simmer until done, about 2 hours. Makes 3–4 servings.

Gravy: The liquid normally does not require flour-thickening—the flour on the chicken does the trick.

Smothered Hen

Prepare as above, cooking about 3½ hours. Makes 4-plus servings.

Oven-Smothered Chicken

This is an easier-to-do version. Melt enough fat to generously cover bottom of baking dish. Add diced onion and arrange over it, in a single layer, parts of young chicken rolled in seasoned flour. Add cold water to almost cover. Cover and bake in preheated, hot 400° F. oven until done, about 1½ hours. For crusty browning, uncover last 15 minutes of cooking, and increase heat, if necessary, to very hot, 450° F. Makes 3–4 servings.

Egg-Laced Chicken

In Belgium, this is called *waterzooi*. Southerners know it as a "smother." The technique intrigued me, because my freezer always holds uncooked chicken parts and I always bewail the loss of flavor, succulence, and food value when thawing is required. Egg-Laced Chicken is not a thing of beauty. To halfway make it so, fling in a handful of chopped parsley before serving.

- 1 young chicken, cut for fricassee
- 1 large onion, diced
- 2 medium potatoes, diced
- ¼ cup butter

Heat a heavy pan until very hot. Drop pieces of frozen chicken into a bowl of cold water, and using both hands, immediately scoop chicken from the water and drop into pan. Cover, turn off heat, and allow to stand 15 minutes.

Bring to boil 1½ cups cold water (or use chicken stock), and add to chicken with remaining ingredients. Cover pan, bring liquid to boil rapidly, lower heat, and simmer about 1 hour, or until chicken is very tender, and has loosened from bones.

Sauce

- 1 egg (or 2 yolks)
- ½ cup milk or cream
- 3 tablespoons chopped parsley

Remove chicken and vegetables to platter to keep warm. Reduce liquid in pan to 1 cup by boiling uncovered, egg-lace*, and when thickened, season to taste. Add parsley, and pour over chicken. Makes 3–4 servings.

Brunswick Stew

It is difficult to know whether this properly is a chicken or a game recipe. In its name, all varieties of chicken and meat bathe in a hotly-seasoned tomato sauce, enhanced with corn and lima beans, to produce a kind of glorified succotash, into which okra also often finds its way.

As far as title source is concerned, in his *American Place Names*, George R. Stewart writes that "George the First held the title of Elector of Brunswick-Luneberg, and Brunswick [the German city] was therefore used for commendatory reasons, as a name associated with kings, e.g. for towns in . . . Georgia."

One source credits the melange to Brunswick County, Virginia, while still another lists it as a basis for dispute with Brunswick County, North Carolina. In any case, it is another example of aristocrat turned plebe, because, kingly title or no, 20-gallon black iron pots of Brunswick stew hung over outdoor fires to feed folk at political rallies which one hopes were fiery enough to match the entree.

A chicken seems to be the only unvarying ingredient. Combine it with ham, pork (and call it *adobo*—"sauce for seasoning"—as the Spanish do), beef, rabbit, squirrel. Add potatoes and onions, and dine regally and democratically. The following is an uncomplicated version.

Add to Smothered Chicken* about 10 minutes before it finishes cooking, 2 cups fresh or frozen corn kernels and 2 cups fresh or frozen lima beans (or use frozen succotash). Continue cooking until chicken is tender and vegetables are done and season to taste. Makes 4 servings.

VNC Brunswick Stew

This simplified version takes ample advantage of convenience products.

1 young chicken, cut for fricassee
2 tablespoons fat
1 small onion, diced
2 teaspoons salt
1 teaspoon pepper
½ cup flour
Quick-browning aid, optional
½ cup drained canned tomatoes
½ cup chicken stock, approximately
⅓ package frozen okra
1½ packages frozen succotash

Prepare as for Deep-South Smothered Chicken* adding tomatoes with chicken stock. Simmer only about 40 minutes or until chicken is just done. Add unthawed okra about 20 minutes before chicken finishes cooking; unthawed succotash about 15 minutes before chicken finishes cooking. Season to taste. Makes 4 servings and may be frozen.

Baked Chicken Perlo

Almost every country where rice is a staple quickly learned its affinity for extending scarce and costly ingredients and its inclination to absorb flavorful liquids. Webster lists the combined result as "pilau," from Persian and Turkish "pilaw." South Carolinians promptly corrupted the word to *perlo,* and elsewhere in the South it is called "pillow."

Pillow-cooked rice will not emerge "grain for grain," but to avoid a pasty mass, choose long grain or converted rice. Today's young birds speed a pillow to table and the following method adds the pleasure of crisp crustiness.

4 tablespoons butter
1 young chicken, cut for fricassee
1 medium onion, diced
¼ cup diced ham, optional
¼ cup flour
1 teaspoon salt
1 tablespoon paprika
¹⁄₁₆ teaspoon cayenne pepper
1 cup chicken stock
1 cup rice

Preheat oven to hot 400° F. and place butter in baking pan to melt. Roll chicken in butter, and pour off and reserve any excess. Place onion and ham in baking pan and dredge chicken with flour mixed with seasonings. Add chicken, skin side down and bake 20 minutes. Bring chicken stock to boil; remove chicken and add stock, reserved butter, and remaining ingredients to pan. Top with chicken pieces, in a single layer, skin side up, and bake about 30 minutes more, adding additional chicken stock if mixture seems dry. Makes 4 servings.

TURKEY

Today, our own native bird bears about as much resemblance to its early ancestors as we do to Neanderthal man. Now, it sashays around the continent in a multitude of convenience forms that make it easy to cook and serve in Southern ways, and on 365 days of the year.

Frozen whole breasts or dark meat quarters are an especial blessing because, coming from huge birds that have been allowed to plump to perfection, they offer a world of succulence and flavor.

Roast Turkey

Our marvelous abundance of turkeys has provoked some re-think on the part of the U.S. Department of Agriculture home economists. The "new" technique they currently recommend is the old-fashioned method of roasting a turkey covered, in a hot oven. This procedure can save up to half the cooking time, especially with large birds and you can always expect more flavor and succulence from turkeys weighing at least 10 pounds.

To Roast: Allow about ¾ pound turkey per serving—a little less with large birds. If roasting covered, brush with quick-browning aid (optional) and set on rack, breast side up, in preheated very hot 450° F. oven. Allow about 15 minutes per pound for a bird weighing up to 14 pounds; about 12 minutes for one weighing up to 18 pounds; about 10 minutes for larger birds.

Uncover the last 15 minutes, baste, and then if it is not as brown as you would like, increase oven temperature to very hot, 500° F. The same method can be used for turkey parts.

Turkey In Made Dishes

Similarity to chicken allows turkey to be prepared in most of the same ways—"pressed," "saladed," and "hashed." The word hashed derives from French for hatchet. Hopefully, your turkey will be tender enough to require a less powerful tool. Whatever you use, cut large chunks rather than mincing turkey to the vanishing point.

Potted Turkey

Almost all of the Southern states looked to England for guidance in elegance. This recipe and title combined food of the new world with old-world ways. However, it probably traveled to England from France as "paté." Way back when, directions called for "pounding" the meat (doubtless using the *side* of the hatchet) to paste consistency.

It is a marvel as a sandwich spread or an hors d'oeuvre, and shaped, looks engaging garlanded with watercress on a buffet table. For attractive serving and added richness, spread the top with a thin film of melted butter, preferably clarified.

Prepare potted turkey with poached turkey parts; turkey roll; or even leftover roast turkey. In no case will it be dry, and the proportions may be increased or decreased at will.

- ¼ pound cooked ham
- 1 pound cooked turkey
- ¼ pound butter, creamed
- 2 tablespoons Cognac, optional
- ¼ teaspoon mace or nutmeg, optional

Remove excess fat from ham and grind with turkey. Combine (easiest, if kneaded by hand) thoroughly with butter, add remaining ingredients, and season to taste. May be frozen.

Goldsboro Turkey Hash

Charleston's way reflects French ancestry, being composed of a thickened sauce (a sort of Bechamel) made with ¾ cup veal stock and ½ cup cream. Chicken stock* may be substituted for veal stock, and the heavier the cream, the more satiny the sauce will be. Prepare as for Thickened Sauce*, first sautéeing ¼ pound mushroom slices in the butter—3 tablespoons, and thickening with 3 tablespoons flour. Season with grated lemon rind and mace. Add 2 cups turkey chunks, and simmer covered until hot. Add about a dozen oysters and their liquor and continue to simmer covered until oyster edges ruffle. Season to taste. Makes 4 servings.

GOOSE AND DUCK

Interestingly, the South made geese sing for their supper. The birds, called "weeder geese," were put to graze in the cotton, peanut, and strawberry patches, where they proceeded to gulp the weeds.

Uncle Martin spoiled me for any except a non-weeder goose personally fattened by him. This treasure always arrived from his Southern farm just in time for Christmas, and I have never been able to buy a goose that approximated its rich, succulent meatiness.

If you are the fortunate recipient of a similar dream bird, you know the ways of roasting it—and like me—probably consider an affront, all but a thrusting of onion, tart apple, or orange into the cavity.

I also feel that duck is best roasted without any dressing, and unless lean, wild duck (coot) was intended, I also worry about recipes directing that duck be stewed with additional fat.

STUFFINGS

Whether or not they were reassuring, recipe directions in days of old were forceful. One ends a dissertation on stuffing turkey by stating,

"The same stuffing will answer for all wild fowl. Water Fowls require onions." And indeed they do—to counteract the often fishy flavor of their diet. Any of the following dressings also may be used to stuff bland meats, such as pork or veal.

As far as quantity is concerned, despite weight variation, a bird's body cavity does not vary proportionately, so allow about 1 cup bread for each pound of poultry.

Because stuffing can be baked separately, it is wise to exaggerate the amount, and if you enjoy crisp-brown skin, top a put-away-for-another-day casserole of dressing with flaps of leftover poultry skin before baking.

Any stuffing recipe may be increased or decreased at will; the herbs varied at whim. Commercial seasonings for stuffing include sage, thyme, and marjoram. Some also contain rosemary; some add allspice and ginger. With this in mind, put together a personal selection of dried herbs and powdered spices.

Not surprisingly, Southerners add pecans, chestnuts, ham, and giblets, to stuffings and moisten them with stock or oyster liquor. Louisiana cooks choose to embroider dressings with truffles and *paté de foie gras*.

Puffed Stuffed Poultry

For a long time I was dead set against stuffing poultry on the valid grounds that the dressing absorbed the bird's juice, and because stuffings increased cooking time (food finishes cooking in the inner center last), the poultry would be dry. But knowing that stuffed chicken and turkey were a firmly entrenched Southern tradition, I tested in various ways in an attempt to overcome the obstacles.

One secret, I discovered, is to stuff a bird taken out of the refrigerator as soon as the dressing has finished cooking, and to roast it immediately. The second—use a moist stuffing. The third involves stuffing the skin area—a trick that produces a majestic-looking chicken or turkey.

To Stuff: Begin at the back (drumstick) end, and loosen breast skin almost *to* the neck area by sliding your fingers under it, palm side down. Loosen around top of drumsticks, and lightly force stuffing under loosened areas. Fill cavity ⅔ full.

To Truss: This procedure helps prevent drying even if bird is not stuffed. Sew openings or fasten with poultry pins. Backlock wings, and tie ends of drumsticks tightly together with twine.

To Roast: Brush either a young bird or a roasting chicken with quick-browning aid (optional), and place breast-down on rack in shallow pan. Roast in hot, preheated 400° F. oven for a young chicken (moderate 350° F. for a roasting chicken) 25 minutes. Turn breast up, and roast 20 minutes more. Cut and remove leg twine, and continue roasting until done, about 20 minutes longer for a young chicken, 30 minutes for a roasting chicken. A capon is prepared the same way, but will take about 20 minutes longer to finish cooking.

A young bird will serve 4; a roasting chicken, about 6; a capon, about 8.

Convenience Cornbread Stuffing

Packages of cornbread stuffing have infiltrated Northern markets, making it convenient for Damn Yankees to enjoy this splendid Southern variation. I combined my favorite way with stuffing with the crumbs.

¼ pound butter
½ cup water
2 eggs, beaten slightly
1 package (8 ounce) Corn Bread Stuffing (about 3½ cups crumbs)
1½ cups (about 4 stalks) celery, diced
1½ teaspoons instant minced onion
1 teaspoon dried parsley
½ teaspoon dried thyme
1 teaspoon dried summer savory
1/16 teaspoon cayenne pepper
Giblets from 2 chickens (heart, liver, gizzard)

Heat butter in water until melted, and mix with eggs. Empty package of stuffing in large bowl and add celery, onion, and herbs. Cut giblets into ¼-inch pieces (easy with a cleaver), and add with egg mixture.

Mix thoroughly, and add enough additional water (about ¼ cup) for moist consistency, and season to taste. Makes enough for 2 chickens and may be frozen.

Kettle-Cousin Cornbread Stuffing

Kettle-cousin is Georgia colloquial for uninvited relatives who show up at mealtime. With stuffing this irresistible, no wonder! An 8-inch pan of baked cornbread makes about 4 cups crumbs and the cornbread should be at least a day old. Unless the cooked chopped giblets and liver are sacred to the gravy, add them to the stuffing mixture, too. If you do not live in a kettle-cousin neighborhood, a whole turkey probably will not be required. Bake turkey parts on a casserole of this.

- 4 cups cornbread crumbs
- ½ to ¾ pound Homemade Pork Sausage*
- 5 tablespoons butter
- 1 onion, diced
- 2 cups celery (about 4 branches), diced
- 1 teaspoon dried thyme
- 2 tablespoons dried parsley
- Dash cayenne pepper
- 1 tablespoon paprika
- ½ cup chicken stock or water, approximately
- 1 egg, beaten slightly

Crumble cornbread into fairly fine crumbs. In skillet over medium heat, fry sausage, breaking it up into particles. Pour off excess fat, if necessary. Remove sausage to bowl and melt butter in pan. Add onion, celery, thyme, parsley, cayenne pepper, and paprika, and cook covered until vegetables soften, about 5 minutes, stirring as necessary. Mix with sausage and cornbread crumbs. Stir ¼ cup stock into egg, and blend into mixture, adding more stock if necessary to achieve moist consistency—stuffing should hold together when pressed lightly. Season to taste—it should be peppery. Yields about 8 cups stuffing; enough for a 12-pound bird—with some to spare.

Cornmeal Stuffing

Even before beginning this book, I had been vaguely disappointed to find that cornbread stuffing recipes always called for cornbread, rather than cornmeal. Research finally produced one, with the laconic instruction: "Dry it [cornmeal] down and let it be done before stuffing fowl." I took off from there and put the recipe together my way. Meanwhile, in another Southern cookbook, I discovered a recipe called Cornmeal Cakes, identical to the stuffing. Testing all the variations, I produced a diner's chorus of: "Delicious!"

The mixture freezes successfully only if reheated by baking.

2 tablespoons lard
Dash cayenne pepper
2 tablespoons chopped parsley
1 tablespoon dried thyme
1 teaspoon dried sage
1 large onion, diced
4 cups water
1½ cups cornmeal
1 egg

Melt lard in large saucepan. Add seasonings, herbs, and onion, and cook covered until onion is transparent, about five minutes, stirring as necessary. Add half the water, and stir in cornmeal. When smooth, add remaining water and cook uncovered until water evaporates and cornmeal tastes done, about 30 minutes.

Beat egg slightly in bowl. Gradually beat in small amounts of hot cornmeal mixture. When egg warms, stir vigorously into main mixture and correct seasoning. Yields 4 cups, enough for 3–4 pound young chicken.

Cornmeal-Stuffing Cakes

Remove Fried Chicken* to platter and keep warm. Drop spoonfuls of above mixture into fat in which chicken was fried. Flatten with spoon to make "cakes" and turn to brown both sides. Remove cakes to absorbent paper to drain, and pour off excess fat in pan. Prepare Cream Gravy* in same pan.

Double Cornmeal-Stuffing Cakes

Turn cornmeal stuffing mixture into oblong pan and chill. Slice ½-inch thick and dip in cornmeal. Fry in hot lard. Enjoy as a base for creamed chicken.

Orange Stuffing

This Southern specialty fills—and magnificently perfumes—the breast skin (see Puffed Stuffed Poultry*) and cavity of a young chicken.

   Chicken giblets (heart, gizzard, liver)
   6 cups stale bread
   ½ teaspoon each cinnamon, nutmeg, mace
   4 tablespoons butter, melted
   1 cup pecans, broken coarsely
   ½ cup orange juice
   1 egg, beaten slightly
   ½ cup Sherry, approximately

Cut giblets into ¼-inch pieces (easy with a cleaver). Pick bread and crust into crumbs and place in bowl. Add spices to butter; heat, and add pecans. Cook until nuts begin to brown, about 3 minutes. Add giblets and cook, stirring, only until red color disappears. Add to crumbs with orange juice and egg blended with ¼ cup Sherry. Add enough additional Sherry for moist consistency and season to taste.

A WAVE OF SEAFOOD
A GROUSE OF GAME

The seafood the South puts into its pans comes from coasts bordering areas longer than they are broad. Inland waters—the Mississippi, Lake Ponchartrain, numerous bayous and coves, yield estimable catches, and it is said that river shrimp have more delicate flavor than those from ocean or lake.

Cooks preside over stoves holding fish in plenty, with wonderful names—paddlefish, walleye, blue runner, grunt, spadefish, tripletail, wahoo!, and silversides (interestingly, what Britain calls corned beef); while crab, lobster, shrimp, and oysters are the darlings of coastal families.

The beautiful shad flicks its tail through Southern waters, but probably the most admired fish there is the sparkling, silver-blue pomano, accorded appropriate haute cuisine treatment in *Pompano en Papillote.* Mark Twain drolled that the New Orleans way with it was as delicious as the less criminal forms of sin. Next in esteem is the red snapper, which New Orleans folk call "king of the fish market."

New Orleanians accused of having the "fancy appetites of the French," also were bequeathed enjoyment of frogs' legs. Do as they do and bread, or batter-dip them, to fry, or treat the meaty legs to a buttery-garlicky sauce such as Provencale. Virginia brags of spots—tiny sea fish, *a la Russe,* garners herring and sturgeon, and turns the Spanish *seviche* or *escabeche,* for pickle, into "caveach."

Because that miracle—modern transportation—travels oceans, lakes, and rivers of seafood to your door, it is fortunate that it is necessary to master only a few cooking rules and regulations. All varieties respond to basic methods: Frying, broiling, baking, a semi-braising technique, and poaching. And because seafood is naturally tender, the only concern is overcooking. Comparatively lean, let it bask in rich sauces and accompaniments.

The recipes that follow are here by virtue of their strictly Southern airs, but Damn Yankees can prepare them with seafood most likely to be found in Northern markets. Realize, too, that any light-in-color, delicately flavored fish can be substituted for shellfish, while clams, oysters, and mussels are interchangeable in recipes. On a day when you feel like astonishing your family, you can always present them with an old-time darling—Eel Pie.

Fried Fish

Seafood, South or North, is lean, so whole fish, fillets, and steaks take perfectly to frying. Dipping before frying provides a crust, and while its main purpose is to absorb surface moisture, it also seals in juices. Cornmeal is especially good for crunch, and the yellow colors it gold. A combination of flour and cornmeal may be used, and lard makes a perfect frying fat.

If the outer surface is dry, dip the fish in water or quick-browning aid, so any coating will adhere.

To Sauté

A heavy pan just large enough to hold the fish produces best results.

- **2 pounds fish: ¼- to ½-inch thick**
- **2 teaspoons salt**
- **½ cup cornmeal; or half cornmeal, half flour**
- **½ teaspoon paprika, optional**
- **Dash cayenne pepper**

Heat about ¼ inch fat just to the smoking point over medium high heat, and place a whole fish in it, belly-down first. Cook fish 2 to 3 minutes, depending upon size. Cover pan, remove from heat, and let stand 2 minutes. Turn fish and cook uncovered over medium high heat, until browned, 3 to 5 minutes more. Makes 4 servings.

To French Fry

Proceed as above, frying fish in about an inch of fat.

Catfish

This fish which formerly was savored by Southerners alone, currently is a widespread industry. Lovers of the aesthetic shudder when looking upon the fish's cat-like face and whiskers and slippery skin, but all admit that the flesh is sweet. Needle-sharp fin spines make catfish hard to handle when alive, and objects for caution even when dead, because some of the spines contain poison that could irritate the skin. Cutting them off or digging them out is impossible, as is severing the head. The *New York Times,* describing a catfish fry, relates that Northern guests "wound up with a throat full of bones."

Some Southerners suggest that, like corn on the cob, catfish fried in deep or shallow fat be nibbled first on one side, then the other, leaving the main bone in the center. Others advise picking the fish from the bone with fingers. Despite all these problems, the flesh is distinctive, incredibly sweet-flavored, and not at all fishy-tasting, and the cornmeal-crisped skin is good, too. Catfish farmers are raising the fish like wheat—"by the acre"—and profiting handsomely. The farms abound in Arkansas, Carolina, Louisiana, Mississippi.

Shad and Roe

The beautiful shad is a very bony proposition. Part of its high cost in market is the labor involved in filleting; part, transportation. But any cost seems small for this delectable first sign of spring. Offer it with asparagus and strawberries, and bless the earth and the waters.

Shad and/or roe, may be fried, broiled, or baked, and Southerners often poach and cream the roe.

Seafood Ravigote

Purloined from the French, of course, and *en Français,* ravigote means "to buck up." It certainly adds zest to seafood.

    1½ cups cooked lobster; diced
    1   cup medium-size cooked shrimp
    1   large cucumber, peeled, seeded, and diced
    ½ teaspoon dried tarragon
    Ravigote Sauce*

Toss ingredients with sauce, and season to taste. Mound in center of round chop plate, and spread plain mayonnaise over. Sprinkle with paprika and circle salad with cooked artichoke leaves with points out. Or, alternately, half-circle with watercress sprigs and arrange a half-circle of avocado wedges opposite. Makes 6 servings.

CRABS: SOFT AND BLUE

Crabs and the coastal South are deliciously synonymous. In Maryland, the lady crab is called a "sook;" her gentleman, a "jimmie." New

Orleans has entrancing descriptive nomenclature, too. The smallest crabs are called "forty-eight to a dozen." Choose "three for ones," for the thirty-six to a dozen size; "three for fours" for eighteen to the dozen. Say, "twelve to the dozen," when you want "counters" or "jumbos." And speak lagniappe when you hope for a thirteenth for free.

"Busters" are crabs caught while in the process of molting. At this stage, the back shell is soft enough to be cracked by hand. Soft shell crabs, having lost their shells, are defenseless and, therefore, easy to eat. Southerners dip them in cornmeal before frying.

Considering the work involved in retrieving the meat from a hard crab, it is fortunate that they have found their way to supermarket refrigerators—diligently cooked and picked for you—at a deservedly fancy price. Unfortunately, there is only about a tenth of a pound of meat in a 1-pound hard crab. Crab meat goes into salads, scallops, Creoles, etc.

The best crabbing comes in spring and summer just before shrimping, which precedes trapping on Southern calendars.

Shellfish Boil

Like women, seafood responds to gentling—as in rich cloaks—and to overpowering as in spicy seasonings. Hot and spicy are the packaged seasonings available for a Boil, a Southern specialty.

New Orleans provides a whole-spice assortment; a Maryland spice company is famous for an already-ground variety, which has the advantage of blending into sauces. Both are somewhat less trouble than starting from scratch and are interchangeable.

A Boil is a no-nonsense cooking method for crab and shrimp, and niceties, such as tying whole spices in cheesecloth, can be forgotten. All that is required for serving a Boil are crackers for the claws, a newspaper "tablecloth," and guests who enjoy singing for their supper.

Crab Boil

If thyme doesn't grace your back-door herb garden, substitute 1 tablespoon dried thyme, and use vinegar only if you enjoy a pickley flavor.

  6 pounds live hard crabs
  24 whole allspice
  4 sprigs fresh thyme
  3 bay leaves
  2 red pepperpods or 1 tablespoon crushed red pepper
  1 tablespoon celery seed
  1 teaspoon mustard seed
  1 teaspoon black peppercorns
  2 teaspoons salt
  ½ cup white vinegar, optional

Add all except crabs to 2 quarts water, and bring to boil. Add live crabs, head first, and simmer until bright red, about 20 minutes. Rinse with cold water immediately to stop the cooking, and serve promptly.

To make your own grind, whir above spices and seeds to a powder in blender.

SHRIMP BOIL

Substitute 4 pounds unshelled shrimp for crab in the above, and cook below a simmer until pink, about 20 minutes.

To Pick Hard (Blue) Crab

Take heart, this is more difficult said than done.

Twist claws off. With small knife, pry up and pull off "apron" (the small loose shell running to a point at approximately middle of the under-shell). Remove and discard spongy material underneath, but do not remove tomalley or roe. Grasp body in both hands, and break it horizontally in the center. Dig out the lumps of meat, each from its own section and crack claws to remove meat.

Hot Shrimp

This recipe takes advantage of ground seasoning (see Shellfish Boil*), and buying frozen shelled shrimp adds convenience.

Provide cucumber wedges so those who are affected by the hot and spicy can do as the East Indians do—take refuge in their cucumber—or serve with Watercress Mayonnaise*.

    1 tablespoon ground seafood seasoning
    2 cups water
    1 pound (about 42) frozen shelled shrimp

Add seasoning to water, and bring to boil. Add unthawed shrimp, cover pan, and cook over very low heat until done, about 10 minutes. Allow to remain in liquid until cold. Drain, refrigerate, and serve cold. Makes 4 servings.

Deviled Cream Crab

One can not think of Maryland without thinking of deviled crab. The recipe usually calls for a sog of bread crumbs in the mixture.

This creamy version uses eggs to take up the slack, with a crumb topping for crunchy brown contrast, rather than as an eker-outer.

Mustard and cayenne provide the devilish duo of seasoning, and many recipes suggest the addition of Escoffier Sauce. If you have invited the "Ladies Literary" to lunch, serve deviled crab with a Shakespearean quote: "The devil hath power to assume a pleasing shape."

    1 tablespoon butter
    2 tablespoons flour
    1 cup cream
    ½ teaspoon dry mustard
    ¼ teaspoon Worcestershire Sauce
    Dash cayenne pepper
    1 pound cooked crab meat
    2 hard-cooked eggs, chopped

TOPPING

    Fine dry bread crumbs
    Butter
    Paprika

Prepare first three ingredients as for Thickened Sauce* and "Add seasoning" as an old book directs, "making 'hot' according to your taste." Fold in crab meat and eggs, and put in attractive baking dish or individual cocottes. Sprinkle with crumbs, dot with butter, sprinkle with paprika, and bake in preheated, hot 400° F. oven until heated and browned, about 20 minutes. Makes 4 servings and may be frozen.

Wind Song Crab Cakes

These Maryland specialties deserve the world's most extravagantly-glowing adjectives. This recipe—the epitome of crab cakes—is hard on a budget but with picked crab meat being so costly, you might as well treat it rich.

- 1 pound cooked lump crab meat
- 1 tablespoon flour, approximately
- 1 egg
- ¼ cup cream
- Dash cayenne pepper

Dredge enough flour over crab to give it a dry appearance. Beat remaining ingredients together, add to crab, and mix gently. Season to taste. Heat about ¼-inch fat (half butter, half lard is a perfect combination) in heavy pan and drop large spoonfuls in. Cakes should measure about 3 inches. Cook over medium high heat, turning to brown both sides—it will take about 5 minutes. Drain on absorbent paper. Makes 8 cakes, which may be frozen, but will not be as delectable when reheated.

Howard Scallop

Scallops are part of Southern living, and interchangeable with shrimp, lobster, and crab. If you use them in this dish, you can call it a "Scallop Scallop." A Baltimore Howard gave lobster its elegant due in the original 1800s "receipt." called "Scalloped Lobster."

A Damn Yankee's usual "scallop" is made with milk, and a glut of bread or cracker crumbs, but "Mrs. Howard's Way" leans heavily on a sauce made with chicken stock, similar to a *Sauce Poulette,* and deliciously high on Sherry. The recipe readily converts to any cooked shellfish or fish, cut into ¾-inch pieces, if necessary. Tuck it into lobster shells, coquilles, or the like.

- ¼ cup flour
- 2 tablespoons butter

¾ cup chicken stock
¾ cup cream
2 egg yolks
¼ cup Sherry, approximately
2 cups cooked seafood
Dash cayenne pepper

TOPPING

Fine dry bread crumbs
Butter
Paprika

Prepare Thickened Sauce* with first 4 ingredients and Egg-Lace*. Add Sherry to taste, being careful not to thin the sauce too much. Stir in seafood and season to taste. Fill lobster shells, or other attractive baking container, sprinkle with fine dry bread crumbs, dot with butter, sprinkle with paprika, and bake in preheated, hot 400° F. oven until hot, and bubbling, about 20 minutes. Makes 4 servings.

LOBSTER

New Orleans cooks took advantage of lobster by preparing it in haute cuisine French ways. A school of Maryland cooks fiddled with something called "Lobster Chops"—lobster croquettes molded into chop-shape with a small lobster claw tucked into the pointed end of each croquette "to represent the chop bone."

A 1-pound live lobster makes a serving, and yields about ¼ pound (½ cup) edible meat. If economy is on your mind, lobsters are least expensive in May and June. Lobster tails always may be substituted (as can any delicate-flavored cooked seafood). A 6-ounce lobster tail yields about ¼ pound edible meat.

OYSTERS

Oystermen do not consider sailing over the bounding main in their "oyster dredgers" a thing of joy. They are the last of the commercial fishermen "under sail," and the work is hard and cold. Interestingly, the oystering techniques taught to our forefathers by the Indians are still in use—the oysters are dredged from their beds with thirty-foot long raking poles in a process called "hand tonging."

Your work begins with shucking the oysters. Skill and expertise are required even with knives made for the purpose. However, the freezer can come to your aid. Simply wash the shells and pop oysters in (a trick that works with clams, too). About an hour before needed, plop the shellfish into a bowl of water and in a few minutes, the shells will open sufficiently to allow insertion of a paring knife. Use it to scrape loose the frozen shellfish and juice.

As an alternate shucking method, spread oyster or clams on a shallow pan in a single layer and heat in preheated, moderate 375° F. oven about 5 minutes.

Depending upon where you live, these pearls of Southern cooking are available innumerable ways and vary in size. As a help in adjusting recipes to super- or fish-market supplies, the following measurements are for shucked oysters.

Standards, sometimes called stewing size oysters are the smallest. Eight fluid ounces (½ pint) yields about 20 oysters—1 cup oysters and their liquor.

Selects are the largest oysters. Eight fluid ounces (½ pint) yields about 10 oysters—1 cup oysters and their liquor.

Pickled Oysters

The South pickles almost everything—from figs to tripe. One "Pickle" —called Soused Fish, is attributed to Maria Bachman, who provided the backgrounds for many of Audubon's paintings. The method provided a means of preservation, and the following New Orleans way with oysters could as well be called spiced oysters. As always, shellfish or fish may be substituted. Serve pickled seafood cold as an hors d'oeuvre, make it a first course at dinner, or set it out on a buffet table.

    1 **pint (about 24) shucked stewing oysters**
    ⅔ **cup wine vinegar, divided**
    ⅛ **teaspoon hot red pepper**
    ½ **teaspoon allspice**
    ¼ **teaspoon mace**
    1 **small lemon, sliced**

Place oysters and their liquor in saucepan. Cover and cook over very low heat until edges ruffle, about 10 minutes. Remove oysters with slotted spoon and add half the vinegar and spices to liquid. Boil until reduced to approximately 2 tablespoons, about 5 minutes, and strain. Add remaining vinegar, bring to boil and pour over oysters. Cool quickly, season to taste and add lemon.

Oyster Roast
Seafood Stew

This stew, called a roast, is actually a soup. Spicy and scarlet, it traveled from the South to become a specialty of the Oyster Bar in New York's Grand Central Station.

Choose any other seafood, singly or in combination, and sup sumptuously. Allow about 2 dozen shucked clams, or shelled mussels; ½-pound of any of the following: medium size shelled shrimp; crab meat; shelled lobster (or lobster tails), cut in 1-inch cubes; fish steaks or fillets, cut in 1-inch cubes. Allow about 3 minutes for cooking shellfish; about 5 minutes for fish.

- ½ teaspoon celery salt
- ½ teaspoon paprika
- ¼ cup butter, melted
- 1 pint (about 24) shucked stewing oysters
- 1 tablespoon Worcestershire Sauce
- 6 tablespoons chili sauce
- ¼ cup clam juice, optional
- 1½ cups milk
- ½ cup cream

Add celery salt and paprika to butter. Add oysters, cover pan, and cook gently until almost done, about 3 minutes. Add remaining ingredients and bring to boil. Serve immediately, sprinkling servings with additional paprika. Makes 4 servings.

Baked Oysters

If demands for filling the pan with rock salt in baked oyster recipes mystify you, know that the main purpose is to keep the oysters from tipping over. The salt also holds heat in—an advantage only if the pan is taken to table.

No oyster has ever reproached a cook who bought it already shucked, and baked it in a coquille (scallop shell). And inasmuch as anyone who admires oysters will certainly down the three or four that can be cozily snuggled into a single coquille or ramekin, it seems a sensible solution.

Oysters Rockefeller

This New Orleans specialty—licorice-flavored and spinachy—is a variation of *Sauce Verte,* originally thought up for snails. Frozen chopped spinach makes things easy. Even easier—sit yourself down to table at Antoine's, the restaurant that thought of substituting oysters, and gave it its rich name. The dish there is a veritable green sauce, adding chives, tarragon, parsley, lettuce—and a soupçon of anchovy paste to the spinach.

There are many variations—all delectable. Add a squeeze of anchovy paste, top with bacon bits, or sprinkle with buttered bread crumbs, mixing them, if desired, with parmesan cheese.

- 2 tablespoons instant minced onion
- ½ pound butter
- ½ cup frozen chopped spinach, drained
- 1 teaspoon anise-flavored liqueur, optional
- 24 (about 1 pint) large oysters

Add onion to melted butter and stir into spinach, from which as much liquid as possible has been squeezed. Add liqueur (lemon juice may be substituted), and season to taste. Arrange oysters in half-shells on rock salt or arrange shucked oysters in coquilles. Top with spinach mixture, allowing about 1 tablespoon per oyster. Bake in preheated, very hot 450° F. oven until hot and browned, about 10 minutes. Or, broil under medium high heat.

Oyster Loaf

If you have read "Pepys Diary," you know the need for a "Mediator"—the dish erring husbands tiptoed home to their wives in the wee small hours. Whether or not a "three penny" oyster loaf soothed any savage English bosom or not, the custom traveled to New Orleans. There it is called "the Peacemaker."

The hollowed loaf makes a basket to hold fried oysters (Oyster Fritters in Maryland), and other fried seafood may be substituted. Nuggets of batter-fried sweetbreads are often tucked in with the oysters. (For utter convenience, choose fish sticks.)

Some recipes call for a final pour of hot cream or thin cream sauce, defeating, it seems to me, the sole purpose of the crusty-toasted bread and the crisp-cloaked oysters. As an alternate, the oysters can be "ruffled" in a cream sauce. Oyster Pye, a variation, ruffles oysters in their liquor, with onion and mace, before baking them in a pie shell.

Serve an oyster loaf as finger food (or with toothpicks), and if the sauce idea appeals, pass it in a help-yourself pitcher. Some recipes arrange the oysters in layers with chopped pickles (capers would do as well) and tartare sauce. Strips of bell pepper can provide additional color and crunch.

1 loaf bread
Melted butter
24 (about 1 pint) large oysters
2 eggs
Fine dry bread or cracker crumbs
Fat for frying

Cut top crust from bread (French or home made) and remove inner crumb, leaving a 1-inch thick shell. Remove crumb from sliced off top. Brush inside and out with butter, and place in preheated, hot 400° F. oven to brown and crisp, about 15 minutes. Drain oysters (reserving their liquor) and place on absorbent paper to dry. Season bread crumbs with salt and paprika, and spread on waxed paper. Beat eggs with 2 tablespoons oyster liquor and season with cayenne pepper, if desired. Dip oysters in egg, coat with crumbs, and fry until brown in deep, hot fat, about 4 minutes in all, turning once. Drain on absorbent paper. Fill loaf with fried oysters and serve hot. Makes about 6 servings as an entree; 8-plus servings as hors d'oeuvre. Fried oysters may be frozen.

Crab Loaf

Toss picked crab meat with melted butter. Enliven with your choice of: minced onion, cayenne pepper, diced pimento, dry mustard, mace, nutmeg, celery seed. Serve as above.

SHRIMP

I thought that in *Shrimp Cookery* I had included every recipe in the world for the versatile pink curl. I was wrong. There are infinite ways to treat this universally-admired shellfish—South, East, West, and North.

The following recipe comes from an Old New Orleans cook book, and its unusual appeal is its characterful seasoning and the fact that it is not soupy.

Shrimp A La Creole

- 3 tablespoons oil, preferably olive
- 1 tablespoon flour
- 1 small onion, sliced
- 1 clove garlic, diced
- 1 pound raw shelled shrimp
- ¼ cup tomato paste
- 1 small bell pepper, diced
- $\frac{1}{16}$ teaspoon cayenne pepper
- ¼ teaspoon dried thyme
- ¼ cup hot water

In skillet, make a roux* with oil and flour. When brown, add onion and garlic, and cook until onion is slightly browned. Add shrimp and stir until well coated with roux. Stir tomato paste in and toss to coat with mixture. Add green pepper, seasonings, and water. Cover, and cook gently until shrimp are done, about 5 minutes. If sauce seems too thick, dilute with small amount of additional water or dry white wine. Makes 2 servings.

To Butter Shrimps

So easy—so beautiful—and if this is not a work of art, I don't know what is.

- 1 cup white wine, divided
- 2 tablespoons butter
- ¼ teaspoon nutmeg
- 1 pound medium shrimp, shelled
- 4 egg yolks

In wide, flat saucepan, bring to boil ¾ cup wine, butter, and nutmeg. Add shrimp, cover pan and turn off heat. Remove shrimp when firm and pink, in about 5 minutes.

Beat egg yolks with remaining wine and Egg-Lace* pan liquid. When thick, season to taste and serve over rice or other crunchy base. Garnish with additional nutmeg. Makes 4 servings.

Gumbo Gouter

Shrimp added to a variation of the ratatouille theme provides a savory lunch or Sunday supper. One and a half cups canned tomatoes, or one-half cup tomato purée, may be substituted for fresh tomato.

- 2 tablespoons lard
- 1 large eggplant, peeled and diced
- 3 bell peppers, diced
- ¼ pound fresh okra, sliced in ½-inch rings
- 4 peeled tomatoes
- ½ teaspoon sugar
- Dash cayenne pepper
- 1 pound shelled shrimp

Melt lard and add all ingredients except shrimp. Cook covered over low flame 30 minutes, stirring as necessary. Uncover and cook until vegetables are very soft and stew thickens, about 30 minutes. Season to taste, top with shrimp, cover and steam until done, about 10 minutes. Serve hot or cold. Makes 6 servings.

White Bouillabaisse
Bouillabaisse Blanche

Bouillabaisse appears in the earliest Southern cook books and Thackeray is quoted as saying the New Orleans version surpassed any in Marseilles. Indigenous fish went into it and it was served as an entree, rather than as a soup. This one, like a lace-curtain Irish Stew, is composed of white vegetables only, and is appropriately elegant, with a platter of wedges of Belgian endive and avocado, and grapefruit sections. If the fishmonger is kind, he will make you a gift of the bony cod collar. It adds strength to the court bouillon, but any inexpensive large-boned chunks of fish may be substituted.

White Court Bouillon

- 1 bottle (8-ounce) clam juice
- White part of 1 leek, cut coarsely
- 3 stalks celery, cut coarsely
- 1 small lemon, sliced
- Shells from shrimp
- 2 pounds cod collar, approximately, cut up

Boil about 20 minutes to extract flavor.

Shellfish

- 1 lobster, about 1¼ pounds
- ½ pound small shrimp
- 12 littleneck clams, shucked
- 12 bay scallops

Add live lobster to court bouillon. Cover, reduce flame, and simmer until done (when an antenna can be pulled out easily), about 15 minutes. Remove meat from body and large claws. Return legs and shell to court bouillon, and simmer covered 20 minutes. Cut lobster meat into 1-inch pieces. Strain court bouillon, add remaining shellfish in order listed, and simmer covered until done, about 5 minutes. (Return lobster to pan in time to heat.) Remove with slotted spoon.

Sauce

- 1 egg yolk
- 2 tablespoons dry white wine
- ⅛ teaspoon cayenne pepper

Egg-lace* liquid, and add wine. Season to taste, and pour into serving tureen. Makes 4 servings.

To Serve

Make a bed of 2 cups cooked rice (1 cup raw) on platter and arrange shellfish on it.

Egg Sauce to Dress Seafood

This makes a lovely cloak for fish and/or shellfish.

> **Court Bouillon***
> 3 tablespoons flour
> 3 tablespoons butter
> 1 cup cream
> 1 teaspoon lemon juice, approximately
> 3 tablespoons minced parsley
> 4 hard-cooked eggs, cut coarsely
> 3 pounds poached seafood

Reduce to 1 cup Court Bouillon* in which seafood has been poached. Strain and prepare Thickened Sauce* with flour, butter and cream. Add lemon juice and parsley, and season to taste. Stir eggs and seafood in and serve hot, cold, or at room temperature. Makes 4-plus servings.

CAPER SAUCE

Substitute ¼ cup capers for parsley in the above.

A GROUSE OF GAME

So much of our land is now tamed that poaching probably is limited to eggs. If yours is a hunting or trapping family, while you may never have literally eaten crow, you need no instructions for hanging, skinning, plucking, cleaning, or cooking the master's prizes—up to, and including, alligator.

If game comes to your door as a gift, know that it is cooked exactly as for market meat and poultry, and is as delicious plain, as fancy. Sauté, broil, or roast tender cuts; braise or watercook tough cuts.

Spice, sauce, marinate, and enrich at will, realizing that like well-fatted meat and poultry, fat game combines best with lean ingredients. Game with little fat, such as wild duck (coot), requires rich accompaniments.

Rabbit can be substituted for chicken in recipes. Pigeons make a Pye or take a pilaf stuffing. Roasted pheasant, wild duck, goose, and teal, are improved with bacon or salt pork strips laid across the breast. Roast possum is enhanced when a clove-studded onion graces the cavity, and sweet potatoes roasted in the pan with it are a typical Southern accompaniment. Choose piquant ingredients when game is bland and/or to offset gaminess. Venison, deer, bear, and moose are admirable accompanied by currant jelly or the classic Cumberland Sauce.*

Expect purchased game to be costly, and unless you live in a sophisticated metropolis, not readily available. Out-of-season game will, of course, be frozen.

Listing game by name, especially birds, with their colloquial, regional, and pet-name variations, would be of small help. But if you should catch a peacock, do not ruffle its feathers—the bird is properly served with its plumage.

If a wild creature tastes fishy or muddy, unfortunately its diet is to blame. A friend still shudderingly remembers the "garlic" ice cream inadvertently produced with cream from a Bossie who had wandered from pasture.

Roast Pheasant

These are more likely than other game to fly to your market. Check the color of the fat. If it is yellow, the bird will be too old and tough for roasting. The clay pot method produces tender succulence, but pheasant may be roasted as for other poultry. If you come across a game recipe calling for pine needles, and have already quitted the forest, substitute rosemary.

- 6 tablespoons butter, melted
- 3 tablespoons juniper berries, crushed
- 1 tablespoon peppercorns, crushed
- 2 cups Sherry
- 3 whole cloves
- Oven-ready pheasant (about 2¾ pounds)

Combine marinade ingredients and marinate pheasant about 16 hours turning approximately 4 times. Strain marinade, and coat pheasant with solid bits. Roast in clay pot in preheated, moderate 350° F. oven until done, about 2 hours.

A ROUND OF SQUARES

In the Forties, Olive Redfield was a student in my first cooking class. When I wrote my first cook book, she turned the tables, and taught *me* how to put recipes in their places.

Her advice on where to stash those that fit into several categories, but none comfortably, went: Either head a chapter miscellaneous, or throw the recipe away.

Because the following were too wonderful to even think of discarding, I decided to call the delicious misfits square pegs. This chapter provides their round hole. Look here for unexpected pleasures.

EGGS

Flocks of chickens, flocks of eggs, highlight Southern cooking—and cooks display a penchant for poaching. Predictably, in New Orleans, city of *bon vivants,* Eggs Benedict are admired, and poached eggs also set themselves on artichoke hearts, as in Eggs Sardou, where they also combine with creamed spinach to be masked with Hollandaise Sauce.

Artichoke St. Louis, another variation on the artichoke bottom-poached egg theme, cloaks them with Sauce Gribiche—a tartare sauce—which resembles a Remoulade. While Eggs Louisiana is a variation of Italy's Zuppa Pavese—eggs poached in bowls of tomato bouillon to sprinkle with grated cheese.

New Orleans' ubiquitous tomato sauce enlivens eggs in a Creole omelet, and *The Virginia Housewife* suggests an anchovy omelet. The book also offers a recipe for eggs scrambled in a pan holding butter-simmered tomato and onion, and a version of Scotch Eggs, titled "To Fricassee Eggs," which involves breading whole hard-cooked eggs in a nutmeg-flavored coating to French fry, and garnish "with a rich gravy and crisp parsley."

Following are other ways for Spring profligacy when eggs are at their best—and least expensive.

Creole Rice Cakes

This is a sort of Southern rice-addicted *egg foo yung,* ideal for leftover rice and ham, and—a delight for lunch.

- 2 cups cooked rice
- 1 cup cooked ham, cut in ¼-inch dice
- 1 tablespoon freeze-dried green bell pepper
- 2 eggs, beaten slightly
- ¼ teaspoon instant minced onion
- ¼ teaspoon dry mustard

Combine ingredients and fry cakes measuring about 2 inches, preferably in about ¼-inch lard, turning to brown both sides. Makes about a dozen cakes; about 6 servings. May be frozen.

Shirred Eggs With Kidneys

Veal kidneys are not always easy to find in market because butchers have the wit to set these elegant sundries on their own tables. Although many pre-preparation directions are daunting, I have never had to skin, remove tubes, membranes, or the like, from veal (or any other variety of) butcher-bought kidney. Shirred, the elegant word for eggs prepared this way, translates to baked.

Split veal and pork kidneys lengthwise; leave lamb kidneys whole. Brush with quick-browning aid (optional), then with melted butter and place in baking dish. Allow 1 kidney per serving. Break 1–2 eggs per serving in dish, sprinkle with salt and pepper, and dot with butter. Bake in preheated, moderate 350° F. oven until kidneys are cooked (preferably medium rare) and eggs are done, about 20 minutes.

Sausage Hominy

The South shakes hands with Italy in this tomato sauce, substituting sausage meat for link sausages or ground beef; hominy for pasta.

Do it their way, to spoon over any cornbread, or hot biscuits and, if desired, drain fat when sausage browns.

- 1 pound pork sausage meat
- 1 onion, chopped
- 1 tablespoon quick-browning aid, optional
- ¼ cup tomato paste
- 2 tablespoons dry wine, white or red, optional
- 1 can (16-ounce) tomatoes
- 2 tablespoons dried green bell peppers
- 1 teaspoon dried basil
- ¼ teaspoon hot red pepper
- 1 can (1 pound 4 ounce) hominy (about 2 cups)

Heat deep heavy pan and fry sausage, stirring to separate particles. When brown, drain fat, if desired. Add onion and cook until browned, about 10 minutes, stirring as necessary. Add remaining ingredients except hominy, in order listed, and bring to boil. Cook, stirring occasionally, until sauce thickens, about 1 hour.

Add hominy and liquid in can and cook again to desired sauce consistency, about 15 minutes. Season to taste. Makes 4-plus servings. May be frozen.

Link Sausage and Eggs

- 4 link sausages
- 2 tablespoons butter
- 4 eggs

Cook sausages, as above, being careful not to pierce when turning. Pour fat off, and add butter. Increase heat to medium high, break eggs into skillet and arrange browned sausages between them like wheel spokes. Cover, reduce heat, and cook gently until eggs reach desired firmness, about 10 minutes. Makes 2 servings.

Angel Omelet

With cornmeal adding so much to so many good things, I decided to stir a bit into an omelet. It turned out golden and airy with puffy wings, and similar to, but lighter than, a German pancake.

The cornmeal provides a crisp brown crust, and I have enjoyed it with pancake accompaniments, or filled with creamed vegetables, chicken, seafood. Cooked ham, vegetables, grated cheese, and the like may be added to the mixture before frying, and milk—for tenderness, preferably skim—may be substituted for water. If you allow a tablespoon cornmeal for each egg, the omelet will have a kind of "bread" bottom; a custard-like top.

- 2 eggs
- ¼ cup water
- 1 teaspoon sugar
- ¼ teaspoon salt
- 1 tablespoon cornmeal
- 1 tablespoon butter

Beat eggs and stir in all ingredients except butter. (Or whir eggs in blender with all ingredients except cornmeal and butter. Pour into bowl, stir cornmeal in.) If possible, allow to stand about 20 minutes. Melt butter, preferably in 8-inch omelet pan, and heat. Pour egg mixture into pan, cover, and cook over medium to medium-high heat until firm, about 5 minutes. Fold in half and turn out. Makes 1–2 servings and may be frozen.

French Toast
(French-Fried Pudding)

New Orleans calls this Lost Bread translating directly from the French *pain perdu*. But colonials with English blood, who even called a loaf of pork paté a pudding, knew better. Good white bread and the South's glut of barnyard eggs provide a profligate version. Enjoy it in spring when hens are on an egg-laying spree, and realize that the staler the bread, the better the toast. The toast may be baked in a waffle iron.

For a caramel finish, sprinkle with brown sugar, or drizzle with maple syrup before turning to brown second side. Pass a pitcher of syrup and/or a bowl of preserves.

- ½ cup cream
- 8 eggs, beaten slightly
- ¼ cup sugar
- ¼ teaspoon salt
- 12–16 slices stale white bread, depending upon thickness

Combine all ingredients except bread. Dip slices in mixture, then allow to soak until absorbed, about 15 minutes, turning slices occasionally.

Fry on hot buttered griddle, or in heavy skillet, browning both sides. Arrange on platter or individual serving plates in overlapping layers and sprinkle with confectioner's sugar. Makes 4 servings and may be frozen.

VEGETABLE BASKETS

Southern cooks "dress" any vegetable that can be hollowed with a variety of savory stuffings. In addition to the obvious bell pepper, tomato and onion, cucumbers, eggplant, and squash, both summer and acorn, supply baskets to hold leftovers or the newly made.

Onions and herbs are almost invariable flavor providers, and celery often is added. Ground pork or veal, chicken giblets, sausage, and oysters swell the stuffings. And rice, white bread, or cornbread are all called upon to bind the delectable dressings.

Bell Pepper Baskets
(Piments Doux Farce)

Stuffed peppers can be a pedestrian stash for indifferently-flavored leftovers—or this spicily satisfying luncheon entree. If you prepare the dish to take budget advantage of a surplus of ham, hopefully sweet peppers glow green and red in your garden.

For variations almost without end on the following recipe (or any other vegetable basket), substitute for ham, cooked beef; raw ground pork; corn; or cooked, mashed fried vegetables. Moisten bread crumbs may replace rice, and a beaten egg may be stirred in after the filling is cooked. Gravy or tomato purée can supplant the stock, and the peppers may be topped with toasted bread crumbs.

    4 small bell peppers
    1½ tablespoons fat
    3 tablespoons onion, diced fine
    2 cups cooked rice (1 cup raw)
    1 cup (about 3 stalks) celery, diced fine
    ½ cup diced, cooked ham
    ¼ cup parsley, optional
    Dash cayenne pepper
    ½ cup beef stock, approximately

Stem peppers, halve lengthwise, and remove seeds and white membrane. Add 4 of the halves to enough boiling water to cover. Turn off heat and allow to remain in water until softened, about 5 minutes. Remove and drain.

Dice remaining pepper halves and fry in fat with onion in covered pan until lightly browned, stirring as necessary, about 10 minutes. Add rice, celery, and ham, and cook uncovered 10 minutes, stirring occasionally. Season to taste, and stuff remaining halves. Dot with butter, sprinkle with paprika, and add enough beef stock to baking pan to reach a depth of ¼ inch. Bake in preheated, very hot 450° F. oven until peppers are cooked, about 15 minutes. Makes 2 servings as entree.

Basket of Crab

Attributed to Galatoire's Restaurant in New Orleans and as satisfying as the music of Bourbon Street. Vary by substituting shrimp for crab; combining equal parts of each, or substitute softened bell peppers (see Bell Pepper Baskets) for eggplant.

- 1 large eggplant, preferably round
- 4 tablespoons butter, melted
- 1 teaspoon instant minced onion
- 1 tablespoon dried parsley
- ½ pound lump crab meat
- Dash cayenne pepper

TOPPING

Fine dry bread crumbs
Grated cheese, preferably Parmesan
Paprika

Cut eggplant in half from stem end and slash flesh in a crisscross pattern, being careful not to cut through to skin. Bake, flesh-side down in preheated, moderate 350° F. oven until tender, about 25 minutes. Scoop pulp from skin (leave a ¼-inch thick shell) and reserve shells. Purée pulp or whir in blender. Add remaining ingredients, folding crab in carefully, and season to taste. Fill shells lightly and sprinkle with topping ingredients in order listed. Return to oven and bake until browned, about 20 minutes. Makes 2 hearty servings.

Basket of Shrimp

Serve this Creole variation at lunch with tomato slices wilted in butter.

1 medium-size eggplant
¼ cup butter, melted
2 teaspoons instant minced onion
¼ teaspoon dried thyme
1 tablespoon snipped parsley
¾ cup diced, cooked shrimp
¼ cup diced, cooked ham

Prepare eggplant shell (see Basket of Crab, above). Chop pulp. Add remaining ingredients to pulp and season to taste.

Fill shells lightly, and, if desired, add topping as in Basket of Crab. Sprinkle with fine dry bread crumbs and dot with butter. Sprinkle with paprika, and bake in preheated, moderate 350° F. oven until browned, about 30 minutes. Makes 2 servings.

BATTER BREADS
Batter Puddings

I have always been fascinated by unusual recipe titles, and long ago, upon trying one, called Toad in the Hole, that looked to be—and was—simplicity itself, discovered I had produced a Yorkshire Pudding. Now, in this book of recipe ancestry-tracing, I have found that in some parts of the South Toad in the Hole wears a literal name—Sausage and Egg Pudding.

Aptly or not, Virginians call the dish Mugwump in a Hole, thanks to the corruption of the Natick Indian word, "mugwomp" (captain) applied to Southerners who, in 1884, bolted from the Republican party.

Ham and Egg Pudding, "A Spring Diſh," the *Williamsburg Art of Cookery* notes, substitutes sliced boiled ham for sausages, while the same batter, made with half milk, half chicken stock, also poured itself over poultry to make Chicken Pudding.

Confusion over the name of this batter of many uses is rampant. If it produces a pudding, no reason not to call it batter pudding; if a bread, certainly it is entitled to be called batter bread. But balk with me at the misnomer Spoon Bread, which, of course, actually is a kind of soufflé, and smile with me at the Italian title—*Lesso Riffato all' Inglese*—"Boiled meat used up in the English way."

Batter-Bread Pudding

The following batter proportion will allow you to cover about a pound of cooked meat or poultry with glory, and no reason thawed frozen vegetables cannot be included in the array. Plant solid foods, such as sausages, directly in the baking dish. For food in a sauce, proceed as for Beefsteak Pudding. Add a bit of cornmeal if you like, too, as in Cornmeal Popovers.*

In any case, the batter will be more tender if half milk and half water or stock make the liquid, and if it is allowed to rest up to 2 hours before baking. Choose a fat compatible with the food being covered—sausage fat for a "Toad," butter for chicken, etc. And, if you own a prime rib of beef—make Yorkshire Pudding.

For handsome service, bake this multi-purpose bread, batter, pudding in a glass oven container that fits into a footed silver holder. And, about 5 minutes before the dish is done, if you like, sprinkle the top with grated cheese.

¼ cup (2 ounces) fat, divided
¾ cup liquid
2 eggs
½ teaspoon salt
¾ cup flour

Place 1 tablespoon melted fat and remaining ingredients in blender, in order listed, and whir smooth. (Lacking a blender, beat eggs, then beat in milk, the tablespoon of fat, and salt. Add flour and beat smooth.) Melt remaining fat in 8 x 8 x 2-inch baking pan. Add solid cooked meat or poultry and cover with batter. Place in cold oven and bake at very hot, 450° F. 30 minutes. Turn oven off, puncture neck of pudding at corners and allow to dry about 10 minutes. (It can remain in oven at least 15 minutes more.) Makes 4 servings.

Beefsteak Pudding

This is an example of a sauced food enveloped in batter-bread pudding. For make-ahead convenience, and better flavor, prepare the meat filling the day before. If you like things fiery, substitute canned, spiced tomato juice for wine.

- 1 pound top round steak
- 1 onion, diced
- ½ tablespoon fat
- Quick-browning aid, optional
- ¼ cup dry red wine, optional
- ½ cup beef stock, approximately
- ½ teaspoon Worcestershire sauce, approximately
- 2 peeled tomatoes, diced

Have round steak sliced ½-inch thick and remove outer layer of fat. Cut meat into ½-inch cubes. In skillet, brown onion lightly in fat. Toss beef with quick-browning aid and add to skillet with wine and enough beef stock to reach a depth of ¼ inch in pan. Cover pan, bring liquid to boil rapidly, lower heat, and simmer until beef is tender, about 1½ hours.

Pour pan juices into measuring cup and add more beef stock, if necessary, to make ¾ cup. Add Worcestershire, and season to taste. Thicken liquid, using 2 tablespoons flour, and combine with beef and tomatoes.

Prepare Batter-Bread Pudding, above, and pour half into pan. Bake in preheated, very hot 450° F. oven, until puffed and set, about 10 minutes. Spread with meat and gravy, cover with remaining batter, and bake until crisp and golden brown, about 15 minutes longer. Makes 4-plus servings and may be frozen.

Jambalaya

Even though the word derives from *jambon,* the French word for ham, so many ingredients can go into what is basically a rice pilaf, that this Southern staple might better be called jumble-aya. My favorite from way-back-when jambalaya recipe begins, "Skin two coots."

Shrimp and ham are the classic components, but oysters, sausage, rabbit, and game birds (the coots) also are treated to this redolent tomatoey sauce, which is similar to that used for Lobster Americaine.

In New Orleans, jambalaya is served between appetizer and entree. Charleston heats leftover chicken, pork, veal, or mutton jambalaya-fashion.

The garlic in the following can be omitted. The amount to use depends upon your tolerance for it; and the strength of the cloves, determined by size, age, and variety. Test by smelling a peeled clove—and for ease in peeling, crush it, and the skin will lift off.

- 1–4 cloves garlic, diced
- 1 teaspoon salt
- 1 bay leaf
- 1 teaspoon dried thyme
- $\frac{1}{16}$ teaspoon cayenne pepper
- ½ teaspoon cloves
- 4 tablespoons oil, preferably olive
- 1 large onion, chopped
- ¼ cup bell pepper, chopped, optional
- 1 can (6-ounce) tomato paste
- ¼ cup dry wine, optional
- 1 cup rice
- 1½ cups (about ½ pound) cooked ham, cut in 1-inch cubes
- 1 package (10-ounce) frozen shelled shrimp

In mortar and pestle crush garlic to a paste with salt. Add and crush bay leaf and thyme. Add cayenne and cloves. Meanwhile, heat oil in heavy casserole. Add garlic mixture and cook until aromatic, about 2 minutes, stirring as necessary. Add onion and green pepper and cook covered about 5 minutes more, or until softened. Add tomato paste diluted with wine, plus enough water to make 3 cups liquid. Bring to boil. Add rice and ham, cover casserole, bring liquid to boil rapidly, lower heat and simmer about 30 minutes, or until liquid is almost absorbed. Add shrimp, preferably in a single layer, and continue cooking, covered, until rice is tender and shrimp is done, about 5 minutes. If desired, serve dotted with butter and sprinkled with parsley. Makes 4 servings. Jambalaya improves with overnight storage and with every subsequent reheating and may be frozen.

Jambolin

Mississippi gives jambalaya, a name that has the sound of a delightful carnival, a diminutive ending and substitutes the diminutive bacon for ham (jambon). The dish is inexpensive, and reminiscent of both carbonara sauce for pasta and of Spanish rice.

Like so many Southern recipes, it takes care of leftover rice splendidly. Although the butter may seem superfluous, it is a needed enhancement. Serve jambolin as starch or topped with any cooked seafood to offer as an entree.

- 1 tablespoon butter
- 4 strips bacon
- 1 large onion, diced
- 2 cups (1-pound can) tomatoes in tomato purée
- 2 cups cooked rice

In large heavy skillet, melt butter. Add bacon cut in bits (scissors make it easy) and fry covered, over low heat, tossing as necessary until it begins to crisp. Add onion, and fry covered until it begins to brown. Add tomatoes and cook uncovered until mixture thickens to sauce consistency. Add rice and cook covered on very low heat until rice browns, scraping it up from bottom occasionally, and adding a little water, if necessary, to avoid scorching. Allow about 30 minutes for complete cooking. Makes 6 servings; tastes better with every reheating and may be frozen.

Cheese Toast

This cheese dish of English legacy is more unusual than Welsh Rabbit or Scotch Woodcock. It takes economical advantage of stale bread. Serve it at lunch, and, if the bread cupboard is bare, spread the mixture on *biscottes*. Choose any preferred variety of grated cheese, white wine may be used throughout, and the proportion may be increased ad infinitum.

- **1 slice stale white bread**
- **2 tablespoons dry red wine, approximately**
- **1 tablespoon grated cheddar cheese**
- **1 teaspoon butter**
- **2 teaspoons dry white wine**
- **¼ teaspoon dry mustard**

Saturate bread with red wine. Make a paste of remaining ingredients and season to taste. Spread on bread and broil until browned and bubbly. Probably everyone will want at least two of these.

A CREAM OF SAUCES

Numerous is the best word for sauces of the South, many of which include Dixie's favorite spices—mace, nutmeg, cinnamon, and cayenne—all announcing their presence like a clarion.

The cheerfully permissive Mrs. Mary Randolph announces in her *Virginia Housewife:* "You may put as many Things as you choofe into Sauces." Although this might not be considered a completely helpful directive, the lady is perfectly right.

Sauces are internationally similar, and in the South, the word becomes multipurpose—gravy and sauce being used interchangeably. Even unpeeled, sliced green peaches or apples, fried in lard acquire the title. The German affection for ginger is reflected in the directive that ginger-snap crumbs can be used to thicken the gravy for any kind of roast.

Today, tomato paste, purée, and tomato purée with tomato pieces ease sauce-making and happily we are able to purchase the variety of catsups, such as mushroom and oyster, so dear to the hearts of Southern cooks of British heritage.

THICKENED SAUCES

The following chart gives proportions on which most of the world's sauces are based. Because they are proportions, if one ingredient is increased or decreased, so must all the others.

The fat is for flavor alone, and may be omitted. When milk makes the liquid, the result is called "White Sauce."

Unless your preference is for more or less thickening, use the thin proportion for soup or gravy; medium for bisques, creamed meat, poultry, seafood, eggs, vegetables; thick for soufflés and croquettes.

Chart For Flour-Thickened Sauces

Sauce	Fat	Flour	Liquid
Thin	1 tablespoon	1 tablespoon	1 cup
Medium	2 tablespoons	2 tablespoons	1 cup
Thick	3 tablespoons	3 tablespoons	1 cup
Very Thick	4 tablespoons	4 tablespoons	1 cup

The following is a simplified method I developed for putting the ingredients together. For ease and speed, it may be used whenever a roux is not required.

Place fat and most of liquid in saucepan and cook on low heat until liquid warms and fat, if solid, melts. In jar with tight cover (or blender), place remaining liquid (which must be cold), allowing about 2 tablespoons for each tablespoon flour. Add flour and shake (or whir) until mixture is smooth. Pour into heated mixture, and stir constantly until sauce comes to a boil. If storing, cover to prevent skin formation.

EGG-LACED SAUCES

Beat egg yolk slightly. Remove any Flour-Thickened Sauce from heat, and beat about a tablespoon at a time into yolk until warmed sufficiently to prevent curdling. Stir back into sauce, and if not thick enough, stir constantly over low heat until it reaches desired consistency, about 2 minutes. Do not let sauce boil.

To thicken sauces with cornstarch (or arrowroot, a more costly, but not better, substitute), use half the amount of flour called for, and simply stir some of the cold liquid into the cornstarch until smooth. Then add to remaining cold liquid and stir until it comes to a boil. If sauce tastes of raw starch, cover, and continue cooking over very low heat, stirring occasionally.

Roux

A roux gives sauces a comfortable color and a fine toasty flavor. The word is French for "reddish-brown," and roux-making probably reached New Orleans along with the first cooks and their *casseroles a pieds*. The color can range from golden to dark-brown—depending upon the length of time the flour cooks. If you like a very thick sauce, be warned—as flour cooks, its thickening power lessens.

Method If necessary, melt fat. Stir flour in, and using low heat, cook, stirring as necessary, until desired color is achieved. Stir liquid in gradually and stir constantly until sauce comes to a boil (it bubbles in the center).

Onion Roux

Cook sliced or diced onion in the fat, either before or after flour has been added.

GRAVY—SAUCES

Onion Gravy For Poultry

This enhances roast pork or veal, too. In a pinch, substitute water for stock and if desired make about ¼ cup dry white wine part of the liquid. The herbs can be thyme, marjoram, or what you will.

Sage, according to early authors (and I concur) is too strong-flavored for chicken.

> **Chicken Stock***
> 3 onions, sliced
> 1 tablespoon lard
> 3 tablespoons flour
> 1 teaspoon dried herbs
> 2 tablespoons minced parsley

Add enough stock to pan in which poultry was roasted to measure 2 cups liquid in all. Cook, stirring to scrape up brown particles. In covered skillet, brown onion in lard, stirring as necessary—it will take about 30 minutes. Make a brown roux* with flour and add liquid from roasting pan (skimmed of fat, if desired), and herbs. Bring to boil, add parsley, and season to taste. Yields about 2½ cups.

Lemon Butter Sauce

Marylanders clarify the butter and substitute chives for seafood in their version of Maitre d'Hotel Butter. Approximately 2 tablespoons dry white wine may be substituted for lemon juice and rind.

> ½ cup (¼ pound) butter
> 1 lemon
> 3 tablespoons snipped chives

Clarify butter by melting and pouring into bowl carefully, and discard sediment and milky portion that settles on bottom. Add juice and grated rind of lemon, and chives, and season to taste. Serve hot. Yields ½ cup sauce; enough for 4 servings meat, poultry, seafood that have been sautéed, broiled, or baked.

Parsley Butter Sauce

Virginians serve this with steak, beef roast, and/or seafood.

Place ½ cup minced parsley in a sieve and quickly dip in and out of boiling water. Drain and add to ¼ cup butter, clarified as above. Add lemon juice and rind, if desired.

Kill With Kindness Sauce
Egg Dressing

A rich-as-Croesus topping for cooked fish, baked potatoes, asparagus, artichoke bottoms, and what you will. Fabulous cold, too, as an hors d'oeuvre spread.

To cook yolks alone, drop into a pan of boiling water, cover, and cook over low heat until firm, about 10 minutes. Freeze the whites for an angel food cake.

- 2 eggs, hard cooked
- 2 cooked egg yolks
- ½ cup (¼ pound) butter, melted

Chop eggs and yolks, or whir in blender. Stir butter in and season to taste. It can take cayenne pepper. Yields about 1 cup sauce.

Cheese Sauce

Cornstarch used as thickening betrays the French genesis of this Creole sauce for compatible vegetables or potatoes. Escoffier, in a dissertation on sauces says: "It is only habit that causes flour to be still used as the binding element. . . . A sauce made with pure starch such as cornstarch will be clearer, more brilliant and better . . ."

- 1 teaspoon cornstarch
- ½ cup milk
- 1 tablespoon butter
- 1¾ cups American cheese, grated

Dissolve cornstarch in about a tablespoon cold milk. Melt butter in remaining milk and stir cornstarch in. Continue to cook, stirring until thickened and no raw starch taste remains. Remove from heat and stir cheese in. If not hot enough to melt cheese, stir over very low heat and remove as soon as cheese melts. Makes about 1 cup.

Cheese Sauce For Fish

Add ½ teaspoon dry mustard and 1 teaspoon Worcestershire sauce to above, to serve over poached fish.

Celery Sauce

Celery sauces are fine for pouring over veal, chicken, or fish. This one can double as a vegetable if the amount of butter and flour are doubled. Then if you add chopped hard-cooked egg, it makes a delicate and nutritious luncheon entree.

 3 cups (about 6 stalks) celery, diced
 1 cup chicken stock
 ½ cup cream
 1½ tablespoons butter
 1½ tablespoons flour
 ⅛ teaspoon mace
 ¼ teaspoon nutmeg

Discard leaves and cook celery covered in boiling stock, until tender, about 20 minutes. Drain and prepare Thickened Sauce* with drained liquid. Return celery to sauce, add spices, and season to taste, adding a dot of sugar if desired. Makes about 2 cups; enough for 6-plus servings.

Celery Puree Sauce

Flecks of about a tablespoon snipped parsley threaded through the finished sauce enhance appearance.

 1 cup celery, puréed
 ½ cup cream
 1 tablespoon butter
 1 tablespoon flour

Cook celery as above. Prepare Thickened Sauce* with drained liquid and remaining ingredients, and season to taste. Makes about 1 cup.

French-Market Sauce

This is an outstanding example of the wonderful French way with foods. Serve as a sauce or as a dunk for hors d'oeuvre.

1 tablespoon flour
½ cup Pepper Stock*
Vinegar, optional

Add, if necessary, enough fat to pan in which crumb- or batter-coated food has been fried, to measure a tablespoon. Make a brown roux* with flour, and add pepper stock. When sauce comes to a boil, add vinegar, if desired, for piquancy, and season to taste. Yields ½ cup.

TOMATO SAUCES

Southerners like these on the sweet side, and after all, tomatoes are a fruit. In addition, a small amount of sugar helpfully neutralizes the acidity of the tomato.

Creole Tomato Sauce

Flour-thickening makes this a quick and easy multipurpose sauce for baking chicken parts, pork chops, or fish. The optional additions are legion and their flavor—and that final arbiter, your palate—determine delectability.

Roux

1 medium onion, diced
2 tablespoons lard
2 tablespoons flour
½ cup liquid (chicken or beef stock or water)
1 can (16 ounce) tomatoes with tomato paste or 1 can (8 ounces) tomato purée

In large saucepan, add onion to melted lard and cook covered over medium heat, stirring as necessary, until onion begins to brown, about 15 minutes. Make a light-colored roux* with flour, and add liquid and tomatoes gradually. Add any (or all) from the following and cook over medium heat until sauce thickens, about 15 minutes, stirring as necessary.

Optional Additions

- 2 tablespoons dry wine, white or red
- ½ cup freeze-dried mushrooms
- 2 tablespoons dried bell peppers
- 1 tablespoon quick-browning aid
- ⅛ teaspoon hot red pepper
- 1 teaspoon sugar
- 1 tablespoon dried parsley
- 1 teaspoon dried basil
- 1 teaspoon dried thyme
- ½ teaspoon dried marjoram

Barbecue Sauce

The South boasts countless days of perfect barbecue weather, and the many possible additions to what basically is a hotly-spiced tomato sauce, allow every cook to claim her own "secret" recipe.

This one boasts speed, redolent flavor, and is useful on food to be grilled out of doors or roasted or broiled on your kitchen range. It also makes a good table substitute for ketchup.

- 1 can (6-ounce) tomato paste
- ½ cup sharp vinegar
- ¼ teaspoon hot red pepper
- ½ teaspoon salt
- 1 teaspoon sugar
- 1½ tablespoons quick-browning aid, optional

Combine ingredients, and adjust to taste. Yields about 2 cups sauce and may be frozen.

AN EDEN OF VEGETABLES

The rich Southern soil blooms a largesse of vegetables. Perhaps too many for long ago cook book writers, who instructed their readers in gentle deception. Whether or not diners were deluded, green corn fritters supposedly could pass for oysters; fried eggplant for soft shell crab. Old cook books sniffed at snobbery, too. Readers were assured that pumpkin baked with molasses was "better than many things with more reputation."

One of those many things may have been "harty choaks." If rarity connotes elegance, it could not have been broccoli. Because although Damn Yankees of the early 1900s considered the vegetable a new Italian import, at least a hundred years earlier, it was growing so profligately in the South that only the heads were served.

Still strange to Damn Yankees, though, is rappini, the young turnip plant, plucked (as is the scallion) before the bulb develops. It tastes like dandelion greens. The Blue Ridge area of North Carolina celebrates Spring with the ramp, a wild leek a *New York Times* writer described as a high-intensity onion, that is "a pungent mountain delicacy" to its admirers; to others, "an abominable cross of onion and garlic with the worst features of both."

Also foreign to our markets is the mirliton, described as New Orleans' most distinctive vegetable, "climbing" as one author poetically put it, "in wild haste over back fences."

However, we do have turnips to cut into olive-shape for glazing in butter and sugar—as Maryland cooks were instructed. But the price tag of the truffle, for which Williamsburg ladies seem to have reached with abandon, must give us pause.

The following vegetables are Damn Yankee familiars, to enrich in Southern ways, and to add delicious variety and distinction to your table—as they have to mine.

Pot Likker Portmanteau

Of all the Southern classics, this is probably the most famous— and best known as Greens and Pot Likker. Testing on my own, I failed miserably. When I was privileged to watch it done correctly—as follows—I was informed that snap beans, cabbage, parsnips, white and yellow turnip (Swedes and rutabagas), and blackeye peas can receive identical treatment.

Pork neck bones or smoked ham hock can replace streak-o-lean and the liquid left from cooking them can be used for preparing the vegetables. Of the greens often sharing the same pot there is a choice of turnip greens, mustard greens, kale, and collards.

Today even old Southern hands take advantage of frozen greens and soon may be adding to this orchestra, one called Ethiopian rapeseed in European commerce. It has passed successful tests for freezing and canning, and, in addition to nutritional advantage, yields about five tons more per acre than spinach. It claims kin to collards, but with milder flavor—and to mustard greens, but without their pungency. I wonder what rapeseed will be called when it is ready for the retail pot.

In the South, when topped with Cornmeal Dumplings,* platters of greens "flavored with meat," as one author put it are considered an entree. Lemon wedges or vinegar are passed, and menu accompaniments often include rice, sliced tomatoes, and scallions. Cake or pie come on for dessert.

If you find the gross overcooking of the vegetables nutritionally egregious, realize that early on, it was considered impossible to cook any vegetable too much.

- 6–8 ounces streak-o-lean
- 1 package (about 10 ounces) frozen chopped greens
- 2 cups water
- 2 teaspoons sugar

Slice streak-o-lean ¼" thick and cut 2-inch pieces. Place in saucepan with water, greens, and sugar. Cover pan and bring liquid to boil rapidly, breaking up frozen block of greens with fork. When thawed, reduce heat, cover, and cook gently until greens are soft as velvet, about one hour, adding more water if necessary. Season to taste, realizing that Southerners don't add pepper. Makes 4 servings.

ARTICHOKES

In deference to the thistly choke, globe or French artichokes often are called burr artichokes in the South. "Get them young," directs a New Orleans cook book, and "serve with mustard and oil." No better way than with Creole Mustard*. Or prepare in a seemingly inevitable Southern way—baked in a pye.

CORN

Maize, sometimes called Indian Corn, is an American native, and probably our major agricultural contribution to the world. The word derives from *maiz,* via *mahiz,* which comes from the Taino tribe—a group of now-extinct aboriginals.

In the interest of history, Pamunky, an ancient corn variety, currently is being given rebirth by agricultural students at the Virginia Polytechnic Institute.

But there is nothing extinct about maize as a crop, and the spread of hybrid corn, since the late 1800s, is the most spectacular food-production triumph of the twentieth century. Hybrids have been "hand-tailored," to weather storm or drought, pest, disease, and the unthinking rigidity of mechanical harvesting. Much of the thanks for the superior varieties and their abundant yield goes to Henry A. Wallace, who worked with "ancestor seeds" with stunning names such as Copper Cross and Bloody Butcher.

My many reference books all offer varying definitions of the difference between field corn, fodder corn, roasting ears, sweet corn, green corn, and maize. But agreement is universal on dried or parched corn—sweet corn that has been cooked, then dried. Guinea Corn is *durra,* by way of the Arabic—*dhurah,* a variety of grain-yielding sorghum, widely grown as food, in North Africa and Southern Asia.

In buying sweet corn, generally called "green corn" in the South, count the rows. If the cob boasts 14 or more, the kernels will be narrow, deep, and consequently, more tender.

Three medium-sized fresh ears of corn yield about 1 cup kernels; 6 ears of grated corn yield about 1 cup; 1 package frozen cut corn yields about 2 cups kernels.

Krewe Corn

A roux says New Orleans, and I urge you to try this recipe even if it doesn't "sound good." It seems to me, a firm corn devotee, who tested this with turned-up nose, the ultimate in corn as a vegetable —and proof that nature can be improved on.

    1 tablespoon flour
    1 tablespoon lard
    1 tablespoon instant minced onion

4 cups frozen corn kernels
2 cups water, about
Dash cayenne pepper

In large skillet, prepare a brown roux* with flour and lard. Add onion, and stir until chips brown. Add frozen corn and stir until thawed. Gradually stir in enough water for sauce consistency.

Cover and cook until corn heats, about 5 minutes, stirring as necessary, adding cayenne pepper, and in the words of the source, "Season well." Makes 4 servings.

Corn Fritters
Artificial Oysters

If using frozen or canned corn (neither of which needs preliminary cooking), be sure kernels are well-drained before adding them to batter. To pretend, fry them oyster-size, in deep fat, or on a greased griddle as for pancakes. This Damn Yankee serves them with maple syrup.

2 eggs, separated
2 cups cooked corn kernels
¼ cup flour
1 teaspoon baking powder
2 teaspoons sugar
½ teaspoon salt
3 tablespoons milk
¼ teaspoon cream of tartar

Add corn to beaten yolks. Mix flour, baking powder, sugar, and salt, and combine with egg mixture. Stir milk in and fold in egg whites, beaten with a pinch of salt and cream of tartar to soft peak stage.

Fry in deep fat until brown, allowing about 3 minutes on each side. Makes 4 servings.

Corn and Okra

Summer says fresh vegetables. In winter, substitute frozen or canned, and if you like, serve sauced in any season.

¼ pound (about 2 cups) fresh okra pods*
1 ounce streak-o-lean* sliced thin
1 cup fresh corn kernels
½ teaspoon sugar, approximately

Remove stem ends and cut okra into ¼-inch rounds. Over low heat, in heavy covered pan, cook streak-o-lean until enough fat has been rendered to cover bottom of pan. Add okra and cook gently, covered, about 15 minutes, stirring occasionally. Add corn, and cook covered, about 5 minutes or more or until okra is tender, stirring as necessary. Add sugar and season to taste. Makes 4 servings.

Sauce

Shake ½ cup milk in a jar with 1 tablespoon flour. Add to pan and cook, stirring, until it comes to a boil.

Corn Lorraine

In France, a Quiche without a bottom crust is called Creme Lorraine. If the French title pleases you not, call this Corn Custard, as the old books do, and serve the rich elegance as a Quiche. Then to avoid a soggy crust, prepare as follows.

Milk or cream may be substituted for half-and-half and if it's to be a luncheon entree, substitute diced ham (or combine with corn). For Southern guests, replace the Parmesan cheese with a sprinkle of nutmeg before baking and serve cold, if desired.

1 egg and 2 egg yolks, beaten slightly
1½ cups half-and-half
1 cup cooked corn kernels
2 teaspoons salt
1½ teaspoons instant minced onion
1½ tablespoons dried bell peppers
Dash cayenne pepper

Topping

Parmesan cheese
Paprika

Beat a small amount of cold half-and-half with eggs, and scald remainder. Combine with remaining ingredients, and season to taste. Line a 7-inch pie pan with foil, butter it, and fill with mixture. Set in a pan of simmering water up to level of pie-pan rim, and bake in preheated, moderate 375° F. oven until tip of paring knife inserted halfway between center and outer rim comes out clean. Cool and loosen with table knife. Turn out on plate covered with plastic wrap, and remove foil. Top with cold baked 7-inch pie shell and invert plate. Before serving, sprinkle with topping ingredients and bake in hot 400° F. oven until cheese melts, about 10 minutes. Makes 4 servings.

Pauline's Succotash

Long ago, I read that "succotash" was a corruption of the Indian word "m'siqquatash" and originally was made with snap beans rather than lima beans, which were considered an inferior crop. The recipe reflected a twining resulting from the Indian method for growing corn and beans. As explorer, Samuel de Champlain, wrote in 1605: "With this corn they put in each hill three or four beans . . . when they grow up, they interlace with the corn which reaches to the height of five to six feet." Frequently, a dead fish was tucked in to enrich the soil. This Southern recipe was the product of a cook gone deliciously wild—and you can go even wilder by adding okra. If your cream refuses to sour, add 1½ teaspoons vinegar or lemon juice or substitute the commercial variety.

- 2 cups lima beans
- 1 pound snap beans
- 3 large tomatoes, peeled
- 1 cup corn kernels
- 2 tablespoons flour
- 2 tablespoons butter
- ½ cup room temperature sour cream
- 2 teaspoons sugar

Cook lima and snap beans with tomatoes in ¼ cup boiling salted water until beans are tender, about 15 minutes. Add corn and cook until done, about 5 minutes. Prepare Thickened Sauce* with flour, butter, and cream and add to vegetables. When mixture comes to boil, add sugar and season to taste. Makes 8 servings.

Eggplant Matty Winston's Way

Economy of motion and timing mark the professional—and watching one at work is eminently satisfying. Suzanne Winston, one of my favorite performers, married a gentleman of Virginia ancestry, and when eggplants in their garden grew, he glowingly described his mother's way with them. Miz Winston's Damn Yankee daughter-in-law translated correctly and I had the pleasure of being both spectator and diner.

Recipes directing that eggplant be salted before cooking, as this one does, hark back to the 12th century when the vegetable was called *mal d'insana* because the juice supposedly drove men mad. (How hard superstitions die!) Salting sacrifices food value, so the direction need be heeded only as a preliminary to frying, because then, the salt extracts juice, which otherwise would dilute the fat, cause spattering, and make browning difficult.

Peel a medium-size eggplant and slice into circles no thicker than ¼ inch. Stack in a casserole and salt each layer. Allow to stand about 30 minutes, and pour off liquid. Spread slices between paper towels to dry.

In a wide, heavy pan heat lard to depth of about ¼ inch. In a cereal dish, beat an egg slightly with salt, pepper, and about a tablespoon milk. Sprinkle white cornmeal (the Winstons' preference for this recipe) on waxed paper. Use tongs throughout and dip one eggplant slice at a time in egg, then cornmeal. Drop directly into hot fat and fry, turning to brown both sides—at which point it should be just tender.

Spread slices on absorbent paper to drain (do not stack or they will lose their crispness). A medium-size eggplant fried this way *should* be enough for four diners.

Mushroom Caps on Fried Bread

New Orleans mates mushrooms and mace in a lovely luncheon dish.

- ¼ **cup butter**
- ¼ **teaspoon powdered mace, approximately**
- 12 **large mushroom caps (about 1 pound)**
- 4 **slices French bread, cut ½-inch thick**

Melt butter and add powdered mace. Add mushrooms, cap-side down in a single layer, cover and cook gently until done, about 10 minutes. Fry bread in butter, turning to brown both sides and top with mushroom caps. Makes 4 servings.

OKRA

Old recipes warn against cooking okra in iron utensils, because they discolor the vegetable. With iron skillets currently in vogue, take heed.

Any Damn Yankee, unfamiliar with this bright green vegetable, which is such a familiar on Southern tables, should look for 4-inch long, bright green unblemished pods with tips that bend easily. July is peak season. Rinse pods before cooking and overcook only if a gummy consistency is desired.

Stems need not be removed from small pods—cook whole, if desired. Cut large pods into ½-inch slices; small pods ¼-inch thick. One pound makes about 5 servings and 1 pint (¼ pound) equals 2 cups.

Okra is available frozen, too, both whole and sliced. Because it has been blanched, cooking time can be shortened by about half. Canned okra also is available and so is pickled okra, a Southern relish-dish favorite.

Fried Okra

Slice small, fresh, young pods into ¼-inch rounds. Dredge with cornmeal and fry in about ¼-inch of drippings, stirring constantly until browned and crisp, about 10 minutes.

Okra Ratatouille

Cassell's French Dictionary defines ratatouille as a coarse stew. Transplanted French cooks immediately substituted okra for the eggplant of home and achieved a melange with a deliciously different flavor. Mushrooms, corn, beans or whatever you fancy, can join the vegetable throng and the dish may be served hot, as vegetable; cold; as menu-relish or hors d'oeuvre.

- ½ pound fresh okra pods, chopped coarsely
- 1 medium onion, sliced thin
- 2 tablespoons butter
- 1 can (1 pound) tomatoes in tomato purée
- 1 teaspoon sugar, approximately

In pan, preferably heavy, combine ingredients and add 2 tablespoons water. Cover and simmer until okra is very soft and sauce thickens—from 20 to 45 minutes. Season to taste. Makes 4 servings.

PARSNIPS

If you have never tasted a parsnip, realize that it is the whitish-brown root supermarkets tuck into bags of "soup vegetables" in winter. Because it is sweet, do not add a whole parsnip to your stock pot.

Taste a thin slice raw and peel as for carrots in the interest of appearance. If you like, serve sticks or rounds as hors d'oeuvre.

The South, obviously paying no attention to the "butter me no parsnips" cliche, batter-fries sliced parsnip, mashes cooked parsnip "like turnips," or cooks it as for Pot Likker Portmanteau*.

Twin-City Stewed Peas

To differentiate them from blackeye peas, Southerners call them "green English peas." An ancient cook book announces that a quart is enough for a "small mess," and suggests serving them in the "spring of the year" with lamb.

Tennessee Ernie Ford, who refers to himself as a pea picker adds to his vocal distinction the fact that he was born in Bristol, Tennessee —a town whose Main Street cuts a state boundary. Bristol, Virginia, its "twin city" lies on the other side of the street. Obviously, a chicken crossing Main Street is simply taking off for another state.

As in so many "sauced" vegetables, food value is preserved. Here, the liquid is thickened with *beurre manie*.

- 4 cups (about 4 pounds in the shell) shelled green peas
- 1 teaspoon sugar
- 1 tablespoon butter
- 1½ teaspoons flour

Pour over peas and sugar 1 cup cold water brought to boil, and boil, covered, until just tender, about 15 minutes. Blend butter with flour and stir bits in to reach desired sauce consistency. Stir until liquid boils and season to taste. Makes 4 servings.

BELL PEPPERS

Because of their shape, bell, rather than green peppers is their name in the South. It makes sense because, when completely ripe, green peppers turn a glorious red. Although color does not determine use or flavor, look forward to Fall for decking your dishes with scarlet brilliance.

It is aesthetics that direct that seeds and white pulp be removed. Dried bell peppers are a superb convenience and invariably sweet and tender.

IRISH POTATOES

White potatoes are called Irish potatoes in Dixie to differentiate them from sweet potatoes. Although Irish potatoes mostly are prepared in typical ways the meals at which they appear may be unique. "Stewed Irish Potatoes," (creamed potatoes) with a fillip of chopped parsley, a Southern cook book suggests, will serve as "a nice breakfast dish."

Following a recipe for Sweet Potato Pudding (in reality a pie) the *Williamsburg Art of Cookery* allows as how Irish Potato Pudding "is made in the *f*ame Manner, but is not *f*o good."

In one of New Orleans' famous *vieux carre* restaurants, the curious menu-listing, Potatoes Brabant Bordelaise, impelled me to order it. Brabant signifies prepared in the style of a province in the Netherlands; Bordelaise—in the style of Bordeaux. What arrived was a dish of cooked, diced Irish potatoes that seemed to have been deep-fried, tossed with bits of garlic, minced parsley, and butter—in the style of Provence.

The following recipes have French and Spanish, rather than hashed background—and are guest-pleasers all.

Potatoes Au Four

Four is French for oven and in this recipe, peeled potatoes are baked in a covered pan—which distinguishes them from the crisp-crusted Franconia Potatoes. Instead, the potatoes will be browned and chewy.

Choose small potatoes of the same size, or if you have the time and are entertaining guests, choose large potatoes, peel, and cut rounds with the large end of a melon-ball cutter. Potatoes au Four are especially good companions for roasts, and will accept any oven temperature up to 400° F. This, and their size, determine doneness but they will contentedly wait well beyond the approximate 1½ hours required when medium-size potatoes are baked in preheated, moderate 350° F. oven.

For each potato, allow one teaspoon melted fat (lard, or drippings from prime ribs of beef, are especially good). Sprinkle with salt, pepper (preferably cayenne), and paprika; turn in the fat; and bake covered until tender, shaking dish occasionally for even browning.

Potatoes in Brown Butter

This way with potatoes goes hand in hand with Crusted Lamb Chops* or any other sautéed, breaded dish. Simply peel, quarter and boil medium potatoes. When tender, drain, add to skillet after removing fried food and turn, until hot and well-coated with fat and the crisp crumb particles. Butter obviously is a euphemism here.

Potatoes Auvergne

This makes a welcome Creole replacement for the usual baked stuffed potato.

- **6 medium size potatoes**
- **1 small clove garlic, diced, optional**
- **1 teaspoon salt**
- **½ cup cream, approximately**
- **2 tablespoons chopped pimento**
- **2 tablespoons chopped parsley**
- **Dash cayenne pepper**
- **¼ cup butter**

Bake potatoes in 350–450° F. oven, until done, about 45 minutes. Cut in half and scoop out to make a shell. Crush garlic to paste with salt, and mash with potato. When smooth, beat in enough cream for a light fluff. Add pimento, and parsley, and season to taste. Pile lightly into shells, leaving tops rough and dot with butter.

Bake in preheated 450–550° F. oven until browned, about 20 minutes. Makes 6 servings.

SWEET POTATOES
Yams

The true yam, a tuberous root of African origin, weighs about 7 pounds, resembles a semi-deflated football, and is a different plant from the yellow sweet potato with fawn-colored skin (which Ohio Damn Yankees call "Jerseys") and the dark, moist variety with whitish or reddish skin we obviously incorrectly term yams. Spanish markets offer another variety of the veritable yam, which is white-fleshed, and sold cut in chunks.

By any name, they are interchangeable in recipes and all ye need know is that "moist" sweet potatoes take less time to cook. Pumpkin and winter squash share enough similarities to be interchangeable with any of them in recipes.

When recipes call for pre-cooking, for best flavor and food value (they are high in Vitamin A), cook sweet potatoes whole in their jackets. Easy, too—the skin parts readily from cold potatoes. Depending on size, allow about 40 minutes in boiling water; about 50 minutes in a preheated, hot oven, 425° F. And if there's a bonfire, bury them, to bake in the ashes.

Buy sweet potatoes in small amounts and use within a week— especially early in the season. From Mid-November on, they are "cured" to increase storage span.

It appalled me to discover that I had always sliced sweet potatoes incorrectly. The right, and Southern way, is lengthwise, rather than crosswise. It takes strength, is easier to do with a cleaver, and eliminates stringiness.

Yam Crisps

When you taste these plainspeak potatoes, done an old Georgia way, you may never want to glaze or candy them again. They make a breakfast dish to serve with bacon, and Georgians pass a pitcher of molasses. At dinner, let them grace platters of ham, fried chicken, or game.

Peel 2 medium yams and slice about ½-inch thick, the long way. Drop into a bowl with enough cold water to cover. Add 1 tablespoon salt and soak 5 minutes. Heat lard in heavy pan to reach a depth of about ¼ inch. Dry potato slices and fry a few at a time, browning both sides lightly (about 10 minutes), at which point they should be tender. (If too brown, they will become tough and dry.) Drain on absorbent paper. Makes 4 servings and may be frozen.

Savannah Sweets

These are an unbelievable and complete joy.

    4 medium size yams
    1 cup sugar
    ¼ cup butter
    3 teaspoons vanilla, approximately
    ⅛ teaspoon salt
    Dash cayenne pepper
    ¼ cup water
    Nutmeg

Peel yams and cut ¼-inch thick lengthwise slices. Arrange in skillet, preferably heavy, sprinkling layers with sugar and dotting with butter. Add vanilla, salt, and cayenne to water to taste, and pour over potatoes. Grind nutmeg over top, cover skillet, bring liquid to boil rapidly, lower heat and simmer 20 minutes, adding more liquid, as needed, to prevent scorching. When potatoes are tender, if necessary to evaporate liquid, increase heat, and cook with pan only partially covered until it thickens to a syrup, about 10 minutes more. Makes 4 servings and may be frozen.

Benson Yam Puff

Benson is a small farm community in North Carolina—a state that impressed the first white man's expedition with, among other things, its "roots" (native yams). Benson yam farmers celebrate Mule Day, the climax of which is a mule-team sled-dragging contest. The non-obstinate tractor is fast making mules as obsolete as hearth-cooking. But hopefully, this soufflé, which Cubans call *dulce de boniatillo* and spice lavishly with cinnamon, will never vanish. For ease, use a 1 pound 2-ounce can of sweet potatoes.

- 2 cups cooked sweet potatoes
- 1 cup milk, scalded
- 2 tablespoons butter
- 2 tablespoons sugar, white or brown
- ¾ teaspoon salt, divided
- 2 eggs, separated
- 1 teaspoon allspice
- ½ cup broken pecans
- ½ cup raisins, optional
- ¼ teaspoon cream of tartar

Mash potatoes, and when smooth, beat in milk, butter, sugar, and ½ teaspoon salt. Beat yolks slightly and stir into potato mixture. Mix with allspice, pecans, and raisins. Beat egg whites with cream of tartar and remaining salt to soft peak stage, and fold into potatoes. Put into casserole and bake in preheated, moderate 325° F. oven until firm, about 40 minutes. Makes 6-plus servings.

Sweet Potato Pudding
Pain Patatre

Pain Patatre is Creole for Sweet Potato Pudding, alias Sweet Potato Pone. The pain-pone relationship is obvious; *patatre* is French for sweet potato.

Versions of the dish are far more numerous than the titles, indicating that *pain,* pone, pudding is a Southern repertoire imperative. Serve it with poultry or game, and admiring its versatility, bring it on as dessert, lavished with whipped cream.

Concerning the legion of recipes, realize that before pay day, you can use water as liquid and skimp on butter and eggs. Because spices do not cost a pretty penny, choose additions that please—cloves, ginger, nutmeg, cinnamon, mace, or allspice—singly or in combination. If you are an old-fashioned type, you may prefer rosewater; lemon juice and rind can replace orange. Etcetera additions include chopped almonds or pecans, raisins, bits of citron, or coconut flakes.

Orange preserves and brandy to stir with the liquid are further choices, and one glowing author pours a half cup of whiskey over the pudding.

Charley Burtt's Sweet Potato Pone

Following a dizzying number of tests for this dish, none of which pleased me, I yelled for help. Charley, with typical generosity, showed me how to put together a gorgeous rich Gargantua. You can decrease his Carolina version, at will, and add any of the above etceteras. One large raw yam yields about 2½ cups, grated.

- 6 large yams, peeled and grated
- ¾ cup butter, melted
- 5 eggs, beaten
- 1 quart milk
- 3 tablespoons vanilla
- 2 cups sugar
- Grated rind of 1 large orange

Beat butter into yams. Combine remaining ingredients, and stir into potato mixture. Fill a greased casserole ⅞ full, and bake in preheated, moderate 350° oven until firm and browned, about 2 hours. Serve hot or cold. Makes 8-plus servings and may be frozen.

Pecan Yams

These come to table with chicken or ham, and are a result of fiddling with a croquette recipe that refused to work.

- 2 cups (1-pound 2-ounce can) yams, mashed
- ½ cup brown sugar
- 1 egg, beaten slightly
- 1 teaspoon salt
- ½ cup pecans, chopped coarsely

Combine all ingredients except pecans and season to taste. Drop teaspoonfuls onto pecans and roll into balls with another teaspoon. Place on greased baking sheet, and bake on center rack of preheated, hot 400° F. oven, until pecans brown lightly, about 10 minutes. Makes about 1½ dozen and may be frozen.

Yam Dodgers

Central Europeans who settled in the South may be responsible for the substitution of yams for Irish potatoes, and variations of the recipe abound in Southern cook books. But nothing explains why the South calls dumplings "dodgers." Dodge bears some kinship to the German "duck down," but dumpling's root is the Scandinavian *dump*—"to let fall heavily." Let yours dodge, not dump.

> 2 cups (1-pound 2-ounce can) yams, mashed
> ¼ cup brown sugar, approximately
> 1 egg
> 1 cup flour, approximately
> ½ teaspoon salt
> Dash cayenne pepper, optional

Beat into the potatoes, sugar, egg, and enough flour for dumpling consistency. Season to taste and drop from tablespoon into boiling salted water. Boil gently and remove with slotted spoon as soon as they rise to the surface, about 5 minutes. Drain, turn in melted butter and brown sugar. Makes about 1½ dozen.

Fritter Dodgers

Chop 1 cup pecans coarsely. Prepare Yam Dodgers, as above, and drop each from tablespoon into chopped nuts. Fry in about ¼ inch hot fat, turning to brown both sides, and drain on absorbent paper. May be frozen.

SAUERKRAUT

Marylanders bake apple slices (and suggest "applesauce in a pinch"), brown sugar, and onion, with sauerkraut.

SPINACH

Creole cooks chop spinach—"it cannot be too fine"—and add a garnish of hard-cooked eggs "cut in fancy shapes." In early spring, cooks of old were told it was "nice to lay poached eggs on."

SQUASH

Squash, like tomatoes and cucumbers, botanically is a fruit, rather than a vegetable, and Southerners, with agreeable appropriateness, add sugar.

Summer Squash

The varieties, including today's popular zucchini, are interchangeable in recipes.

Alabama "candies" cymlings (the flat, scalloped squash) by dotting layers with butter and sprinkling generously with sugar before baking. Summer squash is often simmered in butter and cream for a "scallop." Sometimes the flesh is scooped, pureed and stuffed back into the shell, while a marvelous dish combines equal parts of mashed squash with corn and beaten egg to bake in a casserole until browned, and to eat PDQ.

Winter Squash

Pie made of squash, pumpkin, or yams—they are interchangeable—is a Southern dessert specialty. The molasses-drizzled recipe that follows is referred to by one author as a "dark sweet finish."

Acorn Squash with Molasses

The small acorn squash is more convenient to prepare and serve than Hubbard squash or pumpkin. Depending upon size of squash —and diner—allow ½ to 1 acorn squash per serving.

Halve squash, remove stringy portion and seeds and place flesh side down on roasting pan. Bake in preheated, moderate 350° F. oven 20 minutes. Turn flesh side up, drizzle with molasses, dot with butter, and bake until tender, about 30 minutes more.

Crusty Tomato Crisps in Cream

On Valentine's Day, call these "Love Apple Crisps" because tomatoes were hailed as love apples way back when, to differentiate them from "madapples," another of the names for eggplant.

The tomatoes must be green or just-ripe, so they will hold shape. Allow 1 medium tomato per serving. Cut into ¾-inch thick slices and dredge in cornmeal seasoned with salt and pepper. Fry in about ¼-inch fat.

A pan gravy, made with milk, always is referred to as cream gravy. For 4 tomatoes, remove fried slices from pan and make a roux* with 2 tablespoons flour. Brown slightly, and stir in 1 cup milk. Cook, stirring until it boils, season to taste, and pour over tomatoes.

Baked Tomato Crisps

This is an easier-to-do and less rich version of fried tomatoes. Slice as above, dip both sides in melted butter, then in seasoned cornmeal. Arrange on foil-lined baking sheet. Bake in preheated, very hot, 500° F. oven until browned, about 20 minutes. If slices stick to foil, allow to cool slightly.

TURNIPS

Georgians boil peeled, diced yellow turnips with "meat"—their word for streak-o-lean—to serve mashed, with the meat on the side.

DRIED VEGETABLES

Pulses are a large family, made up of the edible seeds of leguminous plants. The family seems even larger because so many of them—and they include beans and peas—have countless pet names. Blackeye peas, for instance, may be called cow peas, goober peas, or just plain Southern peas. Pigeon peas (a different variety) are Dixie favorites, too, along with red and marrow-fat beans.

No matter which pulse you have on hand, realize that they enhance themselves by absorbing enormous quantities of flavorful fats and liquids, to produce recipes that although basically the same, can be varied to suit your propensities. Hoppin' John* is a cassoulet version. Dixie cooks are more likely to boil than bake (a-la-Boston) dried vegetables, a fact that indicates that there's no stove hotter to stand over than a hot stove in a Southern kitchen on a sweltering summer day!

One pound dried vegetables (about 2 cups) yields about 5 cups after cooking; approximately 9 servings.

Baked Blackeye Peas

I was exposed to this admirable dish at a sumptuous Mississippi Shackelford Christmas dinner. If you are a fancier of home-baked beans, hurry the recipe into your oven, and to simplify your work somewhat, choose frozen blackeye peas.

To avoid using two pots for the following, cook in a top-of-range casserole throughout.

Parboiling Frozen Peas

- 1 package (10-ounce) frozen blackeye peas
- 2 cups water
- 1 small onion, diced
- 2 ounces streak-o-lean, cut into 1-inch cubes

Pour over peas cold water that has been brought to boil, and add onion and pork. Cover, bring liquid to boil rapidly, lower heat and boil gently until skins burst, about 10 minutes.

Sauce

- 2 tablespoons brown sugar
- 6 tablespoons dark molasses
- 1 teaspoon dried thyme
- ⅛ teaspoon hot red pepper
- ½ teaspoon salt

Season sauce to taste, and add to pot of peas, with enough additional boiling water to almost cover them. Cover, and bake in preheated, very slow 250° F. oven 4 hours, adding water, as needed, to prevent scorching. Uncover and bake about 1 hour longer or until beans are mealy. Makes 6-plus servings.

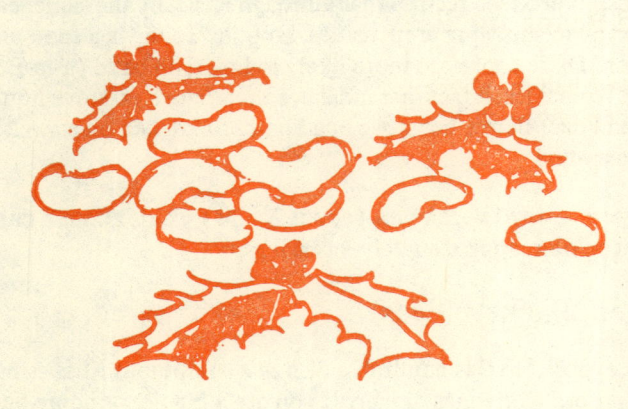

Red Beans

The omnipresent roux typifies this New Orleans treatment and cooks there prefer shallots to onions. A half-pound piece of ham or salt pork may be substituted for the ham bone. Then slice meat and arrange on top of beans. Or top with a dozen fried pork sausages or patties (see Homemade Pork Sausage*).

- 1 pound red beans
- 1 ham bone
- 1 tablespoon fat

- 1 tablespoon flour
- 1 teaspoon dried thyme
- ½ teaspoon dried sage
- 2 teaspoons dried parsley
- 2 small onions, sliced

Wash beans, discard any that are imperfect, and soak overnight in large saucepan in cold water to cover. Next day, add ham bone and enough additional cold water to cover beans. Cover pan, bring to boil, and cook gently until beans are tender, about 1½ hours. Drain, reserving liquid. Melt lard, stir flour in, add herbs and onion slices, and cook until edges of onion begin to brown, stirring as necessary. Stir in 1 cup bean water gradually, and add bits of ham picked from bone. Cook until onions are very soft, about 30 minutes, and combine with beans. Season to taste. Makes 4 cups after cooking; about 6 servings.

Red Beans and Rice

Prepare half the above proportion and combine with 1 cup cooked (½ cup raw) rice.

A TANG OF SALADS
A PIQUANCE OF RELISHES

Recipes for salads appeared as early as 1700. An old Southern cook book indexes green salads under the heading "Fresh Garden Stuff," and herb-enhanced salads dressed with oil and vinegar were piled on plates when gardens obliged.

In some sections, the greens are tossed a la Francais until *bien fatiguee*—completely limp and wilted. A New Orleans friend does not consider dressed greens fit to eat until they have fatigued for at least a day.

Along with green salads, potato, and "pressed" salads also contribute cool antidotes to all the hot summer days—then and now. And a venerable recipe for "gaspacho" begins with a "soft biscuit placed in a sallad bowl."

Yeoman Supper Salad

- 1 tablespoon dried bell pepper
- 1 tablespoon instant minced onion
- ¼ cup sharp vinegar, approximately
- 1 cup cooked blackeye peas
- 2 stalks celery (about 1 cup), diced
- 1 tomato, cut coarsely
- Dash cayenne pepper

Rehydrate peppers and onion in vinegar. It will take about 5 minutes. Add remaining ingredients and season to taste. Makes 4 servings.

Hanover Hominy Salad

The South embraced this German-background salad dressing, which in some regions is called Wilted Salad with Ham, for hominy. Lettuce (then call the salad Wilted Lettuce) may be substituted. The dressing is as delectable with up to 3 cups other tender greens, such as turnip or mustard, or with shredded cabbage.

A further gamut includes cooked vegetables, diced when necessary, such as okra, kale, collards, corn, Brussels sprouts, potatoes, summer squash, beets, snap beans, and turnips. Dice the onion for small vegetables such as hominy or corn, and for diced vegetables; slice it for shredded vegetables. Serve the salad hot or cold, and with hominy salad, pass a bowl of grated cheese.

- 3 strips bacon, cut into bits
- 2 cups cooked hominy
- 1 large onion, diced or sliced
- 1 teaspoon salt
- ⅛ teaspoon cayenne pepper, optional
- ¼ cup sharp vinegar
- ½ teaspoon sugar, optional

Cook bacon bits in covered skillet over low flame. When just crisp, pour bacon and pan-fat, over hominy. Add remaining ingredients to pan in which bacon was cooked and bring to boil. Pour over hominy, toss, and season to taste. Makes 6-plus servings.

Vinaigrette Dressing
Piquant French Dressing

What we call French dressing, the French call Vinaigrette. The following variation from an old Southern book, patronizingly calls it "Poor Man's Sauce with Oil." As opposed to the lavishing of butter in so many Southern sauces, it is indeed frugal. The author claims that it "eats extremely well with cold Lamb, cold Veal, or cold Chicken" and adds that "it may be eat with hot."

- 3 tablespoons oil, preferably olive
- 3 tablespoons vinegar, preferably wine
- ½ cup minced parsley
- 6 chopped scallions

Combine ingredients, adjust oil and vinegar for desired piquancy and season to taste. Yields about ¾ cup dressing.

Mayonnaise Whir

The blender makes this easier than pie.

- 1 egg
- ½ teaspoon paprika
- 1 teaspoon salt
- 2 tablespoons vinegar
- 2 cups vegetable oil, approximately

Place egg, paprika, and salt in blender and whir until mixed. Blend in vinegar. Keeping blender in motion, gradually pour in enough oil to thicken to mayonnaise consistency, and season to taste. Makes about 1½ cups.

Lemon Mayonnaise

Substitute lemon juice for vinegar in mayonnaise, above, and stir in ¼ cup snipped chives. For attractive presentation, pile into pinked lemon halves, and sprinkle with chives, to garnish a seafood platter.

Watercress Mayonnaise

Fold into Mayonnaise Whir, above, 1 bunch snipped watercress leaves.

Hot Water Mayonnaise

This Southern stalwart, dresses poultry, seafood, cooked vegetables, and cole slaw or greens. If nutrition is on your mind, substitute milk or buttermilk for water, and if calories are no problem, use half-and-half.

- **1 cup water, divided**
- **3 eggs**
- **1½ teaspoons flour**
- **1 tablespoon sugar**
- **1 teaspoon dry mustard**
- **Dash cayenne pepper**
- **¼ cup white vinegar**
- **2 tablespoons butter**

Pour 2 tablespoons of the water into broad shallow saucepan. Add eggs and beat only until mixed. Combine in bowl flour, sugar, mustard, and cayenne. Add vinegar and remaining water gradually, stirring to make a smooth paste. Stir into egg mixture and cook over very low heat, stirring constantly until mixture coats spoon rather thickly. Pour into bowl immediately and stir butter in. Season to taste and cover surface with plastic wrap. Refrigerate and serve cold. Makes about 1½ cups.

Old Dominion Sour Sauce

Add 1 cup medium White Sauce* to the above to dress asparagus, Brussels sprouts, broccoli, or use as a dunk for artichokes.

Cream Mayonnaise

Whip ½ cup heavy cream and fold into chilled Hot Water Mayonnaise.

Ravigote Sauce

A marvelous enricher—especially intriguing on seafood.

> 1 cup Mayonnaise Whir*
> 1 tablespoon minced green pepper
> 1 tablespoon minced fresh onion
> 1 hard-cooked egg, chopped fine
> ¼ cup tomato paste
> 1 tablespoon capers, optional
> 1 cup cream, whipped stiff

Fold ingredients into mayonnaise, and season to taste. Makes about 2½ cups dressing.

Remoulade Sauce

New Orleans is famous for this sharp variation of mayonnaise. In some very old books, it is called *Sauce Froide* and suggested as a dressing for fish, while others note that "it is an old salad dressing." An "Oyſter Salad" recipe that begins, "Drain the Liquor from one-half Gallon Freſh Oyſters," advises tossing the dressing "up well with a Silver Fork."

The sauce and its endless variations—chopped celery, pickles, and horseradish are sometimes additions—enlivens any cold, cooked poultry or seafood; is equally at home on a green salad or cole slaw; and provides a perfect dunk for raw vegetables.

> 4 eggs, hard cooked
> ½ teaspoon dried tarragon
> 1 tablespoon dried parsley
> 1 tablespoon freeze-dried chives
> 2 teaspoons salt
> 1 teaspoon dry mustard
> 6 tablespoons oil, preferably olive
> 1 egg, well beaten
> 2 tablespoons sharp vinegar, approximately

Chop egg whites fairly fine. Mash yolks with herbs and mustard. Beat oil in gradually and when smooth, add raw egg. Beat well, and beat in enough vinegar for desired sharpness. Add chopped egg white and season to taste. Yields about 1 cup.

Remoulade Cream

This is a dreamy, creamy variation of Remoulade Sauce*, above. Use it to dress greens—any of the lettuce varieties, escarole, spinach leaves, chicory. For interest combine different greens. Remoulade Cream also can enhance frozen mixed garden vegetables that have been thawed and drained.

The proportions of lemon juice and mustard depend upon your preference for the piquant and the peppery.

- **6 eggs, hard cooked**
- **¾ cup cream, approximately**
- **¼ teaspoon dry mustard, approximately**
- **¼ cup lemon juice, approximately**
- **2 teaspoons instant minced onion, optional**

Whir egg yolks in blender, or chop fine. Chop egg whites fine. Stir into yolks almost enough cream for salad dressing consistency. Add mustard, lemon juice, instant minced onion, and let stand 10 minutes. Season to taste, adding more cream, if necessary for salad dressing consistency. Coarsely tear enough greens for 6 salads into pieces. Toss with dressing, and taste for seasoning, again. Garnish with egg white.

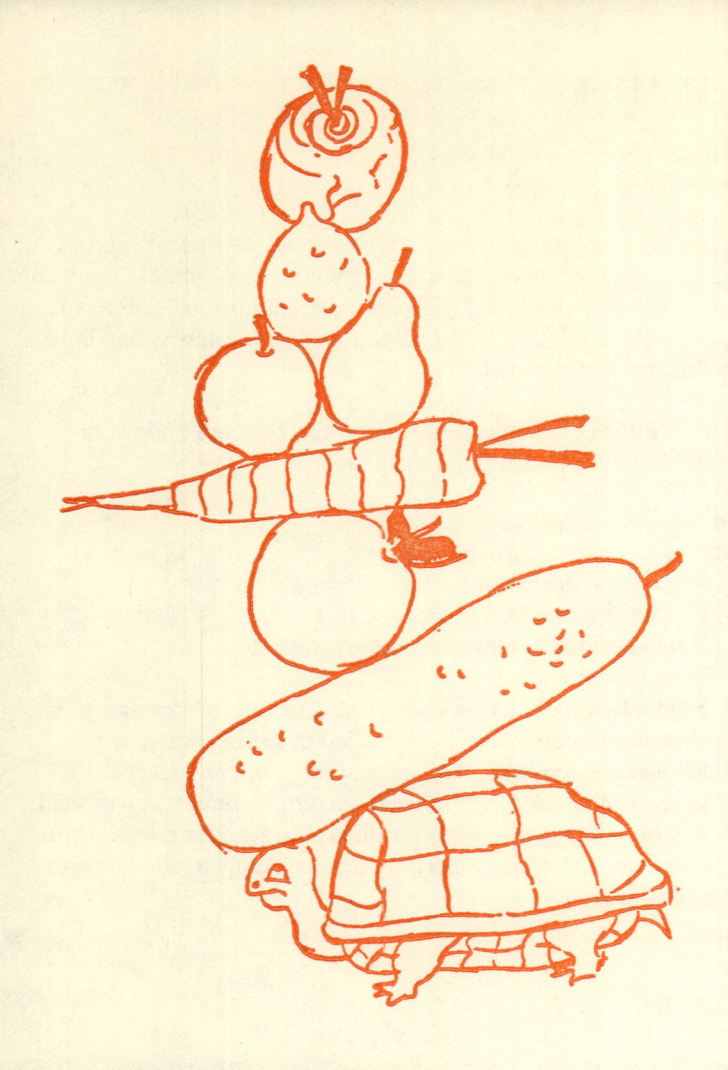

A PIQUANCE OF RELISHES

Peppery relishes and condiments served to pique palates with spicy tang and to counteract the rich meats and lavishly-buttered hot breads that pile Southern tables.

Today, many condiments, such as the various catsups and pickled walnuts, so dear to transplanted English hearts, may be purchased.

Pickled Fruit

To make your own pickled fruit the easy way, buy a jar of watermelon pickle, and spice and sweeten the juice to your taste. It also will take kindly to a spoon of vanilla. Let dried figs or prunes bask in the syrup, and store in the refrigerator, where the pickled fruit will keep indefinitely.

Creole Mustard

Once you have prepared this marvel, you always will want a refrigerator supply. I keep mine in a crystal cruet so it can come to table, too. If ingredients are whirred in blender, it will not begin to separate for at least a week. Otherwise, shake before use—and use with zest.

- ¼ cup dry mustard
- 2 tablespoons hot water, approximately
- Dash cayenne pepper
- 2 tablespoons brown sugar
- ½ teaspoon salt
- ¼ cup vinegar, preferably wine
- ¼ cup olive oil
- 1 tablespoon celery seeds, optional

Dissolve mustard in water. Add remaining ingredients and season to taste. Makes about ½ cup sauce.

Mustard Paste

Serve this as an hors d'oeuvre dunk, but be sure to warn timid types before they dip in because Hot! Hot! Hot! is the South's preference in mustard. Use to spread sandwiches only if you know tolerances to heat. Smooth plastic wrap over surface and store in refrigerator.

- 2 tablespoons dry mustard
- ½ teaspoon sugar
- ¼ teaspoon salt
- 1 tablespoon sharp vinegar
- 1 teaspoon prepared horseradish, optional

Combine dry ingredients and stir vinegar in. Let stand 10 minutes, add more vinegar, if necessary for spreading consistency, and season to taste. Makes about 2 tablespoons.

Garlic Mustard

Crush 1 clove minced garlic with the salt.

Mustard Mayonnaise

Stir any of the above into ½ cup mayonnaise to dress salads.

Lemon Tang Applesauce

Southerners call green cooking apples greenlings. Wait until greenings (the Damn Yankee name) are in season if you make your own applesauce. One pound, about 3 medium apples, purée into 1 cup applesauce.

It is amazing what a difference overnight refrigeration makes.

- **1 cup applesauce**
- **¼ teaspoon cinnamon**
- **½ teaspoon nutmeg**
- **½ lemon**

Combine applesauce with spices, adding more, if necessary, to taste. Bury lemon in applesauce, and refrigerate overnight. Makes 1 cup sauce. Serve as meat or poultry accompaniment.

Spiced Fruit

Sugar 'n spice 'n everything nice is what Southerners made of fruit, to serve along with meat, game, or poultry. Canned fruit may be substituted. Then substitute syrup in can for water and bake uncovered throughout, allowing about 20 minutes to thicken syrup and heat fruit.

- 6 ripe pears or peaches, peeled
- 12 whole cloves
- 1 cup sugar, approximately
- 2 tablespoons butter
- 1 teaspoon lemon juice
- 2 tablespoons water
- 1 tablespoon cinnamon, nutmeg, or mace

Stick each pear or peach with 2 cloves. Place in baking dish and add sugar to taste, depending upon tartness of fruit. Dot with butter. Add lemon juice and water. Sprinkle with spice, cover, and bake in moderate 350° F. oven, 15 minutes. Uncover and bake until tender, about 10 minutes more. Serve hot with meat. Makes 6 servings.

Blue Ridge Chutney

It is marvelous to be able to announce that the chutney is home made. This carried-from-England heirloom recipe can serve as meat or poultry accompaniment or as the star attraction at a curry dinner.

- 1½ pounds apples, preferably greenings
- ¾ pound onions, chopped
- 1 unpeeled lemon, seeded and chopped
- ½ pound raisins
- ½ pound brown sugar
- 1¼ cups cider vinegar
- 1 teaspoon salt
- 1½ teaspoons cloves
- 1½ teaspoons ginger
- ¼ teaspoon cayenne pepper
- 1¼ teaspoons quick-browning aid, optional

Peel apples and chop or grind coarsely with onion and lemon. Combine with remaining ingredients in large saucepan and bring to boil, stirring until sugar dissolves. Cook about 1½ hours or until thickened, stirring as necessary and season to taste. Pack in hot sterilized jars and seal for indefinite keeping. Refrigerate opened jars. Makes about 4 cups.

Carrot Chutney

Easy, pretty, and a fine crunchy accompaniment that is especially good with poultry.

- ½ pound (about 4) carrots, peeled and chopped fine
- 2 tablespoons instant minced onion
- ¼ cup coarsely minced parsley
- ¼ teaspoon mace
- Dash cayenne pepper
- 2 tablespoons honey, approximately

Combine ingredients, adding just enough honey to bind. Season to taste—it should be HOT! Keeps at least 3 days in refrigerator.

Cucumber Bennes

Southerners call cucumbers English cucumbers when they are served unpeeled, as was the British wont. Today, because skins are bred for tenderness, peeling is unnecessary. Slices of white turnip or kohlrabi may be substituted for cucumbers. Then rinse salt off and dry. Carrot sticks, another alternate, do not require preliminary soaking. The sweet pickle keeps at least a week in the refrigerator.

- 1 medium size cucumber
- 1 tablespoon salt
- ¼ cup white vinegar
- 2 tablespoons sugar
- 1 teaspoon benne (sesame) seeds
- ¼ teaspoon ginger
- ½ teaspoon instant minced onion, optional

Slice cucumber thin and mix with salt. Allow to stand until softened and almost transparent, about 2 hours, stirring occasionally.

Strain, place in a cloth, and squeeze hard to remove moisture. Bring remaining ingredients to boil, stirring until sugar dissolves, and pour over cucumbers. Chill and season to taste.

Rosedown Peaches

Summer with this as an hors d'oeuvre or entree accompaniment.

Cut peeled peaches into ¾-inch wedges. Cut wedges in half crosswise. Combine 3 parts fine-grated coconut with 1 part cinnamon and roll peaches in mixture.

Spiced Currant Jelly
Cumberland Sauce

This is an easy-to-make variation of the classic Cumberland Sauce, named for the Duke of Cumberland, third son of King George II. Such a glut of dishes are titled Cumberland that one can only suppose that the duke was either a great gourmet—or a gourmand.

The sauce is an almost invariable accompaniment for game, and as good with meat as with poultry. The original version combines the ingredients with Brown Sauce and Port wine.

½ cup red currant jelly
2 tablespoons orange juice
½ teaspoon ginger
1 teaspoon dry mustard
¼ teaspoon salt
Dash cayenne pepper

In saucepan break jelly up with fork, and melt over very low heat, stirring to prevent burning. Add remaining ingredients, season to taste, cool, and serve when firm.

Optional Additional Spices: Choose ⅛ teaspoon each of cinnamon, nutmeg, allspice, and cloves, and use singly or in combination.

A DAPPLE OF CORNMEAL
A HILL OF HOMINY

There is nothing as artless as corn—nor as complex as its myriad byproducts. Cornmeal takes its color—white or yellow—from the corn from which it is ground, and the white, more scarce, is naturally more expensive.

Grinding still is done in ancient grist-mill ways—stones powered by water granulate the kiln-dried corn, making the terms water- or stone-ground, interchangeable.

Today, the majority of grinding takes place between electrically-powered steel rollers, which unfortunately remove the corn husk and germ almost entirely—a process that, as with wheat and rice, adds shelf-life, but subtracts food value. Many cooks prefer stone-(water) ground meal, which, containing some of the germ, does make for richer flavor.

Southerners unite in their admiration for water-ground white cornmeal. It sometimes cooks in a shorter time, feels more granular, but is interchangeable with cornmeal ground by modern methods, when recipes also contain eggs, baking powder, and flour.

In this book, unless another variety is specified, white or yellow enriched cornmeal may be interchanged at will.

In most cases, yellow and white cornmeal are interchangeable and machine-ground cornmeal, and the various mixes, are standardized and enriched. "Bolted" cornmeal, self-rising cornmeal, and cornmeal mix are not interchangeable with enriched cornmeal.

In the interest of nutrition, be sure both white and yellow cornmeal *are* labeled "enriched." These, and enriched corn grits are recommended by the U.S. Department of Agriculture as part of the Bread-Cereal group of energy foods.

To Cook Cornmeal—White or Yellow

Follow package directions when available. Otherwise, add 1½ teaspoons salt to 2 cups cold water and bring to boil. Add 1 cup cornmeal to 1 cup cold water, and pour into the boiling water, stirring constantly. When it comes to a boil, cover, and simmer until meal is thickened and does not taste raw, about 20 minutes. The meal may be allowed to continue to cook, covered, over very low heat, up to an hour.

For even creamier consistency, add cornmeal directly to cold water and bring to boil slowly, stirring constantly and continue as above. One-half cup cornmeal yields about 1½ cups cooked.

To Cook Grits—White or Yellow

Proceed as for cornmeal, above, and expect the same yield.

To Reheat Cornmeal or Grits

With plate scraper or spoon, mash cold cooked cereal and add small amounts of water, until smooth. Cover, and simmer until hot.

Storing Cornmeal and Grits: They will keep at least 3 months on a cupboard shelf. Smell before use, to test staling or rancidity. Either cooked as above, or baked, the cereals will keep about 5 days in refrigerator and may be frozen.

CORNMEAL MUSH AND GRITS

Mush is only one of the names for plain cooked cornmeal. Early on, it was called *sagamity*. By any name, it, and grits were and are a staff of life food in the South. The many forms, both when just cooked and when left over, help give variety to meals and Damn Yankees who have never enjoyed these charmers of delicate flavor have a treat in store.

Fried Mush

Pour cooked cornmeal (or grits) into mold and refrigerate. When cold, slice ½-inch thick. Coat cornmeal slices with cornmeal; sliced grits with grits; and fry, preferably in lard, over medium heat, on griddle or in skillet, until browned and crisp. For extra flavor and nutrition, dip slices in beaten egg before frying. (Then do not coat with cereal.)

Serve with maple syrup, molasses, jelly, etc., for breakfast or lunch.

Cornmeal Pap

This variation of mush is for palates that admire sour-sweet flavors.

Stir 3 tablespoons buttermilk in heavy pan until heated. Add 1 tablespoon corn meal very gradually, and stir until thickened. Serve as hot cereal with butter, milk, and sugar. Makes 1 serving.

Terrebone Parish Couche Couche

When I described this curiously-named Louisiana recipe to Ann, my Southern right hand, she laughed and said, *"That's* mush! for when there isn't any food money in the house!"

Couche Couche is an obvious corruption of the Arabic *cous cous,* a dish the French took from the Algerians. Middle Easterners and Africans admire the fluffy golden grain. The yellow bits of cornmeal prepared as follows pebble like egg barley and do resemble cous cous. Couche Couche does not deserve to be limited to tables of penury. It is perfect served with poultry or ham, and onion gives it great flavor.

- **1 cup yellow cornmeal**
- **1 cup water**
- **1 teaspoon salt**
- **1 egg, beaten**
- **1 onion, diced**
- **2 tablespoons fat, melted**
- **Dash cayenne pepper**

Stir cornmeal into water. Add salt and bring to boil, stirring constantly. Cover, and cook over low heat, until water is absorbed. Cool, beat in egg and season to taste. In heavy skillet, brown onion in fat. Spread cornmeal over it, and cook until a thin brown crust forms. Scrape crust back into batter, and continue procedure until mixture crumbles into small particles, adding small amounts of water if it appears very dry. Pile into serving dish and top with a generous blob of butter. Makes 4 servings and may be frozen.

CORNBREAD

The South calls cornbread "bread." White bread (and rolls) are light bread, wheat bread or yeast bread. Recipes for cornbread are so diverse they seemingly depend upon when, or if, the cow was milked, because some call for water. They also can depend upon how the hens were laying, and how the larder was fixed for fat.

Whether white or yellow cornmeal is specified, seems to depend upon "what mama used to make," and further variations encompass the "sugar"—"no sugar" controversy.

Some recipes combine cornmeal and flour, with the proportion varying from equal parts of each to as little as ¼ cup flour to 1¼ cups cornmeal. The color of cornbread containing flour is lighter, the flavor more delicate; the texture smoother.

Along with its amiability is the fact that, although cornmeal can be gussied up with butter and cream and eggs, it is equally good as a primitive bread, made only with the addition of water and salt.

As with any recipe, specific measures—teaspoons, tablespoons, cups—cannot cope with the variability of the food itself. That is the cook's job, and it may take a try or two with cornmeal before your hand is sure. If you can, take the opportunity, to watch someone who knows how.

But realize that cornmeal is so agreeably adaptable, it is almost impossible to achieve the inedible—and the imperative buttering while hot can cover a multitude of sins.

Containers for Cornbread

Old black cast-iron frying pans had "legs" (*casseroles a pieds* to the French), that enabled baking of cornbread directly over hot coals. These were called "spiders"—which they do indeed resemble. When ranges replaced these leggy skillets, the pans kept their name, "Spider Corncake" being a *mot juste* recipe title.

Cast iron, long out of vogue, is currently fashionable, now available in cornstick pans, as well as in an eight-section skillet that produces self-contained wedges and eliminates cutting the bread. But any baking utensil may be used—custard cups, muffin- or cornstick-pans, or, for elegance, a glass baking dish that fits into a silver-footed holder that can be taken directly to table.

A one-cup cornmeal proportion recipe will fill one 9-inch square or round pan or about eight custard cups.

CORN PONE

Our impatient forebears quickly shortened the Indian word *apone* to *pone* and the Algonquin (sometimes spelled "Algonkian") word *rockahominy* to *hominy*. To add confusion, sweet potato pone contains no cornmeal at all.

From William Strachey's *Historie of Travell into Virginia Britania,* we learn that the Indians "Receave the flower in a platter of wood, which, blending with water, they make into flatt, broad cakes . . . they call apones, which Covering with Ashes till they be baked . . . and then washing them in faire water, let dry with their own heate."

According to the *American Heritage Cook Book,* ash cake was the name for cornbread baked in the ashes; pone when it was kept out of the ashes. Hoecake was baked on a hoe over an open fire. Ashes were raked out, the small cakes were put on the hoe and the hoe was put into the bottom of the fire and covered with ashes. After about five minutes on the fire, ashes and splinters were brushed off, and the cake was washed with warm water. It had to be eaten HOT. This is the lowest common denominator of baking—but high on the list of heart-warming foods. A final note—Tennessee folk call pone scratch backs.

To complete this historical prowl, in 1766, during the dispute over the Stamp Act, Benjamin Franklin penned a paean of cornbread praise which was published by a London newspaper, *The Gazetteer*. He called cornmeal "one of the most agreeable and wholesome grains in the world."

Oven-Baked Corn Pone

Pone should be crusty on the outside, moist on the inside, and it accepts slathers of butter. The recipe is so simple that printing a proportion seems like putting on the dog. As far as the exact amount of water is concerned, any Southern cook will tell you—"It should be stiff, like a pone."

- **1 cup cornmeal**
- **1 teaspoon salt**
- **Dash cayenne pepper, optional**
- **2 cups water, approximately**

Stir cereal with salt and pepper. Add warm or boiling water gradually, and stir with a spoon until moistened but firm enough to hold together. With hands, shape ½-inch thick oblong pones, measuring about 3 x 2 inches. Place on greased cooky sheet and bake on top rack of preheated, very hot 450° F. oven until browned, about 15 minutes.

Carolina Ash Cake: Charlie's Way

The primitive version translated from flames to oven can provide rainy-day cooking amusement for children. It certainly will allow them to gulp goodies and history at the same time.

Allow ¼ cup cornmeal for each cake. Stir in ⅛ teaspoon salt and enough water, about 2 tablespoons, to make an easy-to-mold dough. Shape as above. Wet brown paper (or a cut-up paper bag) thoroughly and wring out.

Place individual pones on paper and wrap tightly. Bake on top rack of very hot 450° F. oven (preheated or not) until done, about 20 minutes. Unwrap, drench with butter, and eat hot. If the pone sticks, moisten the paper with warm water.

ANN'S CORNBREAD

For more than twenty years, Mrs. Burtt—Ann—who inhabits so many of these pages has been no stranger to those who have come to my door. During that time, she has captained my house, my work, and certainly my life. She is a transplanted Columbus, Georgia, peach—a child of prejudice and poverty—an inflexible woman of great ability, intelligence, and style, with a wide, warm, welcoming smile.

Considering my encompassing world of food and spirits, Ann is an anomaly. She hates to cook. Until this book, she disdained putting together so much as a sandwich, and pretended not even a nodding knowledge of kitchen craft.

But when I began testing, she sighingly looked necessity straight in the eye, because the need to show this Damn Yankee how was so apparent. Her knowledge, skill, impeccable sense of taste, and golden hands have led mine authentically through the realm of down-home dishes.

Cornbread is one. When I asked Ann to demonstrate her way, she appeared with a package of self-rising white cornmeal mix. "You don't!" I exclaimed. But, yes, she did, deviating from package directions only by using for the fat called for, the lard and crackling brown bits left in the pan from the just-fried chicken.

The cornbread was good. But I could not think, even in this day, when saving time seems to take precedence over saving money, of letting this book out of my hands without a recipe for cornbread, made with cornmeal alone and prepared from scratch. The following is my favorite, chosen from the countless ways and shapes of cornbread.

Buttermilk Cornbread

From-scratch preparation of this, as opposed to a mix, necessitates reaching additionally only for soda, salt, and measuring spoons —procedures not calculated to tax your energy grievously. Buttermilk (sour milk may be substituted) produces a light and lovely cornbread and yellow cornmeal gives it the color of sun slanting in a window.

1 cup cornmeal
1 teaspoon baking soda
1 teaspoon salt
2 cups buttermilk
1 egg, beaten slightly
2 tablespoons butter

Mix cornmeal, soda, and salt. Mix buttermilk with egg, add cornmeal, and stir smooth. Place butter in baking pan and melt in preheated, very hot 450° F. oven. Add cornbread mixture and bake on top rack until well-browned, about 30 minutes. Preferably serve hot, and, if desired, pass the syrup.

Reheating Cornbread: Sprinkle the top of the bread lightly with cold water before reheating.

Apple Pone

Guests at my table frequently object to the fact that they never are served anything that isn't a test. Others enjoy the critics' position of judging a recipe on its way to perfection. Sylvia Schur, a favorite guest and a consummate food perfectionist, is as prolific of ideas as there are leaves in an apple orchard. Tasting the apple pone, she said thoughtfully, "Why don't you do this with sliced apples and sugar as an upside down cake . . ." Sylvia—and all others—why not indeed.

Add to Buttermilk Cornbread, above, 2 tablespoons sugar and 2 medium apples peeled, cored, and diced in ¼" pieces. Serve, if desired, with sugar to sprinkle on after buttering or before reheating.

Cracklin' Bread

The crisp bits of pork left when diced salt pork has been rendered are appropriately named cracklings, and waste-not-want-not cooks added these crunchy bits to their cornbread. Fried pork rinds, available under various trade names may be substituted.

The same procedure—with results as delectable—can be accomplished by adding some of the fat and crumbs that result from frying chicken. Short'nin' (for shortening) is another name for crackling bread. Inasmuch as there is no "authentic" recipe, add about ⅓ cup cracklings to any cornbread mixture.

Hush Puppies

I doubt if there is a Damn Yankee who doesn't know that these humble delectables are so-called because they originally were thrown into the kettle at fish fries, to feed to obstreperous dogs. In North Carolina, the recipe title sometimes wears an elegant name—Lacy Corn Bread.

I have made the bread with a simple batter of cornmeal, water, and salt. The following fancies things up.

- 2 cups corn meal
- 1 egg
- 1 teaspoon salt
- 1 small onion, diced, optional

Mix cornmeal, egg, and salt and add enough boiling water, about 2½ cups, so mixture holds to spoon. Drop tablespoonfuls into deep hot fat.

Johnny Cake

"Rich man, poor man, Indian chief" carried this long-keeping bread on travels, hence, journey-cake—according to one source. Another insists that Johnny is a corruption of Shawnee.

- ½ teaspoon salt
- ¼ teaspoon baking soda
- ½ cup sour milk
- 1 cup cornmeal, approximately
- 6 tablespoons melted butter, approximately

In bowl combine salt and soda. Add milk, and enough cornmeal to make a soft dough. Line pan, measuring about 8 inches, with foil, and grease bottom and sides. Layer of dough should be about ½-inch thick.

Bake in preheated hot 400° F. oven until it begins to brown, about 20 minutes. Brush with 3 tablespoons melted butter. After 10 minutes brush with remaining butter. Bake about 40 minutes in all, or until cake tester inserted in center comes out clean. Break, rather than cut Johnny Cake, and serve hot with honey, jam, etc.

Corn Flowers

These are crisp as crackers—fine for hors d'oeuvre or with soups. Add interest by sprinkling them with cayenne pepper and/or paprika, instant minced onion, or seeds—dill or celery—before baking.

- 1 cup cornmeal
- 1 tablespoon fat
- ½ teaspoon salt
- 1 cup boiling water, approximately

In bowl, place cornmeal, melted fat, and salt, and stir in enough boiling water to make a mixture firm enough to shape into balls. (If too thin, add more cornmeal.) Allow a tablespoonful for each ball, and place about ½ inch apart on greased baking sheet. Pat into 3-inch rounds and score deeply with fork tines, making a criss-cross pattern.

Bake on top rack of preheated, very hot 450° F. oven until firm and lightly browned, about 20 minutes. Preferably, serve hot. Makes about 20.

Cornmeal Biscuits
Corncake

This glorious baking powder biscuit variation is my adaptation of an old Southern recipe *Gourmet Magazine* printed. Unable to leave well enough alone, I garnished the biscuits with a variety of toppings as in Corn Flowers, above. Cornmeal Biscuits also can be topped with dried herbs. They will be welcomed as hors d'oeuvre.

- ½ cup butter, divided
- 1 cup flour
- 1 cup white water-ground cornmeal
- 1 tablespoon baking powder
- 1 teaspoon salt
- ⅔ cup milk, approximately

Cut 5 tablespoons butter into mixed dry ingredients as for pie dough, and add enough milk for soft, but kneadable, dough. Knead lightly, but only until dough leaves sides of bowl. Roll into a ¼-inch thick square between 2 sheets of waxed paper. Cut 1½ inch squares and make a deep crease in center of each with the back of a knife.

Melt remaining butter and dip both sides of biscuits. Place on cooky sheet, garnish if desired, and bake on top rack of preheated, hot 425° F. oven until browned, about 20 minutes. Makes at least 12 triangles. Serve hot.

Cornmeal Popovers
Corn Batter Bread

In my family, as far as cooking was concerned, the feeling was "the more, the better." Therefore, after I had prepared a voluminous chart of the proportions of ingredients in the legion of recipes for cornbread, I immediately tested the following, which boasts milk and eggs, and that *La Cuisine Creole* directs be baked in "tin molds" and served at breakfast.

I found I had made a popover! The *Williamsburg Art of Cookery* calls it Soft Egg Bread. The cornmeal adds interesting texture, grits may be substituted, and today, the blender mixes it in seconds. As with any Batter-Bread Pudding,* it can stand about an hour before baking.

- 3 tablespoons cornmeal
- 3 tablespoons flour
- 1 teaspoon salt
- ½ cup milk
- 2 eggs

Stir cornmeal, flour, and salt together. Whir milk and eggs in blender just until mixed. Add dry ingredients and whir only until mixed. Lacking a blender, beat eggs, beat milk in, add dry ingredients, and beat smooth. Pour into 3 or 4 well greased custard cups or muffin pans, filling them at least ¾ full. Place in cold oven, set thermostat at very hot, 450° F., and bake 30 minutes. Puncture four sides of neck to let out steam. Turn oven off, and allow to dry 10 minutes longer. (If necessary to hold an additional 15 minutes, turn them on their sides.) Serve hot with plenty of butter.

Green Corn Spoon Bread

Southerners automatically serve this marvelous mighty-like-a-souffle accompaniment for chicken or ham in place of a starch. The following version also eliminates the need for a cooked vegetable.

- ⅓ cup cornmeal
- 2 cups milk, divided
- 1 cup cooked corn kernels
- ¾ teaspoon salt, divided
- ¼ cup butter, melted
- 1 tablespoon sugar, optional
- 2 eggs, separated
- ¼ teaspoon cream of tartar

Add cornmeal to ½ cup cold milk. Bring ½ cup milk to boil. Add corn, and stir cornmeal in gradually. Add ½ teaspoon salt, and cook 5 minutes, stirring constantly. Remove from heat and beat in butter and sugar. Beat egg yolks well, and stir remaining milk in. Add to corn mixture and fold in egg whites beaten to soft peaks with ¼ teaspoon salt and cream of tartar. Pour into greased casserole and bake in preheated, moderate 325° F. oven until firm, about 45 minutes. Makes 6 servings.

Grits Spoonbread

Cornmeal and grits companion compatibly in this simple to put together entree accompaniment. As always, there are many variations and titles range from Hominy Bread to Baked Grits.

- ½ cup grits
- 1 cup cornmeal
- 1 tablespoon sugar, optional
- 2 teaspoons salt
- 2½ cups water
- 3 tablespoons butter, melted
- 2 cups milk
- 4 eggs, beaten

Stir grits, cornmeal, sugar, and salt into water. Add butter, and milk, and cook over very low heat, stirring, until slightly thickened, about 10 minutes. Gradually stir into eggs and pour into greased 9 x 13 x 2-inch baking pan. Bake in preheated, hot 400° F. oven until firm, about 45 minutes. Makes 6 servings and may be frozen.

Cheese Pudding

Over the years I have harvested many superb and unusual recipes from collections put together by various women's organizations. This favorite Southern dish came to my attention through Cleveland artist Winston McGee. It was included in a recipe booklet his mother sent to him from their Columbia, Missouri home. Her inscription, signed, "Love, Mother," read:

There are many things,
I enjoy to do,
But one is cooking
Good things for you.

Thanks to the amount of protein, the pudding wins a nutritional plus. It can be held about two hours before baking, reheats superbly, and may be frozen either before or after baking. A half pound cheddar cheese equals about 1¾ cups. Grated cheese will keep indefinitely in the freezer.

- ½ cup grits
- 1¾ cups grated cheddar cheese, divided
- ¾ cup milk
- 2 tablespoons butter
- ¾ teaspoon salt
- Dash cayenne pepper, optional
- 2 eggs, beaten slightly

Cook grits in saucepan, and stir in milk and butter gradually. Add all except ¼ cup cheese, keeping heat low and stirring until melted. Remove from heat and mix with eggs. Pour into greased baking dish, sprinkle with remaining cheese and, if desired, with paprika. Bake in preheated, moderate 375° F. oven until knife inserted in center comes out clean, about 30 minutes. Makes 6 servings.

Cheese Puff

For a soufflé-like texture, separate eggs in Cheese Pudding, above, and add yolks to grits mixture. Beat whites to a soft peak with ⅛ teaspoon salt and ¼ teaspoon cream of tartar, and fold in at end. Bake immediately; serve pronto.

Cornmeal Crunch

This is a great make-ahead starch accompaniment for a dinner party that features "smothers" or gumboes.

- **1 cup yellow cornmeal**
- **½ cup butter**
- **Dash cayenne pepper**
- **½ cup Parmesan cheese, approximately**
- **3 cups cold water, divided**

Cook cornmeal, half the butter and add cayenne. Remove from heat, and add cheese, gradually, stirring in enough for good flavor and season to taste.

Rinse 8 x 8 x 2-inch pan in cold water, and fill with mixture—layer should be approximately ½-inch thick. Smooth with wet spatula, cover surface with plastic wrap, and refrigerate. Melt remaining butter in baking pan and cut cornmeal into 1½-inch squares. Dip all sides in butter and place about ½-inch apart in pan with low sides. Sprinkle with paprika, and bake in preheated, hot 400° F. oven until crusty, about 20 minutes. Makes about 4 dozen squares; 6–8 servings.

HOMINY

Hominy comes from the mature kernels of regular field corn, and takes its color from the corn—white or yellow. (The white is more expensive.) Removing the hull produces hulled (shelled) hominy, which sometimes is called lye hominy, because a solution of water and lye (in days of old, obtained by pouring water through wood ashes) loosens the hulls. The process is used commercially today to remove potato skins.

When the hulled hominy is broken into large fragments, it is called coarse grits, pearl hominy, samp, or groats (also the name for coarsely-ground buckwheat).

A fine grind produces "meal" or grits. Two fast-cooking varieties —quick- and instant-grits are more costly than regular grits and, unfortunately, to obtain the desirable fine, creamy consistency, they take just as long to cook.

If you choose hominy as a change from other starches, realize it has an affinity for riches such as butter, cheese, and the like. A special Charleston breakfast treat is Shrimp Smother (shrimp simmered in seasoned butter) to serve with hot hominy.

Damn Yankees who fancy whole kernel hominy needn't be told it comes in cans (and therefore is cooked). A 1-pound 4-ounce can yields about 2 cups hominy; 1½ cups liquid.

Dried Whole Kernel Hominy

Soak one cup hominy overnight in enough cold water to cover, about 2½ cups. Use the same water for cooking, and add 1 teaspoon salt, and enough more water to cover hominy. Cover pot, bring liquid to boil rapidly and boil gently until tender, adding more water as necessary to prevent scorching. Avoid stirring during cooking and cook from 30 minutes to 2 hours, depending upon length of time hominy has been stored. Makes 4 servings.

To Cook the Same Day

Place 1 cup hominy in large saucepan, add enough cold water to cover, about 2½ cups. Cover pan, bring liquid to boil rapidly and boil 2 minutes. Remove from heat, let soak 1 hour and continue as above.

Hominy can be reheated as for any dried vegetable, and like Cornmeal,* will keep, refrigerated or frozen.

Hominy Crisp

Choose salt pork, steak fat, or bacon and a sharp or mild cheese—and try this even if you don't like—or never have tasted—hominy.

- 2 cups cooked hominy
- ½ cup grated cheese
- 4 tablespoons fat, diced fine

Mix hominy with cheese and season to taste. Spread in single layer in heat-proof serving dish. Sprinkle with fat, and bake in preheated, extremely hot 500° F. oven, or broil at medium temperature until fat browns, and hominy is hot, about 15 minutes. Makes 4 servings.

Plantation Hominy

Corn kernels may be substituted for hominy in this sort of non-mashed version of refried beans.

2 small green peppers, diced
1 small onion, diced
2 tablespoons fat
2 cups cooked hominy
1 cup grated cheese

In skillet simmer pepper and onion in fat until softened, about 5 minutes. Add hominy and fry until browned. Just before removing from fire, stir in grated cheese, and season to taste. Makes 4 servings.

A PEEL OF BREADS • A FLOW OF BATTERS

"Take two and butter them while they're hot," a Southern hostess bids guests who are strange to baking powder biscuits. An obviously verbose visiting lecturer vowed that, on his Mason-Dixon circuit, the directive kept him from tasting a biscuit at all. Every time he was about to bite into one, pooled with golden butter, he was asked a question. To answer, he politely put his biscuit down. It cooled. Just as he picked it up, his hostess commanded, "Take two and butter them while they're hot."

Biscuits are not the only superb Southern bread, and in the interest either of variety, or of use-'em-up prudence, indigenous foods—sweet potatoes, winter squash, pumpkin, hominy, rice, peanuts, pecans—are tucked into batters and doughs.

Baking powder biscuits rolled thin to sandwich peanut butter or marmalade before baking, are a variation the Browns in *America Cooks* attribute to Mississippi.

Additional variation comes from the way doughs are cooked. For instance, squares of baking powder biscuit dough often are dropped into fat after chicken has been fried, in a hush-puppy kind of way. And bread dough may be baked on a griddle.

A recipe for one such, called Apoquiniminic Cakes, appears in an ancient tome. I think I would rather eat than pronounce one.

Fist Biscuits

This is an instance of don't tamper with a classic. The dough is equal perfection when rolled and cut to bake on a griddle. Or, in the interest of speed, any baking powder dough simply may be cut into squares.

Old-school Southern cooks often melt the fat to add to the milk and they do not roll the dough at all. They pinch off bits to shape into balls between their palms. Holding a ball of dough in one palm, they flatten it with a swift fist-stroke of the other hand.

- **2 cups flour**
- **1 tablespoon baking powder**
- **½ teaspoon baking soda**
- **1 teaspoon salt**
- **2 tablespoons lard**
- **¾ cup buttermilk, approximately**

Stir dry ingredients together. Cut lard in and add buttermilk slowly, stirring with a fork until dough is soft and fairly moist. Knead—but lightly—if desired. Pat or roll about ½-inch thick, shape as desired, and bake in preheated very hot 450° F. oven until browned, about 15 minutes. Yields about sixteen 2-inch biscuits or top crust for a 4-quart casserole.

Buttermilk Drops

Prepare as above, adding enough buttermilk so they will drop from a teaspoon. The thinner they are, the more like a cracker they become.

Molasses Scones

Once you master baking powder biscuits, these are no trouble at all. Southern cooks would replace the butter with 3 tablespoons lard.

    2 cups flour
    ½ teaspoon salt
    2 teaspoons baking powder
    ¼ teaspoon baking soda
    ¼ cup butter
    ⅔ cup buttermilk, approximately
    1 tablespoon molasses

In bowl, stir first 4 ingredients together and cut butter in. Combine buttermilk and molasses, and stir in. Knead lightly until mixture holds together. Pat to ½ inch thickness on floured board and cut triangles measuring about 2½ inches on all sides. Bake on greased baking sheet in preheated, hot 425° F. oven, until browned, about 12 minutes. Serve hot with butter. Makes about 12 scones which may be frozen.

Potato Scones

    2 cups flour
    1 teaspoon salt
    3 teaspoons baking powder
    3 tablespoons butter
    1 cup cold mashed potatoes
    1 egg, beaten
    ⅓ cup milk, approximately

Mix dry ingredients in bowl and cut in fat, until mixture resembles coarse cornmeal. Blend mashed potatoes in with fork, mixing well. Combine egg and milk, add to potato mixture and stir only until dry ingredients are moistened, adding more milk if necessary. Knead about 10 strokes on lightly-floured board. Divide dough in half, and roll or pat about ¼-inch thick to make a 9-inch square. Cut 3-inch squares, and fry on hot, lightly buttered griddle, turning to brown both sides, allowing about 6 minutes in all. Add more butter to griddle if scones seem dry. Serve hot, for buttering. Makes 18 scones which may be frozen.

Spider Light Bread

Try this recipe, which, if you like, you can call Skillet Bread, when you yearn for the taste of homemade bread but the weather makes lighting the oven seem an affront. It is perfect hot; equally good cold; and if it is around long enough to stale, marvelous for stuffings.

For the batter, half butter and half lard (or oil) make a good combination. The dry ingredients may be premixed in 1-cup proportion amounts to have on hand for speedy put-together, and for that amount, about 1½ teaspoons dried herbs; 1 teaspoon seeds may be added.

A stick-free pan or non-stick coating to spray on, will ease your labors further.

- 1 cup flour
- 1¼ teaspoons baking powder
- ¼ teaspoon baking soda
- ¾ teaspoon salt
- 2 teaspoons dried marjoram
- ¾ cup buttermilk
- 2 tablespoons fat

Mix dry ingredients in bowl. Add buttermilk all at once and stir through quickly, stirring only until liquid is incorporated. Heat fat in 6-inch skillet. Cover with dough, spreading it to sides of pan. Cover skillet, reduce heat to medium low, and cook until firm enough to turn, about 10 minutes. Turn out onto a plate and add about 1 tablespoon additional butter to pan. Place pan over plate, invert, and brown uncooked side, allowing about 10 minutes more. Makes 4 servings and may be frozen.

Boligee Rice Bread

Ante Bellum Alabama ladies arose early enough to bring this on for breakfast. It is an any-meal delicacy—and a marvelous home for leftover rice.

- ½ tablespoon butter, melted
- ½ tablespoon lard, melted
- 1 cup cooked rice
- ½ cup cornmeal
- 1 teaspoon salt
- Dash cayenne pepper, optional
- 1 cup milk
- 3 eggs, beaten

Place melted fats, then rice, in saucepan and heat covered at a very low temperature. Mix cornmeal with salt and cayenne. Stir milk into eggs and stir in cornmeal. Combine with rice mixture, and turn into greased 9 x 9 x 2-inch baking pan, or into 12 muffin pans. Bake in preheated, very hot 450° F. oven until firm when tapped, and well-browned, about 25 minutes. Serve hot. May be frozen.

Beaufort Pudding Bread

This unusual method makes a feather-light bread with a marvelous kind of rice-pudding flavor, and is more than worth the extra time involved. What a way for leftover rice to go!

- 1 cup milk
- 4 tablespoons butter
- ¼ cup cold water
- 1 teaspoon salt
- 2 eggs, beaten
- ½ cup cooked rice
- 1 teaspoon baking powder

In saucepan heat milk with butter. Beat cold water and salt into eggs, stir into milk, and cook, stirring, over very low heat, until thick. Add rice and baking powder and pour into greased 8 x 8 x 2-inch pan. Bake on center rack of preheated, moderate 375° F. oven until cake tester inserted in center comes out clean, about 30 minutes. Cut squares and serve hot. Makes 4 servings. May be frozen but heat before serving.

BREAD SAUCES

The two following sauces are similar to, and a variation on stuffing. They are dear to British hearts, so of course appear in the South, and also are practical ways to extend roasts and to use up good bread (French or Italian is excellent) that has staled.

Orange Bread Sauce

This is an especially fitting accompaniment for duck with orange sauce. Add the peeled chunks of orange to the duck cavity before roasting.

About ½ pound; 8 slices bread, yields 2 cups crumbs.

    2 **cups bread crumbs, packed firmly**
    1½ **cups milk**
    2 **tablespoons instant minced onion**
    Rind of 1 navel orange, grated
    Dash orange bitters, optional
    ½ **teaspoon salt**
    1 **tablespoon butter**
    Nutmeg
    Parsley

Discard crusts of stale white bread and pick into ⅛-inch crumbs. Place onion in broad-bottom pan. Add milk and bring to boil. Add orange rind, bitters, salt, and bread. Mix gently and simmer covered, stirring occasionally until it tastes cooked, about 30 minutes. Add more milk, if necessary for moist-stuffing consistency. Stir in butter, and season to taste. Serve in bowl, sprinkled with nutmeg and garnished with a parsley sprig. Serve hot or at room temperature. Improves with overnight refrigeration and may be frozen. Makes 4 servings.

Claret Bread Sauce

This ancient recipe, suggested for game, sounded so curious it was an immediate challenge. I assumed the color would be strange. But it is close in hue to Cumberland Sauce, that constant companion to game. Don't let the color deter you—or substitute white wine for red.

    2 cups bread crumbs
    1 cup water
    ½ cup dry red wine, preferably Bordeaux
    2 tablespoons instant minced onion
    ¼ teaspoon pepper
    2 tablespoons butter
    4 whole cloves
    Dash cayenne pepper
    ½ teaspoon salt

Prepare as for Orange Bread Sauce, above, and season to taste. Remove cloves, and serve sprinkled with nutmeg or mace. Makes 4 servings.

Dry Bread Sauce

The South really stretches a point by calling this crunchy, toasty elegance a sauce. It is automatically served in the world's haute cuisine restaurants, especially with game.

It is so easy to do. The blender whirs crumbs for you in seconds and they keep indefinitely in the freezer—as does the "sauce."

It also makes an excellent topping for hors d'oeuvre cheese spreads, and for cooked vegetables such as asparagus or cauliflower.

Pass Dry Bread Sauce in a bowl with a spoon, or use it as a "nest" to throne roasted squab, pheasant, partridge—and for adding the word deluxe to baked or broiled chicken.

- 2 tablespoons butter
- 1 cup fine dry bread crumbs
- ½ teaspoon salt
- **Dash cayenne pepper, optional**

Melt butter in shallow baking pan, and stir in remaining ingredients. Toast in preheated, slow 300° F. oven, stirring occasionally, until browned and crumbly, about 25 minutes. Makes 4 servings.

PANCAKES

It should be obvious by now that trying to keep track of the South's many charming names for the same thing is akin to holding an ocean wave. Crepes, or thin pancakes, have been called Saucer Puddings, to indicate their diameter, or, a "Quire of Paper," to denote thin, thin, thin. In many of the old Southern recipes, they are awash with spirits, and cry for chafing dish service. Try, as one long-ago book suggests, heating thin pancakes in mashed peaches, peach brandy, and rum.

In the *Williamsburg Art of Cookery,* the cakes are announced as a must on Valentine's Day, and the receipt, flavored with brandy, is colored pink with beet puree.

A Virginia recipe title, "A Cheap Dessert Dish," adds hominy to griddle cakes for serving with a pour of molasses and butter, warmed until the butter melts. Maple Syrup, treated the same way, Brown Sugar Syrup*, jam, preserves, or fruit, are other admirable toppings for pancakes and waffles.

A measuring cup pitcher is perfect for pouring pancake or waffle batter. A heavy frying pan may supplant a griddle, and after the first filming with fat, if the temperature is correct—moderately hot—it should not be necessary to add more. To test temperature, sprinkle with cold water—drops should bounce and disappear almost immediately.

Pancakes may be frozen in stacks in foil packages to be reheated in preheated, hot 400° F. oven about 10 minutes.

Lace Cakes

It would be a pity not to repeat these swift-to-put-together pancakes from my *Down-on-the-Farm Cook Book.* They have become a looked-forward-to breakfast treat here. The batter is very thin, but the cakes can be turned without difficulty as soon as they have browned. A tablespoon of molasses or a teaspoon of sugar may be added, but a pitcher of maple syrup should satisfy even sweet-tooth types.

    2 eggs, beaten well
    2 cups milk
    1 cup cornmeal
    ½ teaspoon salt
    6 tablespoons butter, melted

Combine ingredients in order listed, and beat smooth. Stir the batter each time before pouring. Makes 4 servings.

Squash Pillows

Squash in a pancake seemed unbelievable enough to try, and, inasmuch as *sumer was icumen in,* I tested with yellow squash. The winter variety does as well and other Southern recipes call for pumpkin or eggplant. Serve hot to accompany chicken or pork, and if you would do as a good Dixie cook does, serve these sprinkled with sugar.

- 1½ cups cooked squash
- ¾ teaspoon baking powder
- 1 teaspoon salt
- 2 tablespoons sugar
- ¼ cup flour, approximately
- 1 egg, beaten

Purée squash or whir in blender. Mix dry ingredients. Add egg to squash and stir in dry ingredients, adding enough additional flour, if necessary, for batter slightly thicker than griddle cakes. Makes about 10 cakes 3-inches in diameter.

Manikin Pecan Perfects

How easy a blender makes things! Two whole eggs may be substituted for the yolks, and Brown Sugar Syrup* and/or red raspberry jelly add the final touch to perfection.

- 4 egg yolks
- 1½ cups milk
- ¼ cup butter, melted
- 1 teaspoon vanilla
- 1 cup cold cooked rice
- ½ cup pecans, broken coarsely
- 1 cup flour
- 2 teaspoons baking powder
- 2 tablespoons brown sugar
- ½ teaspoon salt

Combine ingredients in blender in order listed and whir only until mixed. Lacking a blender, beat yolks slightly. Beat in milk, butter, and vanilla. Stir in rice and nuts, and combine with dry ingredients, beating only until smooth. Makes about 4 dozen 4-inch pancakes. May be frozen.

WAFFLES

Waffle comes from warp, woof, and weave, and indicates a wafer that is honeycombed. A charming 1800s custom involved inviting guests to a breakfast Waffle-Worry. Supposedly, when electric waffle irons appeared, the worry was taken out of waffle-making. Unfortunately, they do not produce waffles as good as the old fashioned, heavy iron top-of-the-range variety which are again available.

Lacking a waffle iron, use the batter for pancakes, and realize that purchased waffles cost three times as much as the home made. It should be necessary to grease waffle irons only for the first waffle in each batch.

Test even a thermostatically-controlled iron for correct temperature (see Pancakes*). Waffles take about 5 minutes to cook; usually are done when an iron stops steaming.

Leftover waffles reheat splendidly in a toaster. If frozen, set toaster at "light," and heat waffles right out of the freezer. Or, spread on a cooky sheet and reheat in preheated, hot 400° F. oven about 10 minutes.

Waffles take the same sweet toppings as pancakes, but Southerners often also sluice them delectably with chicken hash or with other creamy delicacies.

Roanoke
Old Dominion Waffles

It is written that one plantation, famous for its waffles, served tiny ones at tea—and that the hostess never disclosed her recipe. This could have been her delicious secret. Lacking a waffle iron, make pancakes with this batter.

2 teaspoons sugar
1½ teaspoons baking powder
½ teaspoon salt
½ cup white cornmeal
2 tablespoons butter, melted
1 cup boiling water
1 egg
½ cup flour
⅓ cup milk, approximately

Stir sugar, baking powder, and salt into cornmeal. Add butter and stir water in gradually to avoid lumps. Allow mixture to cool. Beat egg in large bowl. Blend in cornmeal, then flour, and add enough milk to thin to batter consistency. Bake and serve waffles hot, with a sprinkle of confectioners' sugar. Makes 6.

FRITTERS

With its penchant for frying, the South turns out multitudes of fritters—even dipping sweet potato slices into batters. The intelligent use of fresh sweet lard for frying results in perfect non-oily fritters. To fry fritters, heat fat, deep enough to float them, to moderate 375° F.—hot enough to brown a 1-inch cube of day-old white bread in 40 seconds.

Most fritters may be frozen and reheated in an extremely hot 500° F. oven, preheated or not, in about 15 minutes, and the batter may be frozen. If it seems too thin after thawing, test-fry a bit and, if necessary, stir in a little more flour.

Feather Fritters

In Louisiana, they make a fritter batter light as the proverbial feather to enhance foods. To make the following even lighter, use skim milk and sour it by filling measuring cup with 1 tablespoon vinegar and adding milk to the 1 cup mark.

½ cup flour
½ teaspoon soda
¼ teaspoon salt
Dash cayenne pepper, optional
1 cup sour milk

Mix flour, soda, salt, and pepper. Add to milk and stir only until dry ingredients are moistened. Batter will appear lumpy. Test-fry a dot and add more flour if batter does not hold together but use only enough to coat food lightly. This amount is sufficient for 1 to 1½ pounds food.

Jefferson Wine Batter

This multipurpose batter is a delicious coating for solid foods, such as cooked ham, and raw foods, such as chicken or shrimp. For fruit, depending upon its sweetness, add approximately 3 tablespoons additional sugar. Spice the batter, too, if you like, with about a teaspoon cinnamon and ¼ teaspoon nutmeg.

- 1 cup flour
- 1 teaspoon baking powder
- 1 teaspoon sugar
- ⅛ teaspoon salt
- 1 egg
- ½ cup dry Sherry
- ½ cup cream or milk

Mix dry ingredients in bowl. Beat egg slightly, beat Sherry in and stir into dry ingredients gradually. Add enough cream for griddle-cake batter consistency and stir smooth. If time allows, for increased tenderness, set batter aside for about thirty minutes. Then add more cream, if necessary, to return to original consistency. Dip foods and fry until browned—at which point raw foods should be cooked through.

Spiced Apple Slapjacks

The only drawback to these is that apple fritters do not freeze well. But they look so pretty and taste so good, leftovers should be no problem.

To add irresistibility, allow apple slices to marinate in a sweet wine about 2 hours. Then drain well before dipping in batter.

The fritters puff up and resemble doughnuts, and inasmuch as mace provides the typical doughnut seasoning, you might want to substitute about ½ teaspoon of it for cinnamon and nutmeg.

Peel and core apples, preferably greenings, and slice rings about ¼-inch thick. A large apple yields about 6 slices. Dip in Jefferson Wine Batter*, above, sweetened and spiced to taste. Serve hot out of the fat—sprinkled with confectioners' sugar, and pass a pitcher of Brown Sugar Syrup* or maple syrup.

Calas

The cry, *"Calas tous chaud!"* through the streets of New Orleans is reminiscent of the hot waffles cry that once was heard in Northern cities. Calas are superb puffy rice fritters. They are simplicity itself to make with an electric mixer. When fried in shallow fat, they resemble pancakes, but are not as proudly puffed nor as delectable.

1 egg
¼ cup sugar
2 cups cold, cooked rice
⅓ cup flour
1½ teaspoons baking powder
¼ teaspoon salt
½ teaspoon cinnamon
¼ teaspoon cloves
¼ teaspoon nutmeg

Beat egg and sugar until mixture is pale and thick. Stir rice in, and add remaining ingredients, mixing them together first. Drop teaspoonfuls into deep fat heated to 375° F., and fry until golden brown, turning once with a slotted spoon. Drain, sprinkle with confectioners' sugar, and eat *tout de suite*. Makes about 18. Both calas or the batter may be frozen.

YEAST BREAD

Despite doting on all the wonders an oven can produce without yeast, the South still admires light bread and cooks are dab hands at turning out soft puffy buns. So devoted are they to yeast doughs, that during the Civil War, when hops were not available, Southern gentlewomen devised a way of making yeast from fig leaves.

Their recipes for white bread and rolls and coffee cakes are not significantly different from Damn Yankee ways—but I do admire the early South's word for the sweet, coiled, cinnamon-sugar rolls that the Germans call *schnecken* (snails)—Coach Wheels.

Bea's Buns

When Bea MacLeod, the *Ithaca Journal* theatre critic, sent me this requested recipe—one of the sensations at a superb dinner party, she added its history.

"I was taught to do these," she wrote, "by a motherly next door neighbor in Washington, during World War II. There were many displaced people to be entertained (we specialized in the Canadian Navy), and party food was hard to come by. My good neighbor insisted that, if plenty of fresh hot little rolls came out of the oven, those officers wouldn't notice that there was more rice than shrimp in the casserole. She was right. We moved to Canada, shortly after the war, and word of the hot rolls preceded us, developing the handle, 'Bea's Buns.'"

　　　3　cups flour, approximately
　　　1　package yeast
　　　¼　cup sugar
　　　1　teaspoon salt
　　　¾　cup milk
　　　¼　cup water
　　　2　tablespoons butter, melted
　　　1　tablespoon lard, melted
　　　1　egg, beaten

In large bowl, mix half the flour with undissolved yeast, sugar and salt. In saucepan, combine milk, water, butter, and lard, and heat gently until warmed. Add to dry ingredients gradually and beat thoroughly. When smooth, beat egg in and add enough remaining flour to make a soft dough. Cover and let rise in warm place 2 hours. Punch dough down, turn out on floured board, and knead until smooth and elastic, about 5 minutes. Roll dough about ¼-inch thick and cut into 2½-inch rounds. Place on greased baking sheet, brush tops with melted butter, cover and let rise until double, about 30 minutes. Bake in preheated, hot 400°F. oven until done, about 15 minutes. Makes approximately 2 dozen.

Yeast Cornbread

Unusual is the word for this sunny-yellow, moist loaf that keeps superbly.

- 3 cups yellow cornmeal
- 5 cups flour
- 3½ cups water
- 2 packages dry yeast
- 1 cup cooked mashed sweet potatoes
- ¼ cup butter, melted
- 2 teaspoons salt

Combine 1 cup each cornmeal and flour, 1½ cups warm water, and undissolved yeast, and stir until blended. Cover and let rise until light and bubbly, about 1 hour. Stir down with wooden spoon and set aside. Boil 2 cups water, pour over remaining cornmeal, stir until thick, cool, and add to first mixture. Stir in sweet potatoes, butter, salt, and 3 cups flour. Add enough remaining flour to form medium soft dough. Knead until smooth, place in greased bowl, cover, and let rise until doubled in bulk, about 1½ hours.

Punch dough down, divide in half and shape into loaves or rolls, as desired. Place loaves in greased 9 x 5 x 3-inch loaf pans, cover, and let rise 30 minutes. Bake in preheated, moderate 350° F. oven until done (bottom or side of loaf sounds hollow when tapped), about 1 hour. Remove from pans and cool on rack. Makes 2 loaves, which may be frozen.

A SEDUCTION OF DESSERTS

Journeying in what, to me, was practically a foreign culinary land, I was struck by the enormous number of dessert and candy recipes. The craving for sugar that hot weather seems to engender may be a reason for so many. Responsible, too, is the fact that desserts were served in plural—a Southern cook pointed to her table with pride only when it held an obligatory cake, companioned by at least one other pudding or pie.

Although I would like to include every last recipe, many of the classics can no longer be considered distinctively regional, and many, such as pecan-bourbon cake, and pralines, can be purchased.

But way back when, even candy-making was one of the cooks' chores. An 1800s recipe for chocolate creams instructs the ladies to distill two gallons of alcohol to one-half. Sampling the potent brew may have twisted *bon-bon* to *bomboon*—the Southerners word for caramels.

With so many desserts to make, there was obvious need to rush, and centuries-old books include desserts titled Hurry-up this and Quick-as-a-wink that. To produce the real triumphs, however, takes time. Expend it to produce the following, letting the mixer and blender make haste for you.

One thing that *can* save time is to omit the traditional savories of English legacy. They followed dessert, and one titled, "An Excellent Relish After Dinner," was to be "stewed at the table." Hopefully, a handsome chafing dish was employed, because the contents can not have provided a feast for the eyes. They included dinner's leftover soup or gravy, vinegar, catsup, wine, and the "broiled legs, liver, and gizzard of a turkey cut small."

FRUIT AND NUTS

Whether Southern cooks of old considered conserving fruit work or play, they frugally canned, candied, brandied, honeyed, jammed, jellied, and pickled the orchard plenty—and also made Fools of it. Wine-marinated fruit topped cup cakes, and sauced fruit was served over puddings and lavished in fillings and on frostings.

Ambrosia is the classic Southern fruit dessert and the mystery of why so much coconut found its way into recipes, is solved when you realize that Barbados was the original home of many of the early settlers, and coconut the obvious cargo for the West Indian trade ships.

Nuts were another part of the South's harvest of plenty. Heavy-ladened pecan trees; trees holding English, and black walnuts; and hickory nuts all grace the Southern countryside, and Georgia has the honor of producing more nuts than any other state.

In dizzying nomenclature, the South calls peanuts ground nuts; earth nuts; monkey nuts; and goobers (possibly from the African *nguba*). But don't look for a peanut tree in the South. This American native is a member of the legume or pea (hence, peanut) and bean family, and the peanuts bury themselves beneath their leafing plants. Virginia peanuts, enclosed in pods, are large and elongated; the Spanish variety is small and round, and, of course, Southern peanut butter was homemade.

Ambrosia

Always oranges and coconut (plus a bit of coconut milk), sometimes pineapple, confectioners' sugar, and a cut crystal bowl, made the original ambrosia of the South. Through the years, cooks, undisturbed by notions of authenticity, added bananas, strawberries, and other seasonal plenty. Some piqued ambrosia with lemon juice; others added an insouciant dusting of nutmeg for this traditional Southern Christmas dessert. Ambrosia can mellow overnight in the refrigerator, where it will keep at least 2 days.

For 2 servings, allow 2 tablespoons shredded coconut for each peeled, sliced orange. Layer oranges in bowl, sprinkle with confectioners' sugar to taste, top with coconut, and continue the layers. End with a frill of coconut, and serve chilled.

Fig Secrets

At a dinner party, I was fortunate enough to sit next to a gentleman with a charming Southern accent, who lovingly reminisced about down-home desserts. He described this as a favorite.

Stem and chop ½ pound (1 cup) black or brown figs coarsely (use blender for ease). Wet hands with cold water and shape 1-inch balls. Drop into about ½ cup bourbon and marinate overnight. Drain just before serving and roll in confectioner's sugar. The balls keep indefinitely and may be frozen. Makes about 2 dozen.

Strawberry Peach

Out of a distinguished Maryland plantation comes this pink-of-perfection dessert which unfortunately loses its bloom when refrigerated overnight. If guests are drinking Champagne, let them add a dollop—and bless both the pressers of the grapes and the freezers.

- 1 package (1 pound) frozen strawberries in syrup
- 6 medium peaches
- ½ teaspoon almond extract
- ¾ cup sliced blanched almonds

Drain berries and boil syrup until it spins a thread from tines of fork. It will take about 10 minutes and almost all the liquid will have cooked down. Meanwhile, skin peaches and slice into serving bowl. Pour syrup over immediately, and add strawberries and extract. Chill and serve garnished with almonds. Makes 6-plus servings and may be frozen.

Green Gage Plum Jelly

These plums are a Southern glory—Damn Yankees usually must pick theirs from a can. Serve with cream or garnish with whipped cream, sprinkled with grated lime rind.

- 1 pound (about 5) fresh green gage plums
- 1 cup water
- ½ cup sugar
- ½ cup dry white wine, divided
- 1 package (1 tablespoon) unflavored gelatin
- Dash orange bitters, optional

Pit plums (do not peel) and cut each into 6 equal wedges. In deep saucepan place water, then sugar. Stir over low heat only until sugar dissolves. Bring to boil and boil 5 minutes. Add plums, cover pan, and cook until tender, about 10 minutes. With slotted spoon, remove plums to serving dish, arranging them in a single layer.

Pour ¼ cup wine in wide-bottomed pan. Sprinkle gelatin evenly over surface and allow to soften—about 5 minutes. Dissolve over low heat, stirring constantly, about 5 minutes. Add with remaining wine to 1½ cups syrup from plums, and add bitters. Pour over plums and refrigerate until firm. Makes 6 servings.

Belle Grove Apple Snow

Watching my stalwart Kitchen-Aid beat this innocent of desserts to a fluff, I could only marvel at the strength of the arms that preceded this machine age. The "snow" is nutritious, an enviable budget-stretcher, and will hold up for several hours. For brown snow, beat in about ½ teaspoon cinnamon and ¼ teaspoon nutmeg.

- 1 egg white
- ⅛ teaspoon cream of tartar
- ⅛ teaspoon salt
- 4 tablespoons sugar, divided
- ¾ cup applesauce
- ½ teaspoon lemon juice, optional

Beat egg white with cream of tartar and salt until fluffy. Beat half the sugar in gradually and when completely incorporated and mixture is fairly stiff, add applesauce. Beat until mixture stands in firm peaks, adding enough additional sugar to taste, and lemon juice to accentuate flavor. Makes about 4 cups.

Amelia Springs Shortcake

This different kind of shortcake should be served hot, lavished with sweetened fruit and whipped cream, between layers and over the top.

- 3 cups flour
- 4 teaspoons baking powder
- ½ teaspoon salt
- 1 tablespoon cinnamon
- ½ cup brown sugar
- ¾ cup shortening
- 1 cup pecans, broken coarsely
- ¾ cup milk
- 2 eggs, beaten slightly

Mix flour, baking powder, salt, cinnamon, and brown sugar. Cut shortening in as for pie dough and stir pecans in. Beat milk into eggs and stir into dry ingredients with fork. Spread in 2 8-inch circles on greased cookie sheet. Bake on center rack of preheated, very hot 450° F. oven until browned, about 10 minutes. Makes 8 servings.

Sugared Pecans

Thanks to undaunted Southern cooks, France's sugared almonds became sugared pecans. The water may be replaced with undiluted frozen orange juice. Then substitute grated orange rind for cinnamon.

Formerly, proportions for the syrup specified an abundance of water and time wasted while it boiled away. This updated version, a non-humid day, and a non-stick skillet are aids to speed and success.

- 1½ cups pecan halves
- ¼ cup sugar, preferably very fine
- 2 tablespoons water
- ¼ teaspoon cinnamon
- ½ teaspoon salt

Combine all ingredients and boil, stirring constantly, until pecans just glaze, about 3 minutes. Do not overcook or sugar will crystallize. Spread on paper—wax or parchment—to cool. If nuts do not dry, place in preheated, moderate 350° F. oven about 5 minutes.

PUDDINGS AND CREAMS

For centuries, the word pudding has been a cover for creams, custards, and a large plus. Doubtless because pudding derives from the word puddle, and includes anything swollen or sticky.

The old South called souffles, "Soufflée Puddings." Their "Apple Pudding" was applesauce baked in a crust, and Indian Pudding, which answered either to the name Choctaw Spoon Bread or Bread Pudding, classily came to table with Brandy Butter.

The popularity of Charlotte Russe and Parisian Pudding, which is Trifle, Tipsy Pudding, Madeira Cream, or, when made with currant jelly, Cardinal Cream, indicated a plenitude of leftover sponge cake. And Naples Biscuits, which cooks were told "to shape carefully into fingers," must have gone begging, too.

An Apple Island was a bavarian cream, made with lemon- and clove-flavored applesauce, surrounded with a moat of custard sauce. Custard also was fried and a Caramel Custard is attributed to a Miss Pidgeon (of the Virginia Byrds?). Burnt Custard (Creme Brulée) was a favorite on Jefferson's table, and the *Williamsburg Art of Cookery* suggests that cooks, "Tip a [cuſtard] about with a little red Currant Jelly."

If you find a market that carries "clouted cream," don't forget to flavor it with rosewater. And, on a really tight-squeeze-for-time day, you might "Butter cottage cheese and serve it with sugar and cream."

Apple Rice Pudding

Leftover rice obviously presented as many problems as leftover sponge cake. One rice pudding, titled "A Dessert For A Delicate Person" may have euphemistically referred to a lady in a delicate condition, a hypochondriac, a convalescent, or an aesthete.

For the simplest old-fashioned version, ¼ cup cream was stirred into a cup of cooked rice and marbled with 2 tablespoons acid jelly—currant, plum, strawberry, or lemon are suggested. Virginia cooks topped the following with melted butter and sugar and passed a pitcher of wine sauce. And, of course, cooked the rice (converted is best) in milk.

½ cup rice
1 egg
½ cup cream, approximately
½ cup applesauce
1 tablespoon butter
3 tablespoons sugar
½ teaspoon cinnamon
¼ teaspoon nutmeg

Cook rice, break egg in measuring cup, and add cream to ½ cup mark. Beat until blended and stir into applesauce. Melt butter in saucepan, add applesauce mixture and cook over very low heat, stirring until thickened. Do not allow mixture to boil. Add rice and season to taste. Serve chilled with a sprinkle of grated lemon rind and pass wine sauce—or cream. Makes 4 servings.

Mrs. Goshae's Bread Pudding

Bread Pudding was "Sippet Pudding" in the long ago South, and recipes called for "a Penny loaf and marrow." It got fancier as time went by—the loaf pan was caramelized and sometimes the egg whites were beaten separately to produce a "Soufflee Sippet

Pudding"—so that making it involved the dubious economics of investing additional cash to avoid wasting stale bread.

This is such a paragon of bread puddings, invest away, and salute Mrs. Goshae, who thought of the vanilla. Sometimes she bakes it in a loaf pan to serve sliced, and she always passes jam and heavy cream. Raisins are the usual fruit, and may be used instead of dates. And if you must, soufflee the pudding by adding the egg yolks to the bread mixture and folding the beaten whites in as for Benson Yam Puff*.

> 1-pound loaf good white bread
> Milk
> 1½ cups sugar
> ½ cup (¼ pound) softened butter
> 4 eggs
> 2 teaspoons vanilla
> 1 cup chopped dates

Pull bread into small pieces and add enough milk to cover. Soak about 2½ hours (or overnight, if desired). Stir remaining ingredients in and turn into buttered 1½-quart casserole. Sprinkle top with nutmeg, if desired, and bake in preheated, moderate 350° F. oven until crusty and brown, about 1 hour. Serve hot or cold. Makes 8 servings and may be frozen.

Syllabub

Spell it Sillibub or Sillabub, as it appears in 1800s dictionaries. Then prepare this beverage-cum-dessert simply, as below, or in any of the thousand and one differing versions found in cook books, South, North, East, and West. The origin of syllabub is noted as obscure, but, inasmuch as it often is suggested as a topping for stale sponge cake, I surmise it may be the British corruption of the Italian *Zuppa Inglese* or *Zabaglione*.

Very early recipes call only for wine (or cider) and milk, but over the years enthusiastic ladies dreamed up versions similar to, and as complex as eggnog. In the garden of a charming restaurant, it was served to me the following way, in a shot glass. Treat yourself to this sweet innocence of cream and wine, and change the kind of jelly at will.

    3 tablespoons guava jelly
    1½ tablespoons Sherry
    1 tablespoon whipped cream

Place jelly in a very small glass. Add Sherry, steep in refrigerator 2 hours, or overnight, and serve topped with whipped cream. Makes 1 serving.

Carlotta Cream

This actually is a bavarian cream that Carolina cooks saw fit to extend with rice.

- ½ cup pecans, broken coarsely
- 1 package (1 tablespoon) unflavored gelatin
- 1¼ cups cold milk
- 1 cup brown sugar, approximately
- ¼ teaspoon salt
- 2 cups cold cooked rice (about 1 cup raw)
- 1 teaspoon vanilla
- 1 cup heavy cream, whipped stiff

Toast pecans in preheated, moderate 350° F. oven until crisped, about 5 minutes. Soften gelatin by sprinkling it over ¼ cup of the milk. Combine remaining milk, sugar, and salt, and heat to scalding, stirring constantly. Remove from heat, add gelatin mixture, and stir until dissolved. Chill until partially set. Beat smooth and stir in rice, vanilla, and nuts. Fold whipped cream in and pour into 1-quart mold, rinsed with cold water. Chill until firm. Unmold on chilled serving dish, rinsed with cold water so mold can be slid into position. Garnish, if desired, with additional whipped cream and pecans. Makes 6 servings.

Coffee Custard

- 2 egg yolks
- 2 cups milk
- ¼ cup cornstarch
- 3 tablespoons sugar
- ½ cup strong hot coffee, preferably chicory*

In broad-bottomed saucepan, beat yolks with a small portion of milk. Add cornstarch and sugar, and stir smooth. Scald remaining milk, add coffee, and stir into cornstarch mixture. Cook just to boiling point, over very low heat, stirring constantly. Turn into serving dish immediately and seal surface with plastic wrap. Refrigerate and serve cold. Makes 4 servings.

Louisiana Snow Eggs
Oeufs a la Neige

Variations of this pretty charmer abound in Southern cook books, and hurried cooks simply beat egg whites with jelly until stiff and dropped spoonfuls of the mixture on sweetened cream.

Coffee Custard makes the "eggs" seem whiter than the snows of the North.

- 2 egg whites
- ⅛ teaspoon salt
- ¼ teaspoon cream of tartar
- 4 tablespoons extra fine sugar
- 1 teaspoon vanilla

Beat egg whites with salt and cream of tartar to a soft foam and beat in sugar, 2 tablespoons at a time. Add vanilla and beat until stiff—mixture holds shape.

Heat milk called for in Coffee Custard*, above, to a simmer and add vanilla. Using 2 tablespoons, shape 2-inch "eggs" with meringue mixture. Poach, covered until firm, preferably turning only once. It will take approximately 4 minutes in all. With slotted spoon, remove snow eggs to paper towel-lined plate to drain. Prepare custard with milk used to poach "eggs" and arrange them on chilled custard. Makes 4 servings.

ICE CREAM

Ice cream was a rare treat in the old South. Making it depended upon the occasional cold spell, frigid enough to produce ice, or a plummeting temperature, which allowed the cream to be hung outside in pails to freeze. When the thermometer descended, the alert *Virginia Housewife* was ready with advice, telling readers that a cream, "when not put into shapes, [must be served in] glasses with handles."

Mississippi's ice cream contains buttermilk, Maryland's strawberry bombe cloaks itself with whipped cream, and the following creamy-cold variations are as Dixie as cool jazz. Purchased ice cream means they can be prepared in a hot lick.

Fig Ice Cream

I knew I was a Damn Yankee indeed when my from-the-South editor asked if I meant fresh or dried figs in a recipe. I had never seen a fresh fig until I came to New York, and invariably ate them out of hand with the awed respect their astronomical price deserved.

Now I know fig trees are as familiar in the South as maple trees in Vermont, and that Southerners can afford the luxury of peeling them. If you are in that fortunate position, do likewise.

Otherwise, simply fold 6 unpeeled, coarsely chopped fresh figs into 1 pint slightly softened vanilla ice cream and freeze until firm.

The peel looks enticingly like the dots of vanilla in French vanilla ice cream. If the figs are peeled and mashed, the ice cream will have a soft pink hue and the seeds will provide interesting crunch. Dried figs, cut small, make another delicious choice.

Mango Ice Cream

Whir 1 cup peeled, chopped mango in blender with about ¼ cup orange-flavored liqueur, and flavor to taste with ⅛ teaspoon mace and ¼ teaspoon nutmeg. Fold into a pint of French vanilla ice cream and freeze firm. Makes 4 servings.

Molasses Ice Cream

Fold ¼ cup molasses and ½ cup chopped pecans into 1 pint slightly softened ice cream. For appearance, marble the molasses, rather than incorporating it completely. Makes 4 servings.

Green Gage Plum Ice Cream

Purée 1 cup pitted coarsely-cut unpeeled plums in blender with ¼ cup orange juice. Fold into a pint of French vanilla ice cream and freeze firm. Drained, peeled, cooked fresh plums (see Green Gage Plum Jelly*) or canned plums may be substituted but the wonderful fresh tartness will be missing.

Mrs. Cook's Brandy Butter
Hard Sauce

Mrs. Cook, the antithesis of her name, favored *no* kitchen operation and, except for this Southern delicacy out of one of her Yorkshire ancestor's past, the food responded in kind.

Use this "Butter," which the South also calls Brandy Sauce, as Southerners do, to complement gingerbread, bread pudding, fruit pies, and the like. And for exceptional use, put it on the buffet table as a dunk or topping for fresh fruit.

Cognac, sweet wine, Sherry, or undiluted frozen orange juice may be substituted for the rum, as may vanilla (or other) extracts.

- 2 eggs, separated
- ¼ pound (½ cup) butter, creamed
- 1½ cups confectioner's sugar, approximately, sifted
- ¼ teaspoon salt, divided
- 1 teaspoon high proof (151 proof) rum
- ¼ teaspoon cream of tartar

Beat egg yolks into butter and when incorporated, beat in 1 cup sugar, ⅛ teaspoon salt, and rum. Beat egg whites with remaining salt and cream of tartar almost to soft peak stage and fold into butter mixture. If sauce is not homogenous, beat in enough additional sugar for smooth consistency. Then, if necessary, add more rum to taste. Makes 12 servings, about 1 cup, and may be frozen.

Brown Sugar Syrup

A heavy non-stick skillet is best for preparing this easy-to-do syrup for ice cream, French toast, pancakes, etc. Melt 1 cup sugar in skillet and cook over high heat, stirring with a wooden spoon until it begins to melt. Lower heat and continue stirring until clear and brown. Pour in ½ cup water all at once, and cook and stir (lumps will disappear) until syrup reaches maple syrup consistency. It thickens further on standing. Store covered in refrigerator—to keep indefinitely. Yield about 1 cup.

AN EXTRAVAGANCE OF PASTRY

Moonshines, to roll "thin as your fingernail," Petticoat Tails, and "Little Hollow Bifkets" were a few of the cookies that frustrated the devil by keeping Southern hands from being idle. The generic names for them—sweet biscuits, wafers, tea cakes—reflect British heritage and the Georgian English tradition of entertaining at tea.

In the early 1700s, cookies were rampant with seeds—cardamom, coriander, and benne (sesame). Elegant Virginians fancied cookies topped with caraway seeds and also proffered Pecan Confections—meringue kisses confected with molasses and pecans. Kisses made with white sugar enclosed a dot of currant jelly for a kiss surprise.

An inadvertent surprise were Chocolate Cakes—cookies containing no chocolate at all. They were made with brown sugar and baked on a griddle, then cut into 1-inch plate-size strips. Hostesses were instructed to serve these on the plate for which they were measured, "in rows to checker each other." "Tavern Biscuits," not surprisingly, contained brandy or wine. Long ago, diamond shapes of rolled-thin biscuit dough were fried, to make "diamond Bachelors." The author coyly added to her receipt the fact that ladies were "very fond of them."

And a pressed-for-time cook made "Spread Cakes," by pressing dough for a rolled cooky onto the back of a baking pan; pressing chopped nuts into that, and sprinkling the dough with sugar and cinnamon. Almonds entitled these cut-into-squares delights to the name "Spread Almond Fancies."

"Empire Biscuits" of the 1700s sound as much trouble as holding an empire together. After baking, cinnamon-flavored cookies clasped currant jelly—of course, homemade. They were topped with a white icing, put together after frenetic sugar-pounding, and decorated with angelica or cherries—and you know who did the candying.

Thumb Run Tea Cakes

In the interests of a cool kitchen, the original recipe specified frying these on a griddle. Oven-baking turns them into cookies with a cake-like consistency, but they harden rapidly. If day-old cookies are a significant problem at your house, expect to dunk.

The griddle-baked version may be frozen. I substituted my favorites—diced dates—for the raisins or currants called for in the Welsh-ancestry original. You'll have about a dozen and a half cakes in either instance.

- 1 cup flour
- ½ teaspoon baking powder
- ¼ teaspoon salt
- ¼ cup sugar
- ¼ cup shortening
- 1 egg
- ¼ cup diced dates
- 2 tablespoons milk, approximately

Stir dry ingredients together and cut shortening in as for pie dough. Stir in egg with a fork, and add dates. If dough is too stiff, stir in a small amount of milk; if too soft, lightly knead in additional flour. Shape as for Fist Biscuits* and place about 1 inch apart on hot, greased griddle. Reduce heat and fry slowly, turning to brown both sides.

To bake, shape as above and place about 1 inch apart on greased cooky sheet. Put on center rack of preheated, moderate 365° F. oven and bake until browned, about 10 minutes. In either case, serve hot, to butter.

Rout Drop-Cakes

The word, rout, to denote a company of select persons is obsolete now, but happily these cookies are not. This old, old recipe directs that the cookies be dropped from a spoon—almost an impossibility with today's ingredients. If the dough is too sticky to roll, refrigerate about an hour or put in freezer about a half hour.

The cookies are crisp, brown-edged, and look pretty snowed with confectioners' sugar. For variety, substitute benne (sesame) seeds for poppy seeds, but check both before use for rancidity and to keep them fresh, store in the refrigerator.

- 2 tablespoons brandy
- 6 tablespoons butter, creamed
- ½ cup sugar
- 1 egg
- 2 egg yolks
- 2 cups flour, divided
- ¼ teaspoon salt
- ¼ cup poppy seeds

Beat brandy into butter. Add sugar gradually and beat until light and fluffy. Beat egg and yolks in. Combine flour with salt and poppy seeds and beat in with enough additional flour so that when dough is touched lightly with an unfloured finger it comes away clean. Roll dough into 1-inch diameter balls (flour your palms lightly, if necessary), and place about ½-inch apart on greased cookie sheet. Press down into rounds with fork tines (dipped in flour, if necessary) and bake on top rack of preheated, moderate 365° F. oven until browned, about 15 minutes. Makes about 3½ dozen 2-inch cookies.

Sesame Seed Cookies
Benne Wafers

Benne seeds are considered good luck tokens and may be the oldest condiment known to man; records of them date back to 1600 B.C.

The rich seeds (they contain about 50% oil) come from an annual herb, are indigenous to Africa, and were carried to America in the 1700s.

This is a rich can't-stop-eating confection, so perhaps you had better double the recipe.

- ¼ cup benne seeds
- 1 tablespoon softened butter
- ½ cup brown sugar
- 1 egg yolk
- 1 teaspoon vanilla
- ½ teaspoon salt
- 3 tablespoons flour

Using heavy pan, stir seeds over moderate heat until slightly browned. Combine butter and brown sugar, add sesame seeds, and stir in egg yolk, vanilla, and salt. Add flour and mix well. With wet hands shape 1-inch diameter balls. Place at least 2 inches apart on foil-lined cookie sheet. Bake on top rack of preheated, moderate 350° F. oven until firm, about 10 minutes. Allow to cool completely, and peel foil off. Makes 24 cookies about 2½ inches in diameter.

CAKES

Cake, being an obligatory of the many desserts served in the South, it is not surprising that recipes are legion. Miss Harper Lee's enchanting *To Kill a Mockingbird* alerted Damn Yankees to the eight-egg Shinny Cake. Dolly Varden's name is given to a cake marbled white and spice-brown. An Angel Food was called White Sponge Cake (but sponge cake was called Savoy Cake, or Palais Royal, when "baked in small paper molds"). Lemon Jelly Cake, also attesting to the profligacy of eggs, is a jelly roll filled with lemon curd.

Fruit cakes, which cooks were directed to "season to taste," were frequently flavored with rose water. New Orleans cooks topped their version with almond paste and a glaze, while Black Fruit Cake boasted a chocolate batter. Lane Cake, an almost inside-out fruit cake, was filled with, and sagged under, a whiskey-laced frosting containing pecans, raisins, candied cherries, and coconut. The Tennessee Smokies honored brides with Stack Cakes—each guest contributing a layer.

A "Hard-Times Cake" called for a half-pound of butter, a pound of sugar, six eggs, and a "bit of brandy." "Plebeian" gingerbread contained no sugar. But when baked for those above the salt, brandy went into it, too. Southerners shaped yeast dough into

"Cakes the Size of a Half Dollar," fried them in "boiling lard," and called them, "Dough-Nuts—a Yankee Cake."

FROSTINGS AND TOPPINGS

I find that guests are awed most when I end a dinner party with an imposing cake. An impatient "froster," I have devised serve-on-the-side calorie-tempters to replace icings. It is a short cut which ladies of old would have cheered—especially while occupying themselves in pulverizing blocks of castor sugar to a powder. They were advised to make, rather than buy this "flour sugar," because the available confectioners' sugar was "adulterated with the white earth called 'Terra Alba,' which causes it to harden like stone."

Fortunately for pulverizers, most long-ago Southern frostings were primarily orange- or lemon-flavored meringue froths, and did not depend upon confectioners' sugar.

My favorite direction—for a chocolate icing—indicates that cooks were asbestos-fingered as well as busily versatile. It instructed them to test the boiling sugar syrup so that, "when pressed with the fingers [it] would present the appearance of strong glue."

Snow Hill Silver Cake

A chef taught me to fold egg whites into batters with my hand—almost a must when combining them with a batter as firm as is this typical English "cut and come again" cake.

- ½ cup (¼ pound) shortening, creamed
- 1 teaspoon vanilla
- ½ teaspoon lemon extract
- ½ teaspoon almond extract
- 1 cup sugar
- 1½ cups cake flour
- 1½ teaspoons baking powder
- ½ teaspoon salt
- ½ cup milk
- 4 egg whites, beaten to soft peaks
- ½ teaspoon cream of tartar

Beat extracts into shortening. Add sugar gradually, and beat well after each addition. Stir dry ingredients together and add alternately with milk. Begin and end with dry ingredients, adding them in about 4 parts, and beat just until incorporated; stir milk in. Fold in the beaten egg whites as for Benson Yam Puff*. Place in greased 9 x 5 x 3-inch loaf pan and bake in preheated, moderate 350° F. oven until cake tester inserted in center comes out clean, about 50 minutes. After about 10 minutes, turn out on cake rack to cool, and serve, if desired, with the following topping.

Chipped Chocolate Cream Topping

2 cups heavy cream
¼ cup confectioners' sugar, approximately
1½ ounces unsweetened chocolate, coarsely grated

Whip cream, and when stiff, fold in sugar to taste. Fold chocolate in, reserving a bit to garnish top. Turn into bowl but do not flatten. Sprinkle with remaining chocolate and pass with cake.

FRUIT CAKE

From a largesse of fabulous Southern fruit cakes, I have chosen the following blonde version to serve at circles—social, or family. It even may soothe the anti-social.

Because fruit cakes normally contain raisins, if you like, substitute up to 2 cups to replace an equal quantity of candied fruit. If your social circle is very rich, substitute sliced almonds for pecans.

Storing Fruit Cake

A fruit cake does not require spiritous storing, but a heavy hand with the Cognac bottle adds incomparable moisture. For storing, I prefer to bake fruit cake in loaf pans, to cut into 2 x 1-inch fingers or into 1½-inch cubes, for eating out-of-hand.

Line a tin box, first with enough foil, then with enough cheesecloth, to extend over the top. Place cake in box in layers and sprinkle each layer with Cognac. Fold cheesecloth over, then fold foil over, and store tightly closed. Occasionally give the cake another drink.

Social Circle Fruit Cake

- 1 teaspoon vanilla
- ½ teaspoon orange extract
- 1 cup (½ pound) butter, creamed
- 1 cup sugar
- 5 eggs
- ½ cup Sherry
- 2 cups flour
- 1 teaspoon baking powder
- ½ teaspoon salt
- 4 cups (2 pounds) diced, mixed glacé fruit
- 2 cups (about ½ pound) broken pecans

Combine first 4 ingredients as for Snow Hill Silver Cake*. Beat eggs in one at a time, beating well after each addition and beat Sherry in. Mix dry ingredients together and stir them into batter gradually. Drain fruit, if from a jar, and add with nuts. Turn into greased, floured 10-inch tube pan, or 2 9x5x3-inch loaf pans. Bake in preheated, slow 300° F. oven until cake tester inserted in center comes out clean, about 1¾ hours. After 10 minutes, turn out onto cake rack. Yields about 4 pounds cake.

Mrs. Governor Floyd's Good but Cheap Cake

Keeping cream from souring must have been an almost insurmountable problem in the South, whereas today, our problem is to get it to sour. Dairy sour cream may be substituted, which of course, removes the adjective "cheap" from this title.

Neither rose nor orange flower water has ever struck me as being particularly characterful, and, in testing, I found that the rosewater called for didn't stand a chance against the mace, so omit it at will. This cake is firm, coarse-textured, and moist, but chocolate frosting with coconut shreds pressed in will give it party airs.

- 1 tablespoon butter, softened
- 1 cup sugar
- 3 eggs
- 1 tablespoon rose water, optional
- 1 cup sour cream
- 1¼ cups flour
- 1 teaspoon baking soda
- ½ teaspoon salt
- ½ teaspoon mace
- 1 cup walnuts, broken coarsely

Beat sugar into butter and add sour cream. Combine dry ingredients and stir in, using as few strokes as possible. Flour clumps should be moistened, but batter will appear lumpy. Stir in nuts and turn into greased 9-inch (round or square) baking pan, and bake in preheated, moderate 375° F. oven until cake tester inserted in center comes out clean, about 25 minutes.

Mincy Devil's Food Cake

Ozark ladies today may be substituting instant mashed potatoes in this recipe of theirs. It works very well and skim milk produces a lighter cake.

- 1 teaspoon vanilla
- 1 cup (½ pound) shortening, creamed
- 2 cups sugar
- 4 eggs
- 2 cups cake flour
- 3 teaspoons baking powder
- ½ teaspoon salt
- ⅔ cup hot milk
- 1 cup hot mashed potato
- 3 ounces chocolate, grated

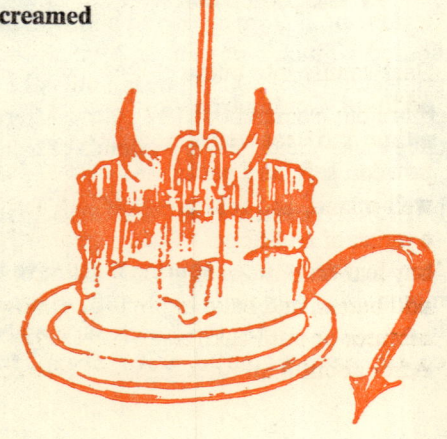

Proceed as for Snow Hill Silver Cake*, but beat eggs in one at a time. Mix dry ingredients and add alternately with combined mixture of milk, chocolate, and potato. Grease a large tube pan all over and put a large dab of butter in top depressions. Press an unblanched almond into butter dabs. Add batter and bake in preheated moderate 350° F. oven about 1 hour. Let rest for ten minutes, turn out, and cool on cake rack. Sprinkle with confectioners' sugar. Makes 12–16 slices. Serve with Chipped Chocolate Cream*, if desired.

Pecan Torte

Germans use ground almonds to make a feather-light torte. Louisiana cooks substitute pecans, choose brown sugar, and call the cake "sweet bread." If you are feeling expansive, offer it as an entree accompaniment. Or double the recipe, top with rum-flavored whipped cream, and serve for dessert.

- ½ teaspoon vanilla
- ¾ cup butter, creamed
- 1 cup brown sugar
- 3 eggs, separated
- 1 cup flour
- 1 teaspoon baking powder
- ¼ teaspoon salt
- ½ cup pecans, ground
- ¼ teaspoon cream of tartar
- ½ teaspoon crumbled bay leaf

Beat vanilla into butter. Add sugar gradually, beating well after each addition. Continue beating until light and fluffy. Add yolks one at a time and beat well after each addition. Mix flour with baking powder, salt, and pecans and add to butter mixture. Beat only until well-mixed, and fold in egg whites beaten to soft-peak stage with a pinch of additional salt and cream of tartar. Sprinkle pieces of bay leaf on bottom of greased 8-inch round or square cake pan, add batter, and bake in preheated, slow 300° F. oven about 30 minutes or until cake tester inserted in center comes out clean. After about 8 minutes, turn out on cake rack to cool.

Richie-Lee's Cider Cake

West Virginia, nestling up to Ohio Johnny Appleseed Country, boasts extensive apple orchards and *syder* was a Maryland staple. Apple juice may be substituted for the cider in this inexpensive-by-Southern standards—but imposing cake. Whipped cream, dappled with bits of pink apple jelly would make a pretty topping to serve on the side.

- 1 teaspoon vanilla
- ½ cup (¼ pound) shortening, creamed
- 1½ cups sugar
- 2 eggs
- 3 cups flour
- 1 teaspoon baking soda
- 1 teaspoon nutmeg
- 1 cup cider

Proceed as for Pecan Torte* adding whole eggs and mixed dry ingredients alternately with cider. Spread batter in greased 9-inch tube pan and bake in preheated, moderate 350° F. oven until cake tester inserted in center comes out clean, about 50 minutes. After about 8 minutes, turn out on cake rack to cool.

Apple-Slice Corn-Cake

This looks angel-innocent—and is as ethereal. Hooray! for canned apples—and other fruits may be substituted. Pass whipped cream or ice cream, if desired.

- ½ cup flour
- 1 cup yellow corn meal
- 2 teaspoons baking powder
- ½ teaspoon salt
- ⅓ cup sugar
- ½ teaspoon nutmeg
- ½ cup (¼ pound) butter, melted
- ¾ cup milk
- 2 eggs, beaten slightly

Topping

- 1 can (1-pound 4-ounce) apple slices, well drained
- 3 tablespoons brown sugar
- ½ teaspoon cinnamon

In large bowl, mix flour, cornmeal, baking powder, salt, sugar, and nutmeg. Combine butter, milk, and eggs, and add to dry ingredients stirring only until they are moistened. Pour into greased 9-inch square pan and cover top with apples, arranging them in rows on batter. Mix brown sugar with cinnamon, and sprinkle over apples. Bake in preheated, moderate 350° F. oven until cake tester inserted in center comes out clean, about 35 minutes. Serve hot or cold. May be frozen.

Tavern Gingerbread

It is nice to update a classic and today's pineapple wine gives gingerbread elegant airs. Skim milk or water may be substituted and lard is excellent as shortening.

- 7 tablespoons shortening, creamed
- ½ cup sugar
- 1 egg, beaten slightly
- 1 cup molasses
- 2½ cups flour
- 1½ teaspoons baking soda
- ½ teaspoon salt
- 1 teaspoon cinnamon
- 1 teaspoon ginger
- ½ teaspoon cloves
- 1 cup pineapple wine

Proceed as for Pecan Torte*, adding egg and molasses to creamed mixture, and adding wine alternately with combined dry ingredients. When smooth and well-beaten, pour into greased 9 x 13 x 2-inch pan. Bake in preheated, moderate 350° F. oven until cake tester inserted in center comes out clean, about 30 minutes.

Pineapple Ginger Topping

2 ounces crystallized ginger, cut in ¼-inch pieces
1 cup crushed pineapple, drained
1 cup heavy cream, whipped

Add ginger to pineapple, and refrigerate overnight. Drain and fold into whipped cream. Serve separately to spoon over gingerbread, spice cake, and the like.

PIE

In New Orleans, they say, "When the mouse is full, the flour is bitter." I can't think of a fuller mouse than one who had downed the ample aggregate of dishes on Southern tables—even before the bringing on of the multiple desserts. An attempt to tantalize satiation may be one of the reasons for the tempting pies lovingly put together by imaginative cooks.

They filled them with fruits and creams and called upon an alphabet of flavorings. They frothed them with meringue or snowed it on as topping. And, today, as then, gave "chop crust" pastries wonderful names. "Puffs"—eight-inch squares of pie dough folded over spicy-sweet mixtures of crushed peaches, to swell and billow in sweet hot fat. Crow's Nest Pie, a kind of apple cobbler, wore a layer of lemon slices beneath its flaky crust. No Matters were rounds of fried pastry, stacked with applesauce between.

And, seemingly, every lady with a jug of molasses in her hand poured a different kind of Stick-Tight Pie—another name for that Dixie extravagance—pecan pie. Some piqued the toothsome filling with cloves, some reached for cinnamon, others folded chocolate in.

Jeff Davis Pie, the traditional June 14th dessert that celebrates Jeff Davis Day, is a variation of pecan pie. According to some Mississippi authorities, the difference is the substitution of dates and raisins for pecans. Other Southerners claim that Jeff Davis Pie is a brown-sugar-flavored custard. Non-constructionists honor the President of the Confederacy with Jeff Davis Pudding—a steamed molasses pudding studded with candied fruit.

On less gala occasions, a large family, and a plenitude of apples may have induced cooks to pay attention to the author of an 1800s cook book. Instructing them in the ways of economy, she suggested Pork and Apple Pie, made by sliding thin slices of salt pork through the layers of fruit as substitute for butter.

On any day, dyspeptics, defined in an ancient dictionary as those "suffering from deranged digestion," were proffered fruit pies in pastries "containing no lard or butter." But an even greater aid to the troubled, appeared in 1885. Miss Parloa, in her *New Cook Book*, said, "An ice cream freezer is a great luxury, and will soon do away with that unhealthy dish—Pie."

Marmalade Apple Pie

Canned apple slices offer more than speed in this simply delicious apple pie. Because they don't shrink, the yawning space between top crust and fruit is eliminated, as is any by-guess and by-gosh figuring out of thickening. But unless the apple slices are uniformly even, better do some cutting.

Marmalade, on the other hand, is variably thin, so be sure bottom and top crusts are securely sealed, and to be on the safe side, place foil under the pie pan. To grate lemon rind easily, freeze shells after extracting juice.

Pastry for an 8-inch double-crust pie
1 can (1-pound 4-ounce) sliced apples
1 teaspoon ginger
2 teaspoons grated lemon rind
¼ cup orange marmalade, preferably Vintage

Line pan with crust, and arrange a layer of apple slices on it. Sprinkle with ginger and lemon rind, and dot with marmalade. Continue layers, filling pan generously, and topping with marmalade. Cut "A" for apple in top crust, and bake on lowest rack of a preheated, hot 425° F. oven, until fruit is tender and crust browned, about 35 minutes.

Ann Elizabeth Rials Chess Pie

If, in searching for Southern antiques, you discover a pine cupboard, with screen doors, you can say knowingly, "Oh, a pie safe," or, "Oh, a pie chest." Pies hibernated here and the word chest became colloquially, ches'. This led to the further corruption of chess—so says one author.

Another author titles a recipe for the dessert, "Cheese Cake (Chess Pie)", and notes that chess is a corruption of cheese; that it is not a cake at all; that it does not contain cheese; and that the filling can go into tart shells. And the naming contentions go on and on.

A third source spells out the method of eating Chess Pie—"in tiny slivers with a piece of good white cake on the same plate." It is so superbly rich it is no wonder that "tiny slivers" are recommended, but not going back for seconds calls for the utmost in will power.

There are, of course, many recipe variations. Few call for lemon; many for cream and nutmeg; raisins or currants are suggested additions; and a meringue topping is sometimes made with the egg whites.

When Richmond, Virginia novelist Harry Woodward learned I was writing this book, with his usual grace, he offered me his grandmother's recipe. Your gratitude, too, will go to him when you taste Miz Rials luxurious lemony dessert.

- ½ cup sugar
- 4 tablespoons butter, creamed
- 3 eggs, separated
- 1 lemon, grated rind and juice
- 2 teaspoons cornmeal, preferably stone-ground
- ¼ teaspoon salt, divided
- ¼ teaspoon cream of tartar
- **Pastry for 8-inch bottom crust**

Add sugar to butter, and beat until light and fluffy. Beat egg yolks in, then lemon juice and rind, cornmeal, and ⅛ teaspoon salt. Beat egg whites to soft peak stage with remaining salt and cream of tartar and fold into butter mixture. Line pie pan with pastry, add filling, and smooth top. Bake on center rack of preheated, moderate 325° F. oven until filling is firm, about 20 minutes. If top browns before filling sets, protect it with foil. Serve at room temperature. Makes quite a few "tiny-sliver" servings.

El Granada Grape Pie

The muscadine, a sweet musky grape is one of the flowers of the South, and history says President Buchanan was responsible for an arbor of them at the White House. However, any slip-skin grape may be used for this pie, which should be enjoyed at least once each autumn.

Pastry for 9-inch bottom crust
4 cups blue slip-skin grapes
1 cup sugar
⅛ teaspoon salt
1 tablespoon lemon juice
1 tablespoon orange juice
1 teaspoon grated lemon rind
1 teaspoon grated orange rind
1 tablespoon quick-cooking tapioca

Line pan with pastry and, if desired, roll strips for lattice top. Pick over, wash, and stem grapes. Slip skins from pulp, and reserve them. Cook pulp until seeds loosen, and press through a colander to remove seeds. Place pulp, skins, and remaining ingredients in bowl. Mix and let stand 5 minutes. Turn into pastry shell, top with a lattice and bake in preheated, hot 450° F. oven 10 minutes. Reduce heat to moderate, 350° F. and bake until juice bubbles and crust browns, about 25 minutes more.

Key Largo Lime Pie

One of Florida's delights, this pie, as some authorities have it, was created by a waiter in a Key Largo restaurant. The tart-sweet taste makes it a perfect ending to a seafood meal, and possibly the reason it is such a great favorite with Keys fishermen.

A baked pastry shell may be used, but a crumb crust simplifies things and although preliminary baking is unnecessary, flavor is improved and then it can be cut without a crumble. Almost any crumbs can be used but chocolate provides a pretty color contrast. (A package of 2¼-inch diameter chocolate wafers yields 40.)

For ease, fill a plastic bag with cookies, place open end toward you and crush to fine crumbs with a rolling pin. Unfortunately, that sensation, the blender, crushes the crumbs to a powder.

Lemon juice may be substituted for lime juice, but only sweetened condensed milk will work. If saving egg whites is not your cup of tea, substitute 2 whole eggs for the 3 yolks.

Chocolate Crumb Crust

- 2 cups (about 24) chocolate wafer crumbs
- 6 tablespoons softened butter
- 2 tablespoons sugar
- Pinch salt

Blend all ingredients and press evenly on bottom and sides of an 8-inch pie pan, foil-lined if desired, making crust about ¼ inch thick. Bake in preheated, moderate 365° F. oven 8 minutes. Cool completely before filling.

Lime Filling

- 2 limes, about 6 tablespoons juice
- 1 can (14–15 ounces) sweetened condensed milk
- 3 egg yolks, well beaten
- 1 tablespoon high proof (151 proof) rum, optional
- Dash orange bitters, optional
- 2 drops green color, approximately

Grate rind of 1 lime; peel rind of second lime very thin with blade peeler (or substitute chocolate curls as garnish). Roll pieces of peel into cigarette shape and cut fine with scissors. (Pieces will curl.) Squeeze lime and measure ⅓ cup juice. Stir milk into egg yolks. Stir in lime juice and grated rind. Add rum and bitters to taste, and tint a delicate green. Turn into baked, cooled pie shell or crumb crust and allow about 4 hours for thickening. Do not attempt to remove pie from pan. Just before serving, top with whipped cream mixture and garnish with lime curls. The pie keeps at least a week in the refrigerator, and may be frozen. If freezing the pie, add topping immediately. Makes 4–6 servings.

Whipped Cream Topping

- 1 cup (½ pint) heavy cream, beaten stiff
- 2 tablespoons confectioners' sugar, approximately
- 1 tablespoon high proof (151 proof) rum, optional

Fold sugar and rum, to taste, into cream.

Pecan Pie
Treacle Pie

Although pecan pie says South to Damn Yankees, the dessert is simply another example of adding the indigenous to a from-home specialty. The British know it as Treacle (molasses) Pie. Virginia cooks replaced the molasses with "brown corn syrup," and set halved pecans neatly on top of the filling about 15 minutes before the pie finished baking.

This recipe for the most magnificent version I ever tasted is called Treacle Pie by Miz Jean Peacock of Mississippi. Her great-niece served it topped with a slather of whipped cream—an added attraction that might be frowned on by Southern purists—and weight-watchers, equipped with the information that, even without the cream, an average size piece contains 490 calories.

- Pastry for a 10-inch bottom crust
- 3 eggs
- 1 teaspoon vanilla
- 6 tablespoons butter, melted
- ⅔ cup dark corn syrup
- ⅓ cup very dark molasses
- ¾ cup brown sugar
- ¼ teaspoon salt
- ¾ cup broken pecans

Line pie pan with pastry and flute rim if desired. Beat eggs slightly, and whisk in all remaining ingredients except pecans. Pour into crust and add pecans. Bake on center rack of preheated, moderate 375° F. oven, until top crust cracks toward edges but filling jiggles slightly in center when pie is shaken, about 30 minutes.

A BRIO OF BEVERAGES

In the index of an old cook book containing a section titled "Chef d'Oeuvres," of the thirty-four listed, only six are not alcoholic beverages. So it does not appear that water was man's most vital quaff. However, witching for water was, and is, still done. Whether or not this means of locating a subterranean source was practiced by the Miccosukee Indians, whose reservation is on the Tamiami Trail, until recent days they had no pure water. As a result, they drank what they call *sofkee,* a beverage that combines water with corn (or other grains), and is kept continually hot over an open fire. The Creek Indians call hominy *sofky,* a shortening of *osafki.*

235

In complete antithesis to this imperative and frugal thirst-quencher were the rich-with-cream eggnogs characteristic of plantation entertaining—entertaining that in days of old began with a breakfast tray holding eye-openers of Bourbon. It is said that once upon a time, a guest, declining a servant's early-morning offer of a third julep, was warned that no other drink would be served before breakfast.

The splendid plantations must have needed an ocean of alcohol for imbibing at what was seemingly a constant round of levees, fetes, soirees, theatricals, routs, socials, squeezes, and *conversaziones.*

In 1841, Miss Leslie's *House Book,* discussing the social order of the day, notes, "There is great reason to hope that the period is fast approaching when large, crowded, and extravagantly luxurious parties will become obsolete; at least in those classes of American society that are or ought to be the most distinguished for good taste and refinement."

The author continues, "The most eligible manner of keeping up social intercourse, is to see your friends frequently but in small number . . . instead of asking every one you may happen to know (and consequently many whom you do not care for), and incurring a great and sometimes very inconvenient expense, and a vast deal of fatigue, for a purpose that, after all affords no real pleasure, either to the family or their guests."

The lady suggests twenty to thirty as a nice number of guests. If her advice was followed, how coolly empty those great halls must have seemed. But even that number must have put a strain on wine cellars, inasmuch as six wines at dinner were part of plantation living.

Thomas Jefferson, founder of the Democratic party, is closely associated with wine and the good life. He tried unsuccessfully to develop a good Virginia wine and the cellar he provided for Monticello is still one of the sights of that beautiful Virginia home. He was a confirmed inventor and you can marvel at one of the mantelpieces he contrived there. It conceals dumbwaiters for bringing wine bottles up from the cellar and returning the empties.

Reputedly, Jefferson's favorite wine was a French Margaux—indicating a cultivated palate indeed. Patrick Henry complained that Jefferson was "so Frenchified that he abjured his native victuals."

Madeira was so closely associated with early colonial history that wines from there were referred to as wines of the new world, but the South produced its own quaffs, too. A wine was made with geraniums, while a sweet beer—*biere douce*—was frugally put together with the skin and eyes of pineapple, rice, and sugar. Molasses and corn made another beer, and panada or *panade* (from French, *pain*, for bread), also occupied cooks, who assembled it from wine, rum or vinegar, bread crumbs, butter, sugar, spices, and boiling water.

Unless, of course, they were involved with a Chicken Panada, made of white meat pounded, seasoned, and boiled to "consistency liked [but] it should be such as you can drink, though tolerably thick."

Creole country is responsible for many superb beverages, including Café Noir (chicory coffee), and its dramatic presentations in a blue blaze of flame. Supposedly the word cocktail, elsewhere called whets, comes from New Orleans' French Quarter, and a Colonel Creecy in 1834 sneered that Creoles could do more with a bottle of poor claret, smiles, bows, shrugs, and grimaces, than a Virginian of the first family could with a dozen superior sparkling Champagnes worth twenty dollars. It also is said that New Orleans ladies sipped orange blossom syrup and Eau Sucre—sugar-water—gossipy tidbits I find difficult to believe.

Virginia claims Bourbon, the corn-mash whiskey named for its birthplace—Bourbon County, which now is part of Kentucky. Enthusiasm for France during the Revolution, provided the name—as tribute to the royal family.

Of the other beverages, the South busied itself with the production of perry (cider made with pears), mead, made with honey from the blossoming gallberry and tupelo gum trees, and cordials (also called ratafias and elixirs). And, was never at a loss in finding charming names for drinks—as witness Shrubs, Shams, Flips, Fizzes, Bounces, Caudles, and Creams.

Stephen Vincent Benét sang of moonshine, that white lightning, in his poem, "The Mountain Whippoorwill," which, in part, goes:

> "I started off with a *dump-diddle-dump*.
> (*Oh, Hell's broke loose in Georgia!*)
> Skunk-cabbage growin' by the bee-gum stump,
> (*Whippoorwill, yo're singin' now!*)
>
> "Oh, Georgia booze is mighty fine booze,
> The best yuh ever poured yuh,
> But it eats the soles right offen yore shoes,
> For Hell's broke loose in Georgia."

Apple Tea

According to the *New Yorker's* apocryphal railroad buff, Ernest M. Frimbo, iced tea is "the proper Southern breakfast drink." Invalids however, were served apple tea—which an old book lists as "a grateful and cooling drink."

Being hale and hearty when I tested, I can not vouch for its curative powers, but found the beverage far more fascinating with the addition of a dollop of rum.

- 1 apple
- Peel of ½ lemon
- 1 cup boiling water
- 1 teaspoon sugar, approximately

Cut unpeeled apple in thin pieces and add lemon peel cut small. Pour water over and refrigerate until cold. To serve, strain, and sweeten to taste. Makes about 1 cup.

Raspberry Shrub

This is the loveliest refresher I know—and so perfect of itself that only a flavorless vodka should be added if a spike is desired.

- 1 box (10 ounce) frozen raspberries in syrup
- ¼ cup wine vinegar

Thaw raspberries in blender container. Bring vinegar to boil and pour over raspberries. Whir smooth and put through strainer. (Lacking a blender, force mixture through a sieve.) Store in a refrigerator. Yields about 1 cup. To drink, dilute to taste with about 1 part water or club soda to 2 parts shrub.

Royal Chocolate

This marvelous mixture can be increased indefinitely, and makes an excellent chocolate sauce. The above preparation may be frozen before or after the whipped cream is added.

- 2½ ounces unsweetened chocolate
- ½ cup cold water
- ¾ cup sugar
- ¼ teaspoon salt
- ½ teaspoon vanilla
- ¾ cup heavy cream, whipped stiff, divided
- 6 cups hot milk

Melt chocolate in water and stir smooth. Stir in sugar and salt and cook, stirring until sugar dissolves and mixture thickens, about 4 minutes. Cool and add vanilla. Fold in cream, reserving about 6 tablespoons. Allow 1½ tablespoons mixture for each measuring cup of milk. Stir together and pour into cups. Top with a puff of reserved whipped cream. Makes 6–8 servings. The above preparation, without whipped cream, yields about 6 tablespoons.

COFFEE CUP AND BOWL

Probably the South's most famous and unusual coffee is the New Orleans dark brew made with chicory. The black-as-night color comes from the long roasting of the beans (as in scorched toast) and, to me, chicory gives the beverage a chocolatey flavor. The eighteenth century Dutch were the first to combine coffee and chicory, and although the method supposedly was a closely guarded secret, an alert Frenchman discovered the way, and from France the method emigrated to New Orleans.

Chicory coffee *is* coffee in New Orleans and if not to your taste, specify *pure* coffee—a beverage New Orleanians sneeringly refer to as "Yankee" coffee.

Of the two types of chicory, the large-rooted variety is used. The root alone is roasted, then ground, and sometimes in its pure form makes a coffee substitute. The leaves of this variety are called Witloof chicory or French endive, neither of which is a U.S. familiar. (The other botanical chicory produces Belgian endive. It is familiar—for delicate flavor, fat chartreuse-tipped stalky heads, and astronomical price.) Interestingly, chicory coffee is said to benefit digestion.

A prepared blend of chicory and coffee is available canned. It also is possible to purchase dark-roast coffee, and chicory separately and blend your own. Then, the amount of chicory and coffee can be adjusted to taste. Serve blazing hot, in demitasse cups.

Chicory Coffee

- **4 tablespoons dark roast coffee**
- **1 teaspoon chicory**
- **1 measuring cup water**

Brew, preferably using drip method. Yields about 4 demitasse cups.

Cafe Au Lait

Combine equal parts of the above with hot milk. Pour them in at the same time, high enough over cups to froth.

Cafe Diable

New Orleans coffee aficionados raise horrified eyebrows at the idea of adding milk, cream, or sugar to the brew; then not letting the right hand know what the left is doing, fire up two sweet spicy drinks. Elegant New Orleans restaurants and some homes prepare this one—and Café Brulot, which is similar—in huge, chased silver bowls adorned with devil gargoyles. Grape is the brandy used; Cognac its finest flower.

    8 lumps sugar
    4 whole cloves
    4 thin slices orange peel
    4 thin slices lemon peel
    ¼ cup brandy
    Dark-roast coffee

Place all ingredients except coffee in flame-proof bowl and warm until brandy ignites. Ladle high with a flourish until flames die, and add enough hot coffee to fill 4 demitasse cups.

Cafe Brule

Antique sterling silver brandy-burning spoons to hook over the edge of coffee cups are collector's items and make this drink sure fire. Otherwise a steady hand is required. To perform either way, place a lump of sugar in a spoon, and fill with warmed Cognac. Light Cognac and stir flaming into a cup of demitasse coffee.

Cafe Royale

"Coffee grows on a white oak tree, the river flows sweet brandy-o," says a song from the late 1800s. Here it is in a cup.

Pour about 1½ teaspoons Cognac into a demitasse cup and fill with dark-roast coffee.

Bourbon Coffee

Combine equal parts Bourbon and coffee.

Meringue Torch

Meringue obliges in many ways edible; disobliges as far as word derivation is concerned. Eric Partridge, the notable knower of word origins, dismisses it with the three o's that mean origin obscure. Another authority explains the name as a variant of Marengo—the site of a Napoleonic victory.

The epicurean French carried the idea to Louisiana and whole, unhulled strawberries and/or cookies make singularly gala accompaniments. Choose the extract to complement the beverage the meringue is topping, realizing that lemon or orange are particularly good with fruit drinks. The meringue will hold up at least two hours. Bake any leftover for ice cream shells or for kisses.

- 1 egg white
- 1/8 teaspoon cream of tartar
- 1/8 teaspoon extract
- 4 tablespoons sugar (preferably very fine)

With rotary beater or in electric mixer, beat egg white with cream of tartar and salt to soft peak stage. Sprinkle no more than 2 tablespoons sugar over surface at a time and beat until completely blended after each addition. When all the sugar has been added, add flavoring extract and continue beating until mixture mounds and holds shape. Yields about 1 cup meringue. Note: Sugar may be increased or decreased depending upon the recipe for which the meringue is being used and upon taste-preference.

To Serve

Fill glasses or cups with any preferred beverage just before serving. Top with meringue, allowing about ¼ cup for each serving and make a depression with the back of a teaspoon. Pass a pitcher of high proof, 151 proof rum (alcohols of lower proof will not flame without immediate preliminary warming), and let guests pour about a teaspoonful into the hollow and light the rum. Allow it to flame a few seconds—just long enough to brown the meringue lightly, then stir into the drink.

Claret Cup

Claret is England's name for Bordeaux and comes from the French, *clairet,* meaning light in color. The cup, similar to Sangria, is such a delicious import, whether it journeyed to our South from England, France, or Spain, is of little significance.

A gladsome through-the-meal beverage, let the gentleman of the house make it a table performance by providing him with a pretty pitcher, a muddler, and a bottle of dry red wine, obviously not of a *premier cru* variety. A California jug wine such as Zinfandel is more than adequate.

Perrier water is an immeasurable improvement over club soda; the orange may be replaced, or used with, any other seasonal fruits; white wine may be substituted for red.

- 1 orange, sliced thin
- 24 ounces (3 cups; 1 bottle) dry red wine
- 3 ounces (6 tablespoons) orange-flavored liqueur
- Dash orange bitters
- 4 ounces (½ cup) Cognac
- 2 cups club soda, approximately

If desired, for attractive appearance, flute orange peel. Combine liquid ingredients, muddle, add orange slices, and serve in capacious (6–8 ounce) wine glasses. Hopefully, this amount will be sufficient for four diners.

White Hall Tavern Punch

The South can reach out its hand to pluck musky aromatic grapes for this cool, colorful thirst quencher. A trip to the supermarket provides us with a reasonable facsimile and a day of mellowing improves flavor.

Serve in punch bowl or pitcher and provide brandy, rum, gin, or vodka, to please guests who prefer a spirited punch.

- 2 cans (6 ounces each) frozen lemonade
- 1⅓ cups water
- 1½ cups grape juice
- Dash orange bitters, optional

Shake ingredients until well-mixed or whir thawed lemonade in blender with part of water and add remaining ingredients. Serve over ice cubes. Makes 4-plus servings.

Fish House Punch

This reputedly is a 1732 classic, originally put together for members of the famous Pennsylvania fishing club called, The State in Schuylkill (schoolkill). By 1862, according to the *Williamsburg Art of Cookery*, it had swum to a Taylor family in Norfolk.

Because it takes to mellowing, it is a good party punch and the following as a one-serving proportion to multiply by the number of guests—and their capacity, who can heed, or not, the warning of Colonel Walter Herron Taylor, Adjutant General of the Army of Northern Virginia: "Look out for *f*well Head next Morning."

- 1 teaspoon sugar
- 1 tablespoon lemon juice
- 3 tablespoons water
- ½ ounce (1 tablespoon) peach liqueur
- 1½ ounces (3 tablespoons) dry white wine
- ½ ounce (1 tablespoon) Cognac
- 1 ounce (2 tablespoons) rum, white or gold label
- **Dash orange bitters**

Combine ingredients and allow to mellow about 2 hours, stirring occasionally. Serve in punch bowl over block of ice or in glass with ice cubes. Yields 5 ounces, about 1½ drinks in a 6–8 ounce glass filled with 2 ice cubes.

Planter's Punch

Brisk trade with Jamaica makes any rum drink a Southern indigene. Virginia, goodness knows, a plantation planter's paradise, is credited with this punch. The storied past has it that one planter dashed his drink with red pepper. Another, supposedly topped his with a float of claret.

Any except high proof, 151 proof, rum, can be used, and brandy, rye, or gin can be added. Lemon juice may be substituted for lime, and some recipes call for grenadine (pomegranate juice), which adds a lovely pink color.

- 3–4 ounces (6–8 tablespoons) rum
- 1 teaspoon Sugar Syrup*, approximately
- **Juice of 1 lime**
- 1 slice each of orange and pineapple

In tall glass muddle rum, syrup, and lime juice. Fill with cracked ice as for Mint Julep* and stir until glass frosts. Garnish with fruit, adding a maraschino cherry (green, for good color contrast), and serve with straws. Makes 1 drink.

Mint Julep

It is not possible to complete a Southern cook book without a dissertation on mint juleps, and I would like to preface mine with a name-dropping tale.

In Kentucky, I was the guest of a Bourbon company. Following a tour of the distillery, I was taken to lunch at a Louisville hotel. Among the several local celebrities at table were his honor, the Mayor. Early on, I was taught that when in Rome, one did as the Romans, so when asked whether I would like a cocktail, I knew enough to request a Mint Julep.

There was a small silence and then my host asked the waiter if he thought the bartender knew how to make one. The waiter was not sure. . . .

I was served a saccharin-sweet, utterly undrinkable combination which I sipped politely. However, when asked if the drink was all right, decided honesty was the best policy and said—"It is dreadful!" "Take it away," the waiter was ordered, "and bring her whatever else she would like."

Inasmuch as I was the only person who had ordered a Mint Julep, I asked why no one else had requested "the wine of the country," and was told that, in Louisville, no one ever touched them. So much for what is obviously a legend that is having a hard time dying.

Incidentally, the word Julep, comes from the Persian *gulāb* (*gul* for rose plus *āb* for water). Also informative is the fact that, according to the Browns in *America Cooks,* a bellman at the Greenbrier Hotel in West Virginia was responsible for a glorious julep. If your garden grows mint, his seems the least troublesome of the usually-listed long-ways 'round procedures. For it, your bar should grow the very best (bonded) Bourbon.

> **5 large crisp mint leaves**
> **1 teaspoon Sugar Syrup,* approximately**
> **1½–2 ounces (3–4 tablespoons) Bourbon**

Crush mint in bottom of glass and add syrup to taste. If possible, allow to steep with Bourbon 15 minutes. Pack glass tightly with crushed ice dried in a towel. Stir until glass is frosted and thrust in a sprig of mint. Add a straw, if desired, so short that the nose can be buried in the mint to inhale the aroma. Makes one drink.

Sugar Syrup

For a lazy-way substitute, simply use granulated sugar and water, or confectioners' sugar, but realize that confectioners' sugar contains cornstarch, which clouds drinks.

> **1 cup water**
> **1½ cups sugar**

Place water, then sugar in saucepan and bring to boil, stirring only until sugar dissolves. Boil 5 minutes and cool. Yields about 1 cup and keeps indefinitely in the refrigerator.

Ramos Gin Fizz

It is a fact of life that the seemingly simple always turns out to be complex. When I vacationed in New Orleans, I "slept in," as New Yorkers put it, rising only in time for brunch—*déjeuner a la fourchette.*

No matter when I sat down to it, I ordered Oysters Rockefeller, and a Ramos gin fizz, congratulating myself on being treated to glories that also contributed nutrition.

Back on Damn Yankee soil, I assayed the drink, using what was purported to be the one and only original and correct formula—and failed. Further research revealed any number of additions to the one and only original formula.

Following numerous tests, I discovered that the quality of the gin was not important, that the quantity could be within the limits listed below, and that although lime juice added a bit of *je ne sais quoi,* the drink was perfectly good with lemon juice alone. I found, too, that confectioners' sugar did as well as sugar syrup, that cream made a smoother drink, and that a splash of club soda—about a tablespoon—improved a made-with-milk fizz but did not add much to a cream-based fizz. Orange bitters can not be substituted for orange flower water—and the amount of orange flower water can be increased.

As further information, 1 egg white equals about 2 tablespoons; my ice cubes *are* cubes, measure 1½ inches, and melt to 3 tablespoons liquid.

The following proportion yields about 1¾ cups—just right for 2 servings in 6–8 ounce glasses. Better make it twice for 2 drinkers, and if the formula is not to your taste, adjust any of the ingredients at will.

There *was* a Ramos in New Orleans, and purportedly he had a bar, where this drink was passed down a line of a dozen barmen, each of whom gave the shaken shaker several additional shakes. The blender replaces everything except those gentlemen's warm smiles. Lacking a blender, crack 3 ice cubes, then dry them in a towel.

The drink can use a touch of decor. An unhulled strawberry, slit to hook on the rim of the glass is pretty, or use a half orange or lemon slice, or a twist of the peel of either. The frothy white left at the bottom of the glass is wonderful for coating fruit, so serve a fruit plate of strawberries, to hull and plop into the froth. Spoon, to coat and eat. Blueberries are good, too.

2½ ounces (5 tablespoons) milk or cream
1–2 tablespoons confectioners' sugar
½ ounce (1 tablespoon) egg white
2–3 teaspoons lemon juice
1 teaspoon lime juice, optional
1½–2 ounces (about 4 tablespoons) gin
½ teaspoon orange flower water
3 ice cubes
Splash of club soda

Place all ingredients except soda in blender in order listed and whir until smooth, or shake vigorously and strain into glasses. If made with milk, top glasses with soda.
For extra added attraction, before filling, dip glass rims in lemon juice, then in confectioners' sugar.

ABSINTHE WHETS

Whets, the wonderful old-fashioned word for cocktails is appropriate here, because so many Southern drinks include this storied licorice-flavored liqueur. The stories are macabre—absinthe supposedly drives drinkers insane, cuts down the birthrate, and can kill—and also utter nonsense.

It connects with insanity only insofar as that anyone would be mad to drink it neat, because it can be anywhere from 100 to 136 proof—68% alcohol, which normally is brandy.

Licorice, its most pronounced flavor, results from the anise-flavored ingredients: *artemisia vulgaris* (also called Felon Herb and mugwort); *artemisia mayoris*—Petite Absinthe in French; fennel seeds; and the spice—star anise. The strong-flavored field mint (*Baume des Champs*) goes into it, too, as does the bitter aromatic Hyssop.

Most of the ingredients are highly regarded for medicinal properties so it is not strange that the drink was invented at the end of the eighteenth century, by Dr. Ordinaire, a French exile who fled the French Revolution and settled in Switzerland. The formula was acquired in 1797 by Henri-Louis Pernod, who began its commercial manufacture at 90° proof, and his name is so closely associated with Absinthe that the terms are almost interchangeable.

Anisette, another licorice-flavored liqueur, is a popular French aperitif and is lower in alcoholic content (60° to 80° proof). Marie Brizard's grandmother, famous in her neighborhood for curing the sick, created the formula.

Herbsaint is the trade name the South uses for absinthe, and New Orleans contributes still another licorice-flavored lovely—Peychaud bitters—which also are credited as stomach-soothers.

Absinthe Suissesse

The proportion is normally listed in jiggers. The name obviously comes from Dr. Ordinaire's adopted country. Hospitality measures a 2-ounce jigger; bars usually pour 1½ ounces. Increase anise-flavored liqueur according to your palate, and your capacity for the heady. The drink can be made with skim milk if every little calorie counts.

Anisette is 60° + proof liqueur. Orgeat (orjut) is an almond-flavored sugar syrup from France.

- 1   1½ ounce jigger (3 tablespoons) anise-flavored liqueur
- 1   teaspoon Orgeat
- 1   egg white (about 1 tablespoon)
- 6   tablespoons cream
- ¼   teaspoon Anisette

Shake with cracked ice or whir smooth in blender with 2 ice cubes. Yields about 1½ cups; makes approximately 2 drinks.

The Obituary

The gentleman, a *fin bec* doctor, who first handed me this drink called it a Pernod Martini. Simply mix dry Vermouth and gin in preferred Martini proportion and add a dash of anise-flavored spirit.

Sazerac Cocktail

Blended whiskeys often are called rye. But Straight Rye Whiskey, by law, is distilled from not less than 51% rye grain, and is part of what makes this cocktail a Southern authentic—and a thing of joy. The name of the cocktail has been copyrighted by the Sazerac Company, Inc., which also owns the names Herbsaint and Peychaud bitters.

It is called "the drink that made New Orleans famous," and was born at the bar of the Sazerac Coffee House, and named by Tom Handy, the owner, for the brandy product *Sazerac-le-Forge*. In 1870, absinthe was added and as time passed, rye, which had greater appeal to the American palate, was substituted for brandy.

The built-in ripening feature makes Sazeracs easy to serve to large groups. For an even easier way, simply serve rye on the rocks in a cocktail glass with a dash of anise-flavored liqueur.

- 1 teaspoon sugar
- 1 teaspoon water
- Few dashes Peychaud bitters
- Few dashes Angostura bitters
- 3–4 ounces (6–8 tablespoons) straight rye whiskey
- Few drops absinthe-flavored liqueur
- Lemon peel

Dissolve sugar in water, and add bitters. Add rye and, if possible, let ripen about 2 hours in refrigerator. Pour absinthe-flavored liqueur into wine or cocktail glass and roll glass to coat sides. Add ice cubes and fill with rye mixture. Top with twist of lemon peel. Makes 1 serving.

Brave Noel

Jewel your Christmas with liqueurs and let guests choose what they will. The milk mixture will not separate even when refrigerated overnight, and hopefully the whir of the blender will not drown out the strains of "White Christmas."

> **3 eggs**
> **1½ cups milk**
> **Liqueurs: Peppermint, apricot, etc.**

Whir eggs and milk in blender until mixed and pour into pitcher. Makes about 3 cups; 8 drinks.

For each drink to serve in 8-ounce glass, place in blender container 2 ice cubes and 7 tablespoons milk mixture. Blend smooth and add 1 ounce (2 tablespoons) any desired liqueur. Makes 6–7 drinks. Serve with straws.

And, if none of these Southern solaces pleases, you can always resort to the Damn Yankee specialty, called STRIP-AND-GO-NAKED—pure gin!

APPENDIX: A PRIMER OF PROVISIONS

Even before the days when a recipe was defined as a formula for medicine—usually compounded by the lady of the house blending herbs, and barks, and spices—there has been concern about dining wisely. But neither Southerners nor Damn Yankees of old had one of today's problems. The major concern, as voiced by Dr. Ruth Leverton, adviser to the U.S. Department of Agriculture, is the getting away from "traditional foods prepared in traditional methods."

For us to begin at the beginning with recipes is nowhere near as arduous as it was for cooks in days gone by. So a revival feast is all to the good nutritionally. To make it even easier for you to preserve this epicurean heritage, the recipes in these pages have been adapted to fit today's modes of dining, and they also take advantage of today's mechanical marvels.

I always have disliked wasting words, and the valuable space required for constant repetition of standard procedures. An asterisk (simply consult the Index) will lead you to recipes that are patterns for all others that are similar. In addition, the directions include only departures from the norm: Cover a pan, if so advised; leave an onion unpeeled, when so specified.

If you are an experienced cook, the techniques will be familiar.

If you are a novice, realize that, in the words of an old saying: The more a recipe is used the better it gets. Detailed general culinary information can be found in my *Cooking Without Recipes*. Herewith some facts on foods, many of which are second nature to the South.

You doubtless will have trouble (as cooks of earlier centuries did not), in finding soft water for making soup, and rain- or cistern-water, for preparing vinegar. But for best flavor, unless otherwise specified, begin cooking with cold, rather than with hot tap water, bringing it to a boil when recipes so direct. When sharp vinegar is specified, preferably use white.

TO UNMOLD ASPICS

Gently pull top edge of gelatin away from mold with fingers. Dip mold up to rim in warm water for 10 seconds. Shake mold to loosen and invert on damp, chilled plate.

FATS AND SHORTENING
Grease

Although I go along with the quote from *House Divided:* "You can always recognize greatness in a man by his readiness to taste the joys of life when they're offered him," I must admit I was not intrigued by the idea of frying chicken in bear grease.

I admit, too, that grease, the common Southern word applied to bacon drippings, salt pork, and lard, is unpleasant to Damn Yankee ears. But thrifty cooks keep cans of drippings on hand and treasure lard for the superb results it produces in baked products, and for frying in deep or shallow fat. Lard, in fact, smells like a delicious pie.

Other shortenings can be substituted—use a bit less because lard is a richer fat; and so can vegetable oils—the flavorless cotton or cornseed—peanut, or olive.

FRYING

Frying is a favored Southern cooking technique because early on, compared to open-hearth roasting, less fuel was consumed. When ovens *were* accepted, the red-hot monsters blasted kitchens, already at the boiling point, with a torture of heat. These facts finally wound themselves into a tightly-knit ball composed of the familiar —home and mother's cooking—thus becoming established tradition.

It was a revelation to me that the Southern recipe direction "fry," does not necessarily mean "brown." Frying, as with Pot Likker Portmanteau*, often simply means to cook with fat.

Salt Pork

This Southern favorite has numerous aliases, which to all extents and purposes, are the same thing, and used in the same ways. The aliases include Streak-o-lean, which resembles bacon; White Pork, which is Charleston terminology; Side Meat; Fat Back, which some cooks consider too fat; and Sow Belly, which has tough skin. If any of these products seems too salty, simply rinse the excess salt off.

For different flavor, Streak-o-lean sometimes is available smoked, and then called Back Bacon. Salt Pork sometimes is pickled.

Dairy Products

Half-and-Half is a good substitute in recipes that call for varying proportions of milk and cream. If you prefer, combine milk and cream in any desired proportion, and if calories are of concern, substitute skim milk, or reconstituted powdered skim milk.

Once-upon-a-time, sour cream was exactly that. Use it if you have it, sour sweet cream if you like, or substitute dairy sour cream.

Cornstarch presents no problems, today. In a long-ago cook book, though, following a recipe called Maizena Cake, the author informed readers that, although cornstarch was called for, Maizena (a trade name), was preferable.

However, your baked products will differ slightly from those prepared by Southern hands, because flour sold there usually is softer than that available elsewhere. When recipes in these pages call for flour, all-purpose is intended.

Bases For Foods With A Sauce

In days of old, sops for sauced food were called sippets. Oblongs of bread were fried to serve as pedestals for delicacies such as "oysters and boiled birds." They quickly become unappetizingly soggy, as does toast, so for wonderful crunchy contrast, choose patty shells, *biscottes,* or Chinese noodles. Or, stay on the soft side with rice, noodles, or pasta. *Fried Bread:* Dip slices in drippings from a roast, or fry in greased skillet or on griddle, turning to brown both sides.

SPICES AND SEASONINGS

Spicy sayings abound in old cook books. One, published in 1874, advises: "Gluttony, and the use of spices mingled with food daily, leads more people into the use of brandy and into intemperance than anything else."

Nutmeg

Nutmeg was credited with graver than the above evils. In voodoo circles, a cult born in Dahomey, West Africa, it is considered gris-gris—an amulet. Believers were assured that a bit of nutmeg sprinkled in the hem of a garment plus more gris-gris—incantations—would drive the garment's wearer insane. And, when he was an undergraduate at Harvard, Dr. Andrew T. Weil, a current authority on narcotic use, wrote a thesis on the hallucinogenic properties of nutmeg. But nutmeg happy talk comes from China, where it inspirits tea, and is considered a love spice with restorative powers.

If you oppose nutmeg on the grounds of flavor or aroma (a friend says it smells like a whiskey-drinking cow), chances are you have never tasted it fresh-ground. Eighteenth century ladies sacrificed nails and knuckles on graters, but all you need do, is invest in a nutmeg grinder. Old books directed cooks to buy the largest, heaviest, and most unctuous nutmegs they could find.

In addition to purported magical powers, realize that nutmeg is peppery, so when using it in recipes, taste before adding pepper.

Curry

Inasmuch as Columbus sailed off to sight spices, it is not surprising that curry powder was a demand ingredient of Southern cooking, even way back when. The ladies prepared their own, "beating" the spices in a mortar, and allowing "one teaspoon to ſeaſon any made Diſh."

A blender allows curry powder to be made speedily, and insures freshness. Any of the seeds and powdered spices in the following list may be omitted, others may be added, and the proportions may be adjusted to taste.

Curry Powder

Whir to a powder in blender, 1 tablespoon each: turmeric, coriander seed, cumin seed, ginger, nutmeg, mace. Season to taste with salt and cayenne pepper. Makes about ¼ cup curry powder.

Filé Powder

This is a seasoning that was put together by the Choctaw Indians, long before Columbus made for our shores. Like chili powder and curry powder, it is a combination of ingredients. The base is made with the powdered dried leaves of the sassafras tree, a variety of American laurel, related to the laurel that bears bay leaves.

Creoles consider filé powder an essential in gumbos and combine the ground sassafras leaves with dried okra, and occasionally with allspice, coriander, and sage. They sprinkle it over a tureen of gumbo at table, or into portions as they are served, because if liquids containing filé boil, they become ropy. When cooked lengthily, okra also produces "ropiness," a constituent some admire.

Gumbo with okra and gumbo with filé are as unlike as French onion soup and cream of onion soup. And gumbo recipes minus okra obviously are a contradiction in terms, because the word gumbo comes from the African word for okra (*kombo*).

The approximate proportion of filé powder to use is a tablespoon to 2 cups liquid.

CREOLE COOKING

The word Creole has been traced back to "create" and creative and distinctively Southern this melding of African, French, and Spanish cooking indeed is. Lusty seasonings typify the amalgam, and the herb and spice theme in the recipes recurs as regularly as the refrain of a song. It goes: garlic, shallots, cloves, mace, nutmeg, allspice, pepper, bay leaf, parsley, onion, basil, and thyme. And a roux is second nature to Creole cooks, who are credited with the maxim: An empty sack will not stand up.

Most of the recipes herein call for those conveniences, dried herbs. If you own the fresh, use about three times more than the dried called for.

SEASON TO TASTE

In almost every one of these recipes, season to taste means just that—wield salt shaker and pepper mill to please your palate—and realize that monosodium glutamate is of infinite value as a flavor intensifier.

When using a member of the red pepper family—red pepper, chili-pepper, or paprika—realize that quality deteriorates in about six months, and that in the Gulf States, deterioration is even more rapid. Replace aged supplies of pepper products promptly and for best keeping, store paprika, tightly covered, in the refrigerator.

Brown-Quick, my precooking aid, seasons, and was created in the interest of speeding browning, and intensifying food flavors. It can also reduce shrinkage and help prevent food from toughening. It is referred to throughout as "quick-browning aid," is a high quality soy sauce, for which it may be substituted, and contains herbs and spices.

SWEETENERS

"A few lumps of sugar, dissolved in a glass of pure water, will often relieve dyspepsia, or calm nervous irritation," cooks dipping into the 1866 *Art of Confectionery,* were informed. But molasses was the principal sweetener in eighteenth and early nineteenth century America.

If you have always thought of molasses as being American as apple pie, realize it probably was born in India or China, where sugar cane was first grown. In early America, the molasses jug was as important a table accessory as the vinegar cruet. The kitchen depended upon it for cornbread, doughnuts, puddings, and pies; the table pitcher saw yeoman duty as a pour for bread and pancakes.

To make molasses—a household chore then—sugar cane stalks are pressed to extract the juice, which is boiled until the natural sugar crystallizes. Then the molasses is drawn off; that from the first extraction being the finest table grade. Each subsequent boiling extracts more sugar and produces darker molasses with more pronounced flavor.

Second-boil—light molasses—is used for cake and candy. Third-boil—dark molasses—often called blackstrap, has, according to the *Wise Encyclopedia of Cookery,* "only a commercial value in the manufacturing of cattle feed, the production of alcohol, and other industrial uses."

Treacle is the sticky residual molasses drained from molds used to refine molasses. In days gone by, it was called "sugar-house molasses," and in some parts of the South, it was used both for table and cooking. For admirers of entymological origins, the word treacle stems, by a series of fascinating convolutions, from "wild animal," because it was used to treat bites of those bitten by same.

Sorghum: Corn again! This time, a cane-like grass, resembling broom corn. It yields sugar; and molasses, prepared from the juice, is used as a sweet syrup.

Brown Sugar

This is made by adding molasses to granulated sugar. I have not specified dark brown sugar in recipes, but would not give cupboard space to light brown sugar, which I consider anaemic in flavor.

For accurate measure, pack brown sugar into measuring cups or spoons. Should a small quantity harden, roll it to smoothness with a rolling pin. Soften a large quantity in a very low oven, or flash briefly in a microwave range.

Buying Information

If you have trouble finding any product necessary to a recipe, the following stores will mail-order: B. Altman & Co., 34th Street and Fifth Avenue, New York 10016; Bloomingdale's, Lexington Avenue and 59th Street, New York 10022; Charles & Co., 340 Madison Avenue, New York 10017.

BIBLIOGRAPHY
A GLUT OF KNOWLEDGE

Dipping into the pages of the following books was a revelation—and a learning pleasure, and I also always have found the U.S. Department of Agriculture publications of inestimable value.

In some cases, I have not directly credited my sources—many of which came from the libraries of two of Richmond's museums—The Confederate and the Valentine. I appreciate the privilege given me there of perusing books so old, I feared the pages would crumble at a touch.

If you would like to follow in my research footsteps—and go even further—because material on the South seemingly is endless—these are the sources I found most informative.

General References

Becker, Stephen, WHEN THE WAR IS OVER, Random House, N.Y.

Beecher, Catherine, THE AMERICAN WOMAN'S HOME (and other works), J. E. Ford & Co., 1869.

Bishop, Jim, THE DAY LINCOLN WAS SHOT, Harper & Row, N.Y.

Cahn, William, OUT OF THE CRACKER BARREL, Simon & Schuster, N.Y.

CARRY ME BACK TO OLD VIRGINIA, Virginia State Travel Service, N.Y.

Cash, W. J., THE MIND OF THE SOUTH, Alfred A. Knopf, N.Y.

"Civil War Times, Illustrated," Vol. IX, Nos. 4 and 5.

Dorsey, Leslie and Devine, Janice, FARE THEE WELL, Crown, N.Y.

Giedion, S., MECHANIZATION TAKES COMMAND, Oxford University Press, N.Y.

Goode, Mrs., LITTLE EMILY'S BOOK OF COMMON OBJECTS, Stephen Greene Press, Brattleboro, Vermont.

Hale, Mrs. Sarah J., "Godey's Ladys Book and Magazine," Vol. 7–12, Vol. 67, Louis A. Godey, 1863.

Harper's Bazaar, 100 YEARS OF THE AMERICAN FEMALE, Random House, N.Y.

Hatch, THE BYRDS OF VIRGINIA, Rinehart, Winston.

Horan, James D., MATTHEW BRADY, HISTORIAN WITH A CAMERA, Bonanza Books, N.Y.

Kane, Harnett T., THE BAYOUS OF LOUISIANA, Morrow, N.Y.

Kane, Harnett T., GONE ARE THE DAYS, Bramhall House, N.Y.

Kane, Harnett T., PLANTATION PARADE, Morrow, N.Y.

Kane, Harnett T., QUEEN OF NEW ORLEANS, Morrow, N.Y.

Leach, Joseph, BRIGHT PARTICULAR STAR—THE LIFE AND TIMES OF CHARLOTTE CUSHMAN, Yale University Press, New Haven, Conn.

"Mardi Gras, New Orleans 1968," Official souvenir magazine.

Miers, Earl Schench, ROBERT E. LEE, Alfred A. Knopf, Inc., N.Y.

Mitchell, Margaret, GONE WITH THE WIND, Macmillan, N.Y.

Robinson, Lura, IT'S AN OLD NEW ORLEANS CUSTOM.

Sandburg, Carl, ABRAHAM LINCOLN, THE PRAIRIE YEARS AND THE WAR YEARS, Vols. 1,2,3, Harcourt, Brace & Co., Inc., N.Y.

Stewart, George R., AMERICAN PLACE NAMES, Oxford University Press, N.Y.

Stowe, Harriet Beecher, UNCLE TOM'S CABIN, Doubleday, N.Y.

Washington, Booker T., UP FROM SLAVERY, Dell Publishing Co., Inc., N.Y.

Williams, Ben Ames, HOUSE DIVIDED, Houghton Mifflin Co., Boston, Mass.

Cookbook References

A BOOK OF FAMOUS OLD NEW ORLEANS RECIPES, Peerless Printing Co., New Orleans, La.

Adamson, Helen Lyon, GRANDMOTHER IN THE KITCHEN, Crown, N.Y.

Aresty, Esther B., THE DELECTABLE PAST, Simon & Schuster, N.Y.

Bremer, Mary Moore, NEW ORLEANS CREOLE RECIPES, Dorothea Thompson, Waveland, Miss.

The Browns, AMERICA COOKS, W. W. Norton & Co., Inc.

Brown, Helen Evans, HOLIDAY COOK BOOK, Little, Brown & Co., Boston.

Brown, John Hull, EARLY AMERICAN BEVERAGES, Bonanza Books, N.Y.

Bullock, Helen Duprey, RECIPES OF ANTE BELLUM AMERICA, Heirloom Publishing Co., N.Y.

Bullock, Mrs. Helen, THE WILLIAMSBURG ART OF COOKERY, Dietz Press, Richmond, Va.

Cannon, Poppy, and Brooks, Patricia, THE PRESIDENTS' COOKBOOK, Funk & Wagnalls, N.Y.

Cassina Garden Club, Georgia, COASTAL COOKERY, New England Blue Print Paper Co., Springfield, Mass.

CONFEDERATE RECEIPT BOOK: A Compilation of Over One Hundred Receipts adopted to the Times.

CREOLE CUISINE, Home Service, New Orleans Public Service, Inc.

Dick, Erma Biesel, THE OLD HOUSE HOLIDAY AND PARTY COOKBOOK, Cowles Book Co., Inc., N.Y.

Dull, Mrs. S. R., SOUTHERN COOKING, Grosset & Dunlap, N.Y.

Exum, Helen M., CHATTANOOGA COOK BOOK, *Chattanooga News-Free Press*, Chattanooga, Tenn.

Hammond-Harwood House, MARYLAND'S WAY, Hammond-Harwood House Association, Annapolis, Md.

Hardy, Lady Helen H., and Martinez, Raymond J., LOUISIANA'S FABULOUS FOODS, Hope Publications, New Orleans, La.

HOW TO PLEASE A GOURMET, WWL-TV, New Orleans, La.

Jeffries, Bob, SOUL FOOD COOK BOOK, Bobbs-Merrill Co., N.Y.

LA CUISINE CREOLE, F. F. Hansell & Brothers, Ltd., New Orleans, La., 1885.

Land, Mary, LOUISIANA COOKERY, Louisiana State University Press, Baton Rouge, La.

League of Women Voters, THE VIRGINIA COOKERY BOOK.

Low, Juliette Gordon, CENTENNIAL RECEIPT BOOK, 1860–1960, Girl Scouts of the U.S.A.

McCully, Helen (Ed.), AMERICAN HERITAGE COOKBOOK, American Heritage Press, N.Y.

McMurphy, Harriet S., THE IDEAL RECEIPT BOOK, Peck, Stow, and Wilcox Co., Southington, Conn., 1898.

Ott, Eleanore, PLANTATION COOKERY OF OLD LOUISIANA, Harmanson, New Orleans, La.

Randolph, Mrs. Mary, THE VIRGINIA HOUSEWIFE OR METHODICAL COOK, E. D. Butler & Co., 1828.

Rhett, Gay, and Woodward, 200 YEARS OF CHARLESTON COOKING, Random House, N.Y.

Rosengarten, THE BOOK OF SPICES, Livingston.

Smith, Marie, ENTERTAINING IN THE WHITE HOUSE, Acropolis Books, Washington, D.C.

Soyer, Alexis, SOYER'S COOKERY BOOK, David McKay Company, Inc., N.Y.

Tartan, Beth, THE GOOD OLD DAYS COOKBOOK, Westover Publishing Company, Richmond, Va.

Van Duzor, Alline P., FASCINATING FOODS FROM THE DEEP SOUTH, Gramercy Publishing Co., N.Y.

Helen Worth
April 28, 1972

INDEX

This exhaustive index presents a world of dining pleasure in a deceptively slim book. Thanks for the bounty go to the host of imaginative Southern cooks who adapted recipes from over the seas to their own particular purposes and to the foods of their new land.

Index-stretching also is due to the flexibility of the recipes and to the many regional names for the same dish—a dumpling is a dodger, a pudding is a pone is a cream.

So depend on this index for finding recipes by title. In addition, it lists food by category—soups and sauces, puddings and pies.

Use it as a refrigerator and freezer aid by looking up Sandwiches, Roasts, Chops, and the like. Depend on it, too, for taking care of food surpluses (leftovers) such as chicken or rice under those headings, and reading: "Cooked."

Other headings will tell you when you can transform entree recipes into hors d'oeuvre; sauce recipes into entrees; vegetable recipes into desserts.

A

Absinthe
  ingredients, 250
  Suissesse, 250
  Whets, 249–50
"A Certain Light" (poem), *see* Acknowledgments
Acorn Squash with Molasses, 148
Adobo, see Brunswick Stew
Afton Villa Brains, 61
Agriculture, United States Department of
  nutrition, *Dr*. Ruth Leverton, 252
  (of) cornmeal, 166
  pork: safe cooking temperature, 24
  publications: Bibliography reference, 260
  turkey (roasting method), 81
Alcoholic beverages
  Southern names for, 237
Ambrosia, 201
  recipe, 202
Angel Omelet, 111–12
Ann Elizabeth Rials Chess Pie, 230–31
Ann's Cornbread, 172
Antoine's Restaurant, 100

Apéritif, *see* Absinthe Whets
Appendix, 252
Apple, Fritters, *see* Spiced Apple Slapjacks
  Pie, Marmalade, 229–30
  Pone, 173
  Rice Pudding, 208
  Sauce, Lemon Tang, 160
    yield per apple, 160
  Slice Corn-Cake, 226–27
    Slices (Yield), *see* Spiced Apple Slapjacks
  Snow, Belle Grove, 204–5
  Tea, 238
Artichokes, 131
  dip for, *see* Old Dominion Sour Sauce
  St. Louis, 109
Ash Cake, 170
  Carolina, 171
Aspic, *Boeuf a la Mode*, 43
  Green Gage Plum Jelly, 203–4
  Marbled Chicken, 69–70
  Pig's Tail, 30–31
  Pork, Pressed, 25–26
  unmolding, 253

B

Bacon dressing, see Hanover Hominy Salad
Baked Blackeye Peas, 149–50
   Oysters, 99–100
   Tomato Crisps, 148
Barbecue Brisket, Barnwell, 47
   Sauce, 128
   Spare Ribs, 26
Barnwell, Barbecue Brisket, 47
Bases for foods with a Sauce, 255
   Double Cornmeal-Stuffing Cakes, 87
Basket of Crab, 114
   of Shrimp, 114–15
Batter Bread, 115–17
   ingredients, 116–17
   Pudding, 116–17
     Beefsteak, 117
Bavarian cream, see Carlotta Cream
Bea's Buns, 198–99
Beaten biscuits, 33
Beaufort Pudding Bread, 188–89
Beecher, Catherine (quoted), 23
Beef, 40–64
   (boiled) and Broth, 2–3
     serving Southern style, 4
   Briskets, 45–46
   Dumplings, 48–49
   Fillet with Wine Merchant Sauce, 41–42
   ground, see Ground Beef
   Heart, 62
   Oxtail Stew, Burnt Ordinary, 64
   stews, 45–46
   with Mushrooms, Valcour Aime, 45
Beefsteak Montfort, 62–63
   Pudding, 117
Beer, Southern varieties, 237
Belle Chasse Pot Roast, 44
   Grove, Apple Snow, 204–5
   Lamb Scallops, 56–57
Bell Peppers, 139
   Baskets, 113–14
Benét, Stephen Vincent. "Mountain Whippoorwill" (poem), 238
Benne seeds, 218–19. See also Rout Drop-Cakes
   Wafers, 218–19
Benson Yam Puff, 143–44

Beurre manie, 139
Beverages, 235–52 (See also Coffee; Punch)
   Absinthe Suissesse, 250
     Whets, 249–50
   anisette, 250
   Apple Tea, 238
   Brave Noel, 252
   Chocolate, Royal, 239
   Gin Fizz, Ramos, 247–48
   martini, see The Obituary
   Meringue Torch, 242–43
   Mint Julep, 246–47
   Obituary, The, 250
   Raspberry Shrub, 238–39
   Sazerac Cocktail, 250–51
   Southern varieties, 237
   Strip-and-Go-Naked, 252
   Sugar Syrup, 247
   Syllabub, 210
Bibliography, 260–63
   Cookbook References, 262–63
   General References, 261–62
Biscuits, buttermilk, see Buttermilk Drops
   Cornmeal, 176
   Fist, 185
Bisques, Seafood, 10–11
Blackeye Peas, Baked, 149–50. See also Pot Likker Portmanteau; Yeoman Supper Salad
   parboiling, 149–50
   Soup, 17–18
Blue Ridge Chutney, 161–62
Boeuf a la Mode, 43
Boligee Rice Bread, 188
Bouillabaisse, Petite, 11
   shellfish for, 104
   White, 103
Bourbon, 237. See also Mint Julep
   at breakfast, 236
   Coffee, 241
Brains, Afton Villa, 61
Brandy Butter, Mrs. Cook's, 214
Brave Noel, 252
Bread, 184–89. See also Cornbread; Scones
   Bea's Buns, 198–99
   Buttermilk Drops, 185

Crumbs: preparing; storing. *See* Dry
    Bread Sauce
  Fist Biscuits, 185
  Fried, 255
  Pudding, Mrs. Goshae's, 208–9
  Rice, Boligee, 188
  skillet, *see* Spider Light Bread
  Southern, cooking variations for, 184–85
    ingredients added to, 184
    names for, 168
  Spider Light, 187–88
  "sweet," *see* Pecan Torte
  Yeast Cornbread, 199
Bread Sauce, Claret, 190
  Dry, 190–91
  Orange, 189–90
Brisket, Barnwell Barbecued, 47
  Beef, 45–46
  in Barbecue Sauce, 46
  names for, 3
  pork, 28
  Ragout, 46
Brizard, Marie (anisette), 250
Broccoli, 129
Broth, Beef and, 2–3
Brown, Helen Evans. *See also* Bibliography
  Hoppin' John, 38
Brown-Quick, *see* Season To Taste
Browns, the, Cora, Rose, and Bob. *See also* Bibliography
  biscuit variations, 184–85
  juleps, 247
Brown Sugar,
  measuring, 258–59
  Syrup, 215
  to soften, 259
  variety to use, 258
Brunswick Stew, 78
Buchanan, James (grape arbor), 231
Buns, Bea's, 198–99
Burgoo, 22
Burnt Ordinary Oxtail Stew, 64
Burr artichokes, 131
Burtt, Ann, 172. *See also* Acknowledgments
  Charley's Sweet Potato Pone, 145
Buttermilk Cornbread, 172–73
  Drops, 185

Butter Sauce
  for meat, 124
  for poultry, 124
  for seafood, 124
  Lemon, 124
  maitre d'hotel (for fillet), 42
  Parsley, 124
Buying Information, 259

C

Café au Lait, 240
  Brulé, 241
  brulot, *see* Cafe Diable
  Diable, 240
  Royale, 241
Cake, 220–27. *See also* Fruit Cake
  Apple Slice Corn, 226–27
  Cider, Richie-Lee's, 226
  Devil's Food, Mincy, 224–25
  (fruit), Shortcake, Amelia Springs, 205
  Gingerbread, Tavern, 227–28
  Good but Cheap, Mrs. Governor Floyd's, 223–24
  Pecan Torte, 225
  Silver, Snow Hill, 221–22
  Southern varieties, 220
Cake Toppings, Chipped Chocolate Cream, 222
  Pineapple Ginger, 228
Calas, 197
Canadian Bacon, Toasted (roast), 24–25
Caper Sauce, 105
Capon, *see* Puffed Stuffed Poultry (roasting)
Carlotta Cream, 211
Carolina Ash Cake, 171
  Hoppin' John, 38
Carrot Chutney, 162
  sticks, *see* Cucumber Bennes
Cassoulet, *see* Cottage Dinner; Dried Vegetables; Hoppin' John
Catfish, 91
Celery Sauce, 126
  Puree Sauce, 126
Champlain, Samuel de (quoted), 135
Chancelorsville Chicken Gumbo, 75
Charley Burtt's Sweet Potato Pone, 145

267

Cheese Pudding, 179
  Puff, 180
  Toast, 120
Cheese Sauce, 125
  for Fish, 125
Chess Pie, Ann Elizabeth Rials, 230–31
Chicken, 65–80. *See also* Gumbos; Stews
  baked (recipes for) stuffed Breasts, 70–71
  Breasts, 70
  Brunswick Stew, 78
  VNC, 78–79
  Creole, 74
    Tomato Sauce for, 127–28
  Pillowed, 73
  Celery sauce for, 126
  Colette, 71–72
  Cooked for Made Dishes, 5
    recipes for: Pot Pie, 67
    Pudding, 68
    Sandwich, Louisville (shortcake), 68–69
    Terrapin, 67
  Fried, 72–73
  frozen, *see* Crisp-Poached Chicken
  Gumbo, Chancelorsville, 75
  in Made Dishes, 66–69
  in the Pot, 65–66
    varieties for, 65–66
  Marbled (aspic), 69
  Perlo, Baked, 79–80
  Poached, Crisp, 66
  Pot Pie, 67
  roasting, *see* Puffed Stuffed Poultry. *See also* baked chicken
  Smothers, 75–77
  Soup with English Peas, 6
  Stock, 4–5
  Terrapin, 67
Chicory, 240
  Coffee, 240
Chipped Chocolate Cream Topping, 222
Chitterlings, 58
Chocolate Cream Topping, Chipped, 222
  Crumb Crust, 232
  Royal, 239
  sauce, *see* Royal Chocolate
Chops, Crusted Lamb, 55–56

Lamb Scallops, Belle Grove, 56
  pork, Creole Tomato Sauce for, 127
  stuffed, 24
  See also Ham Hotpot
Choucroute garnie, *see* Sauerkraut and Hocks
Chutney, Blue Ridge, 161–62
  Carrot, 162
Cider Cake, Richie-Lee's, 226
Clams, shucking, *see* Oysters
Claret Bread Sauce, 190
  Cup, 243
Clear Watercress Soup, 6
Coconut, 201
Cod fat, 62
Coffee, 239–40. *See also* Café
  Bourbon, 241
  Chicory, 240
  Custard, 211
  "Yankee," 240
Cole slaw dressings, *see* Hot Water Mayonnaise; Remoulade Sauce
Convenience Cornbread Stuffing, 85
Cookies, Rout Drop-Cakes, 217–18
  seed, 218–19
    Sesame, 218–19
  Southern varieties, 216
  Spread Cakes, 216
  Tea Cakes, Thumb Run, 217
Corn, 131–35
  and Okra, 133–34
  buying information, 132
  Cake, Apple Slice, 226–27
  Chowder, Drum Point, 14
  (cooked), *see* Plantation Hominy
  Custard, *see* Corn Lorraine
  Flowers, 175
  Fritters, 133
  growing, 135
  in spoonbread, 178
  Krewe, 132–33
  Lorraine, 134–35
Cornbread, 167–76. *See also* Spoonbread; Pone
  Ann's, 172
  Ash Cake, Carolina, 171
  baking, containers for, 169
  Buttermilk, 172–73
  Corn Flowers, 175
  Cornmeal Biscuits, 176

Popovers, 177
Cracklin' Bread, 173
Hush Puppies, 174
ingredients for, 169
Johnny Cake, 174–75
  packaged mix, see Ann's Cornbread
  reheating, 173
  sandwich, see Louisville Chicken Sandwich
Stuffing, Convenience, 85
  Kettle-Cousin, 86
Yeast, 199
Cornmeal, 165–68. See also Dumplings; Grits; Mush; Stuffings
baked, see Cornmeal Crunch
Biscuits, 176
Cooking, 166
Couche Couche, Terrebone Parish, 168
Crunch, 180
crust, see Toasted Canadian Bacon
Mush, 167
  Fried, 167
pancakes, see Lace Cakes
Pap, 167
Popovers, 177
storing, 167
Stuffing, 86–87
  Cakes, 87
  Double, 87
  varieties, 166
Cottage Dinner, 37–38
  meat for, 37
Country-Cured Ham, 33. See also Ham
Court Bouillon, 9
  for brains, 61
  White, 104
Cous cous, see Terrebone Parish Couche Couche
Crab, 92–93. See also Seafood
  Basket of, 114
  Blue, see hard crab
  Boil, 93–94
  Cakes, Wind Song, 96
  Deviled Cream, 95
  hard (blue), 93
    picking, 94
  Loaf, 101
  Soft, 93
Cracklin' Bread, 173

Cream, Mayonnaise, 155
  souring, see Pauline's Succotash
Cream Soups
  Chicken, 5–6
  Pumpkin, 16
Creole Chicken, 74
  cooking, 257
  Mustard, 159
  Rice Cakes, 109
  spices used, 257
  Tomato Sauce, 127
Crepes in peach sauce, 192
Crisp-Poached Chicken, 66
Crumb crusts, 232
Crusted Lamb Chops, 55–56
Crusty Tomato Crisps in Cream, 148
Cucumber Bennes, 162
Cumberland Sauce, 163–64
Curry, 256
  Powder, 256
Custard, see Chicken Pudding
Custards, Dessert. See also Puddings and Creams
  Coffee, 211
  Louisiana Snow Eggs, 212

D

Dairy Products, 254
Desserts. See also names of desserts; Sweet Potato Pudding
  Carlotta Cream, 211
  Southern specialties, 206–7
    for Jeff Davis Day, 229
  Syllabub, 210
Dessert Sauces, 214
  Brandy Butter, 214
  Brown Sugar Syrup, 215
  chocolate, see Royal Chocolate
  hard, see Brandy Butter, Mrs. Cook's
  pancake toppings, 192
Deviled Bones, 26
  Cream Crab, 95
Devil's Food Cake, Mincy, 224–25
Dickens, Charles (quoted), 22
Dodgers. See also Dumplings
  Cornmeal, 20–21
  Fritter, 147
  Yam, 146
Dorothy Atkin's Pork and Corn, 27
Double Cornmeal-Stuffing Cakes, 87

269

Dough-Nuts, 221
Dried Vegetables, 149–51
  blackeye peas, 149–50
  Red Beans, 150–51
    and Rice, 151
  Whole Kernel Hominy, 182
  yield, 149
Drum Point Corn Chowder, 14
Dry Bread Sauce, 190–91
Duck, 83
  accompaniments, see Orange Bread Sauce
Dumplings. See also Dodgers
  baking powder, see Sauerkraut and Hocks
  Beef, 48
  Cornmeal (Dodgers), 20–21
    for Pot Likker Portmanteau, 130
  fried, see Fritter Dodgers
  Plain Flour, 19
  Pulled, Elizabeth's, 21
  Queen Bee, 20

E

Egg-Laced Chicken, 77
  Sauces, 123
Eggplant. See also Squash Pillows; Vegetable Baskets
  frying, 136
  Matty Winston's Way, 136–37
  salting, 136
Eggs, 108–12
  Angel Omelet, 111–12
  Balls, 19
    in curry sauce, 20
  Creole Rice Cakes, 109
  Link Sausage and, 111
  Louisiana, 109
  Sardou, 109
  Scotch, 109
  Shirred, with Kidneys, 109–10
  white (yield), 248
Egg Sauce to Dress Seafood, 105
El Granada Grape Pie, 231
Elizabeth's Pulled Dumplings, 21
Entertaining, nineteenth century, 236
Escoffier, see Cheese Sauce
Exum, Helen (roasting ham), 34. See also Bibliography

F

Fats and Shortening, 253–54
  cod fat, 62
Feather Fritters, 195–96
Fig Ice Cream, 213
  fresh figs, 213
  Secrets, 202
Filé Powder, 256
Fillet with Wine Merchant Sauce, 41–42
Fish. See also names of fish; Sauces for fish; Seafood
  (baking) Creole Tomato Sauce, 127
  Celery Sauce for, 126
  Fumet, 9
  House Punch, 244–45
  Velvet, 9–10
Ford, Tennessee Ernie (Southern birthplace), 139
Franklin, Benjamin (quoted), 171
French dressing, see Vinaigrette Dressing
  Market Sauce, 126–27
  Toast, 112
Fried Bread, 255
  in butter, see Mushroom Caps on Fried Bread
  Chicken, 72–73
  Mush, 167
  Okra, 138
  Pigs' Tail, 31
  Tomatoes, see Crusty Tomato Crisps in Cream
Fritters, 195–97
  Apple, Spiced Slapjacks, 196–97
  Corn, 133
  Dodgers, 147
  Feather, 195
  frying, 195
  oyster, see Oyster Loaf
  Rice, see Calas
  Tripe, 60
  Wine Batter, Jefferson, for, 196
Frostings and Toppings, 221–22
Fruit. See also Cake; Fruit Cake; Relishes
  Ambrosia, 202
  Apple Snow, Belle Grove, 204–5
  Fig Secrets, 202

270

fritters, *see* Jefferson Wine Batter
Green Gage Plum Jelly, 203–4
Strawberry Peach, 202–3
Fruit Cake
  Social Circle, 223
  storing, 222
Frying, Southern method, 254

G

Galatoire's Restaurant, 114
Game, 106–7
  accompaniments, *see* Bread Sauce
  cooking methods for, 106
  ingredients for cooking, 106
  Pheasant, Roast, 107
  Southern varieties, 106
Garlic Mustard, 160
Gelatin, *see* Aspics
German pancake, *see* Angel Omelet
Gin Fizz, Ramos, 247
Gingerbread, Tavern, 227
Goldsboro Turkey Hash, 82
Goose, 83
Goshae. *See also* Acknowledgments
  Elizabeth's Dumplings, 21
  Mrs., Bread Pudding, 208–9
Gourmet Magazine (recipe adaptation), 176
Grape Pie El Granada, 231
Gravy. *See also* Ham Slices; Thickened Sauces
  Onion, for Poultry, 123–24
Green Corn Spoon Bread, 178
  Gage Plum Ice Cream, 214
  Jelly (aspic), 203–4
  Pea Family Soup, 15
Greens, for Pot Likker Portmanteau, 130
  wilted, *see* Hanover Hominy Salad
Grits, 166–67. *See also* Hominy
  Beefsteak (with Heart), 63
  Fried Mush, 167
  Spoonbread (baked grits), 178
Ground Beef (recipes), Dumplings, 48–49
  Pompey's Head, 47–48
Gumbo, 12. *See also* Filé Powder
  Chicken, Chancelorsville, 75
  Soup, 13

des Herbes, 28–29. *See also* Clear Watercress Soup
Gouter, 103
Shrimp, 13–14

H

Ham, 32–39. *See also* Pork
  carving, 35
  cooked (recipes for), Basket of Shrimp, 114–15
  Bell Pepper Baskets, 113
  Corn Lorraine, 134–35
  Creole Rice Cakes, 109
  Jambalaya, 119
  Jefferson Wine Batter for, 196
  Potted Turkey, 81–82
  Soup, Green Pea Family, 15
    Tomato, 17
  Stuffings, 84
  Veal with Olives, 51–52
  Country-Cured, 33
  Kentucky, 33
  Smithfield, 33
  Virginia, 33
  for Cottage Dinner, 37
  for Pot Likker Portmanteau, 130
  for Red Beans, 150
  hocks (pork hocks) and Pigs' Feet, Pickled, 27
  and Sauerkraut, 30
  Hotpot, 36
  knuckles (pork hocks), *see* Pickled Pigs' Feet and Hocks
  Loose-Bone, 34
  roasting, 33–34
  Slices, 35
    Gravy, Cream, for, 36
    Red-Eye, 36
  smothered, *see* Yam Hotpot
  Toasted, 34–35. *See also* Toasted Canadian Bacon with Red-Eye Gravy, *see* Ham Slices
Handy, Tom, *see* Sazerac Cocktail
Hanover Hominy Salad, 153
Harvard University, *see* Nutmeg
Hash, Turkey, Goldsboro, 82
Headcheese, *see* Pressed Pork
Heart, 62
  Beefsteak Grits with, 63
  Montfort, 62–63

271

Hen, Smothered, 77
Henry, Patrick (quoted), 237
Herbs, dried, proportion to use, 257
Homemade Pork Sausage, 31–32
Hominy, 181–83
   Bread, see Grits Spoonbread
   canned, and yield, 181
   coarse grits, 181
   Crisp (baked), 182
   Dried Whole Kernel, 182
   Plantation, 182–83
   Salad, Hanover, 153
   Sausage, 110
   varieties, 181
Hoppin' John, 38–39
Hors d'oeuvre, Afton Villa Brains, 61
   Corn Flowers, 175
   Cornmeal Biscuits, 176
   Deviled Bones, 26
   dips, French-Market Sauce, 126
      Mustard Paste, 159
      Remoulade Sauce, 156
      Sour Sauce, Old Dominion, 155
   Egg Balls, 19
   Kill with Kindness Sauce, 125
   Oyster Loaf, 100–1
   parsnips, raw, 138
   Peaches, Rosedown, 163
   Pressed Pork, 25
   quiche, see Corn Lorraine
   topping, see Dry Bread Sauce
   Turkey, Potted, 81–82
Hotpots, 36
Hot Shrimp, 94
   Water Mayonnaise, 155
Howard Scallop, 96–97
Hubbard squash, see Acorn Squash with Molasses
Hush Puppies, 174

I

Ice Cream, 213–14
   Fig, 213
   Green Gage Plum, 214
   Mango, 213
   Molasses, 214
   Southern varieties, 213
Indians, Corn Pone, 170
   oystering techniques, 97

Irish Potatoes, see Potatoes
Ithaca Journal, 198

J

Jambalaya, 118
   ingredients for, 108
   Mississippi, see Jambolin
Jambolin, 119
Jeff Davis Day, 229
Jefferson, Thomas (inventor, connoisseur), 236
Johnny Cake, 174–75

K

Kentucky Country-Cured Ham with Red-Eye Gravy, 36
Ketchup, Barbecue Sauce (as substitute), 128
Kettle-Cousin Cornbread Stuffing, 86
Key Largo Lime Pie, 231–32
Kidneys, Shirred Eggs with, 109–10
Kill with Kindness Sauce, 125
Kohlrabi, see Cucumber Bennes
Krewe Corn, 132–33

L

Lace Cakes, 192
Lamb, 53–57
   Chops, Crusted, 55–56
      (loin medallions) Scallops, Belle Grove, 56
   Stew, 53–54
Lard, 254
   leaf, see Heart
Lee, Harper (cake name from book by), 220
Lemon, Butter Sauce, 124
   Mayonnaise, 154
   rind, grating, see Marmalade Apple Pie
   Tang Applesauce, 160
Leslie, Miss (quoted), 236
Leverton, *Dr.* Ruth (quoted), 252
Link Sausage and Eggs, 111
Lime Pie, Key Largo, 231–32
Liver, Plaquemine Parish, 63
Lobster, 97. *See also* Howard Scallop
Lobster tails, see Lobster
Long, Huey (politician; food popularized), 20

Loose-Bone Ham, 34
Louisiana Snow Eggs, 212.
  See also Huey Long
Louisville Chicken Sandwich, 68

M

MacLeod, Bea (bun recipe), 198
Maitre d'hotel butter, see Butter Sauces
Maizena, 255
Mango Ice Cream, 213
Manikin Pecan Perfects, 193–94
Marbled Chicken, 69–70
Marmalade Apple Pie, 229–30
Martini, see The Obituary
Mayonnaise, Cream, 155
  Whir, 154
McGee, Winston, see Cheese Pudding
Meat. See also under names of meat balls, see Beef Dumplings
Meringue Torch, 242
Milk, skim, to sour, see Fritters
Mincy Devil's Food Cake, 224–25
Mint Julep, 246
Mirliton, 130
Molasses. See also Sweeteners
  Ice Cream, 214
  Scones, 186
"Mountain Whippoorwill" (poem), 238
Mrs. Cook's Brandy Butter, 214
Mrs. Goshae's Bread Pudding, 208–9
Mrs. Governor Floyd's Good but Cheap Cake, 223–24
Mule Day, see Benson Yam Puff
Mulligatawny, 7
Mush. See also Couche Couche; Cornmeal Pap
  Fried, 167
Mushroom Caps on Fried Bread, 137
Mustard, Creole, 159
  Garlic, 160
  Mayonnaise, 160
  Paste, 159–60
  Sauce, 4

N

New Yorker Magazine (Southern breakfast drink), 238
New York Times (catfish fry), 91 (wild leek), 130

Nutmeg, 255–60
Nuts, see Sugared Pecans

O

Obituary, The (Pernod Martini), 250
Okra, 137. See also Filé Powder
  and Corn, 133–34
  buying, 137
  Fried, 138
  Pauline's Succotash, 135
  preparing, 137
  Ratatouille, 138
  Shrimp Gumbo Soup with, 14
Oil, varieties, 254
Old Dominion Sour Sauce, 155
Ollo, 22
Omelet, Angel, 111–12
  Creole Rice Cakes, 109
Onion Gravy for Poultry, 123–24
  Roux, 123
Orange Bread Sauce, 189–90
  flower water, see Mrs. Governor Floyd's Good but Cheap Cake
  Stuffing, 88
Ordinaire, Dr. (inventor of absinthe), 249–50
Orgeat, see Absinthe Suissesse
Oven-Baked Corn Pone, 171
Oxtail Stew, Burnt Ordinary, 64
Oysters, 97–101
  Baked, 99
  Bar (Grand Central), see Oyster Roast
  buying, 98
  Loaf, 100–1
  Pickled, 98–99
  Roast (stew), 99
  Rockefeller, 100
  Sauce, 71
  shucking, 98

P

Pancakes, 191–94
  freezing, 192
  frying, 192
  Pecan Perfects, Manikin, 193–94
  Squash Pillows, 193
  toppings for, 192
Paprika, see Season To Taste

273

Parloa, Miss (quoted), 229
Parsley Butter Sauce, 124
Parsnips, 138
Partridge, Eric (word origins), 242
Pasta in Soup, 18–19
Pauline's Succotash, 135
Peach, Strawberry, 202–3
  Rosedown, 163
Peacock, Jean (pie recipe), 233
Peanuts, 201
  Soup, 15
Peas, dried, Southern varieties, 149
  Stewed, Twin-City, 139
Pea Soup, Blackeye, 17–18
  Green, 15
Pecan Pie, 233. *See also* pie, Southern varieties
  Sugared Pecans, 206
  Torte, 225
  Yams, 145–46
Pepper products, *see* Season To Taste
  Stock, 57–58
Peppers, *see* Bell Peppers
Pepys, Samuel (*Diary*, quoted), 100
Pernod, Henri-Louis (liqueur manufacturer), 249
  See also The Obituary
Petite Bouillabaisse, 11
Pheasant, Roast, 107
Pickled Fruit, 159
  Oysters, 98–99
  Pigs' Feet and Hocks, 27
Pie, 228–34
  Apple, *see* Marmalade Apple Pie
  Chess, Ann Elizabeth Rials, 230–31
  Chicken, 67
  Crumb Crust for, 232
  Grape, El Granada, 231
  Lime, Key Largo, 231–32
  Marmalade Apple, 229–30
  Pecan, 233
  pumpkin, *see* Winter Squash
  Southern varieties, 228
  squash, *see* Winter Squash
  sweet potato (yam), *see* Winter Squash
Pig. *See also* Ham; Pork
  ear, *see* Sauerkraut and Hocks
  Feet and Hocks, Pickled, 27
  knuckles, *see* Pickled Pigs' Feet
  Tail, 30
    Fried, 31
Pilaf, *see* Baked Chicken Perlo
Pillowed Chicken, 73
Pineapple Ginger Topping, 228
Plain Flour Dumplings, 19
Plantation Hominy, 181–82
Planter's Punch, 245
Plaquemine Parish Liver, 63
Plaza Hotel, *see* Cream of Chicken Soup
Poems: "A Certain Light," Rawls
  "Mountain Whippoorwill," Benét
Pokomoke Cider Pot Roast, 44
Pompey's Head, 47–48
Pone, Apple, 173
  Ash Cake, Carolina, 171
  Corn, 170
    Oven-Baked, 171
  Sweet Potato, Charley Burtt's, 145. *See also* Sweet Potato Pudding
Popovers, Cornmeal, 177
Pork, 23–32. *See also* Ham; Pig; Salt Pork
  and Corn, Dorothy Atkin's, 27
  Barbecued Spare Ribs, 26
  breast (brisket), 28
  Canadian Bacon, Toasted, 24–25
  Chitterlings, 58
  Chops. *See also* Ham Hotpot
    Creole Tomato Sauce for, 127
    Tim Turkeys (stuffed), 24
  Deviled Bones, 26
  food value, 24
  for Cottage Dinner, 37
  for Pot Likker Portmanteau, 130
  for soups, 2
  hocks, *see* Pickled Pigs' Feet; Ham hocks
  hog head, smoked, 39
  neck bones, *see* Sauerkraut and Hocks
  Pressed (aspic), 25
  Sausage, Homemade, 31–32
  temperature (cooking) for safe eating, 24
Potatoes, Irish (white), 139–41. *See also* Sweet Potatoes; Yams
  au Four, 140–41
  Auvergne (baked, stuffed), 141

(crumb-tossed) in Brown Butter, 141
Scones, 186
Pot Likker Portmanteau, 130–31
Pot Roast, Belle Chasse, 44
  Boeuf a la Mode, 43
  Pokomoke Cider, 44
Potted Turkey, 81–82
Poultry. See also kinds of poultry;
Cooking Methods for
Accompaniments, see Bread Sauce;
Gravy; Salad Dressings; Sauces
  Onion Gravy for, 123–24
  (roast) Puffed Stuffed, 84
  trussing, 85
Pressed Pork, 25
  Veal, 50
Puddings (and Creams), 207–12. See also Custards, Desserts
  Apple Rice, 208
  Bread, Mrs. Goshae's, 208–9
    Pone, Charley Burtt's, 145
    Sweet Potato, 144
Puffed Stuffed Poultry, 84
Pumpkin. See also Sweet Potatoes;
Winter Squash
  pancakes, see Squash Pillows
  Soup, The Teche, 16
    Cream of, 16
Punch, Fish House, 244–45
  Planter's, 245
  White Hall Tavern, 244
  wine, see Claret Cup

Q

Queen Bee Dumplings, 20
  Victoria (her favorite soup), 15
Quiche, see Corn Lorraine
Quick-browning aid, see Season To Taste
Quick Tripe Creole, 60–61

R

Rabbit, see Chicken Colette; Game
Ramos Gin Fizz, 247–48
Ramp, 130
Rapeseed, Ethiopian, 130
Rappini, 130
Raspberry Shrub, 238–39
Ratatouille, see Gumbo Gouter
  Okra, 138

Ravigote Sauce, 156
Rawls, Eugenia, "A Certain Light" (poem)
Red Beans, 150–51
  and Rice, 151
Redfield, Olive, 108
Relishes, 158–63
  Applesauce, Lemon Tang, 160
  Chutney, Blue Ridge, 161–62
    Carrot, 162
  Cucumber Bennes, 162
  Cumberland Sauce, 163–64
  Fruit, Pickled, 159
    Spiced, 161
  Okra Ratatouille, 138
    pickled, 137
  Peaches, Rosedown, 163
Remoulade Cream, 157
  Sauce, 156
Rice, cooked (recipes for), Apple Rice Pudding, 208
  Bread, Boligee, 188
  Cakes, Creole, 109
  Calas, 197
  Carlotta Cream, 211
  Jambolin, 119
  Pudding Bread, Beaufort, 188–89
  Soup, Tomato, 17
Rice pilaf, see Baked Chicken Perlo; Jambalaya
  Red Beans and, 151
Richie-Lee's Cider Cake, 226
Richmond museums, 260
Roanoke Old Dominion Waffles, 194–95
Roasts, Canadian Bacon, Toasted, 24–25
  Chicken, 85
  Gravy (onion) for, 123–24
  ham, 34
    Toasted, 34–35
  Pheasant, 107
  poultry, 85
  Turkey, 81
Roe, shad, 92
Roquette (rocket, rugula), 28
Rosedown Peaches, 163
Rose water, see Mrs. Governor Floyd's Good but Cheap Cake, 223–24
Rout Drop-Cakes, 217–18
Roux, 123
  brown, 123

275

Onion, 123
Royal Chocolate, 239
Rye whiskey, see Sazerac Cocktail

S

Saint Anthony (and the devil), 26
Salad, Hanover Hominy (for wilted greens), 153
  Yeoman Supper (blackeye pea), 153
Salad Dressings, Mayonnaise Cream, 155
  (Mayonnaise), Hot Water, 155
    Lemon, 154
    Mustard, 160
    Watercress, 155
    Whir, 154
  Ravigote Sauce, 156
  Remoulade Cream, 157
    Sauce, 156
  Sour Sauce, Old Dominion (for cooked vegetables), 155
  Vinaigrette (French dressing), 154
Salted Seeds, 21
Salt Pork, 254. See also Side-dish Sauerkraut; Tennessee Chicken
  names for, 254
Sandwiches, Canadian Bacon, 25
  Chicken, Louisville, 68–69
  (spread for) Mustard Paste, 159
  Turkey, Potted, 81–82
Sangria, variation, see Claret Cup
Sauces, 121–28. See also Bread Sauces; Butter Sauces; Dessert Sauces
  Barbecue, 128
  (base for) Fish *Fumet*, 9
  Bases for Foods served with, 255
  Caper, 105
  Celery (for veal, chicken, fish), 126
    Puree, 126
  Cheese, 125
    for fish, 125
  Chocolate, see Royal Chocolate
  Egg. See also Kill with Kindness Sauce
    Laced, 123
    to Dress Seafood, 105
    for baking meat, poultry, seafood, see Chicken Creole
  French-Market, 126–27
  ketchup, see Barbecue Sauce

Kill with Kindness, 125
maitre d'hotel butter, see Butter Sauces
Mustard, 4
Oyster, 71
Roux, 123
  Onion, 123
  Sour, Old Dominion, 155
  Thickened (chart), 122
  Tomato, 127
  Wine Merchant, 42
Sauerbraten, see Pokomoke Cider Pot Roast
Sauerkraut, 147
  and Hocks, 30
  Side-dish, 30
Sausage and Egg Pudding, see Batter Breads
  Homemade Pork, 31–32
  Hominy, 110
  in Red Beans, 150–51
  Link and Eggs, 111
Savannah Sweets, 143
Savories, 201
Savory Tomato Soup, 17
Sazerac Cocktail, 250–51
Scallop, Howard, 96–97
Scallops, 96–97
Schur, Sylvia, 173
Scones, Molasses, 186
  Potato, 186–87
Scotch Eggs, 109
Seafood, 89–104. See also names of fish and shellfish; Seafood Soups
  Bouillabaisse, White, 103–4. See also Seafood Soups
  cooking methods, 90
  Fish *Fumet*, 9
  fried, 90–91
  Ravigote, 92
  sauces for, Caper, 105
    Egg, to Dress, 105
    Ravigote, 156
    Remoulade, 156–57
  seasoning for a Boil, 93
  soups, Bisque, 10–11
    Bouillabaisse, Petite, 11–12
    Court Bouillon, 9
    Fish Velvet, 9–10
    Gumbo Ingredients, 12–13

276

Shrimp, 13–14
Oyster Pan Roast (stew), 99
Southern varieties, 89–90
Seasonings. *See also* Spices and Seasonings
Season To Taste, 257
Seeds, Salted, 21
  Toasted, 21
Sesame Seed Cookies, 218–19
Shackelford (Christmas dinner), 149–50
Shad and Roe, 92
Shakespeare, William (quoted), 95
Shellfish. *See also* names of shellfish; Seafood
  Boil, 93
Shirred Eggs with Kidneys, 109–10
Shortcake, Amelia Springs, 205
Short'nin' bread, *see* Cracklin' Bread
Shrimp, 102–4. *See also* Seafood
  a la Creole, 102
  Boil, 94
  fritters, *see* Jefferson Wine Batter
  Gumbo, 13–14. *See also* Gumbo Gouter
  Soup with Okra, 14
  Hot, 94–95
  Smother, 181
  To Butter, 102–3
Side-dish Sauerkraut, 30
Silver Cake, Snow Hill, 221–22
Smithfield Ham, 33
Smoked pigs' knuckles, *see* Pickled Pigs' Feet and Hocks
  tenderloin, *see* Cottage Dinner
Smothered Chicken, 74–78
  Hen, 77
Snails, *see* Oysters Rockefeller
Snow Eggs, Louisiana, 212
  Hill Silver Cake, 221–22
Social Circle Fruit Cake, 223
Sofkee, 235
Sorghum, 132. *See also* Sweeteners
Souffle, sweet potato, *see* Benson Yam Puff
Soup. *See also* Seafood Soups
  Blackeye Pea, 17–18
  che*f*tnut, 1
  Chicken, 4–6
    Cream of, 5–6

Gumbo, 13
  with English Peas, 6
Corn Chowder, Drum Point, 14
Mulligatawny, 7
Oyster Roast, 99
Pasta in, 18–19
Pea (Green), Family, 15
Peanut, 15–16
Pork products in, 2
Pumpkin, 16
  Cream of, 16
Tomato. *See also* Pasta in Soup
  Savory, 17
  with Ham, 17
  with rice, 17
  with Vegetables, 17
Watercress, Clear, 6
Soup Accompaniments, 18–21
  Dumplings, Cornmeal (Dodgers), 20–21
  Flour, Plain, 19
  Pulled, Elizabeth's, 21
  Queen Bee, 20
  Egg Balls, 19–20
  Pasta in, 18–19
  Seeds, Salted, 21
    Toasted, 21
Souse, *see* Pigs' Tail; Pressed Pork
Soused Fish, *see* Pickled Oysters
Spare Ribs, Barbecued, 26–27
Spiced Apple Slapjacks, 196–97
  Currant Jelly, 163–64
  Fruit, 161
  Seafood, *see* Pickled Oysters
Spices and Seasonings, 255–57
Spider Light Bread, 187–88
"Spiders (skillets)," 169
Spinach, 147
Spoonbread, 178–79
  Grits, 167
Spread Cakes, 216
  Almond Fancies, 216
Squash, 147
  Acorn with Molasses, 148
  Pillows, 193
  Summer, 147
  Winter, 148. *See also* Sweet Potatoes
Sterne, Laurence (quoted), 4
Stews, Brunswick, 78–79
  VNC, 78–79

277

Burgoo, 22
Chicken, Colette, 71–72
  Egg-Laced, 77–78
  Gumbo, Chancelorsville, 75
  Smothers, 75–76
  Lamb, Lafayette, 53–54
  Oxtail, Burnt Ordinary, 64
Stock, Chicken, 4–5
  Pepper (for sundries), 57–58
  storing, 2
  white, *see* Chicken Stock
Stoves, 22–23
Strachey, William (quoted), 170
Strawberry Peach, 202–3
Strip-and-Go-Naked, 252
Stuffings, 83–88. *See also* Bread Sauces
  amount to prepare, 84
  chicken (base for), 73
  Cornbread, 85–86
  Cornmeal, 86–87
  foods for, 84
  Orange, 88
  Oyster, for Chicken Breasts, 70–71
  Poultry, Puffed Stuffed, 84–85
    under poultry skin, 84–85
  Southern ingredients for, 84. *See also* Spider Light Bread
Succotash, Pauline's, 135
Sugar, Brown, 258–59
  Syrup, 215
Sugar Syrup, 247
Sugared Pecans, 206
Summer Squash, 147
Sundries, 57–64
  Brains, Afton Villa, 61
  Chitterlings, 58–59
  Heart, 62
  Kidneys, Shirred with Eggs, 109–10
  Liver, Plaquemine Parish, 63
  Oxtail Stew, 64
  Tripe, 59–61
Sweetbreads, *see* Oyster Loaf
Sweeteners, 258–59
Sweet Potatoes, 142–47
  buying, 142
  cooking, 142
  fried, *see* Yam Crisps
  fritters, 195
    Dodgers, 147
  Pecan Yams, 145–46

Pone, Charley Burtt's, 145
Pudding, 144–45
  ingredients for, 144–45
  Savannah, 143
  slicing (Southern way), 142
  substitutes for, 142
  varieties, 142
  Yam, Crisps, 142–43
    Dodgers, 146–47
  Puff, Benson, 143–44
  yield of grated, *see* Sweet Potato Pone
Syllabub, 210

T

Taino (aboriginal tribe), *see* Corn
Tamil (East Indian cooking), *see* Mulligatawny
Tavern Gingerbread, 227
Taylor, Colonel Walter Herron (quoted), 245
Tea, Apple, 238
  Cakes, Thumb Run, 217
Teche The, Pumpkin Soup, 16
Tennessee Chicken, 31
Terrebone Parish Couche Couche, 168
Thackeray, William M. (quoted), 103
Thickened Sauces, 122
Thumb Run Tea Cakes, 217
Tim Turkeys, 24
Toad in the Hole, *see* Batter Breads
Toasted Canadian Bacon, 24–25
  Ham, 34–35
  Seeds, 21
Tomato Crisps, Baked, 148
  Crusty, in Cream, 148
  fried, *see* Crusty Tomato Crisps in Cream
  in soup, 19
  Soup, with Vegetables Very Fine, 17
  Savory, 17
Tomato Sauces, 127–28
  Barbecue, 128
  Creole, 127
Toppings. *See also* Cake Toppings
  Whipped Cream, 233
Treacle, *see* Sweeteners
Tripe, 59–61
  Creole, Quick, 60–61
  Crumb-Fried, 60
  Fritters, 60

Tristram Shandy, by Sterne, 4
Turkey, 80-81
  cooked (recipes for), *see* Chicken in Made Dishes
    Hash, Goldsboro, 82
    Potted, 81-82
    Roast, 81
Turnips, 149. *See also* Cucumber Bennes
Twain, Mark (quoted; indirect), 90
Twin-City Stewed Peas, 139

U

United States Department of Agriculture, *see* Agriculture, United States Department of

V

Valcour Aime Beef with Mushrooms, 45
Veal, 49-52
  brisket, 28
  Celery Sauce (for), 126
  Southern veal specialties, 49-50
  with Olives, 51-52
Vegetables, 129-40. *See also* names of vegetables; Dried Vegetables
  Baskets, 112-15
  Bell Pepper, 113
  dressings, *see* Hot Water Mayonnaise; Old Dominion Sour Sauce for Pot Likker Portmanteau, 130-31
  Southern varieties, 129-30
  Stock, 9
  topping, *see* Dry Bread Sauce
  varieties for stuffing, *see* Vegetables, Baskets
Venison, *see* Veal
Vinaigrette Dressing, 154
Vinegar, 253
Virginia ham, 33. *See also* Loose-bone Ham
  Polytechnic Institute (work with corn), 132

Voodoo, *see* Nutmeg

W

Waffles, 194
  irons, 194
  reheating, 194
  Roanoke Old Dominion Waffles, 194-95
Wallace, Henry A. (work with corn), 132
Watercress Mayonnaise, 155
  Soup, Clear, 6
Waterzooi, *see* Egg-Laced Chicken
Weil, *Dr.* Andrew T. (work with nutmeg), 255
Whipped Cream Topping, 233
White Bouillabaisse, 103
  Hall Tavern Punch, 244
  Stock, *see* Chicken Stock
Wilde, Oscar (quoted), 22
Wilted Lettuce, *see* Hanover Hominy Salad
Wind Song Crab Cakes, 96
Wine Merchant Sauce, 42
  punch, *see* Claret Cup
  Southern favorites, 236-37
Winston, Suzanne, 136
Winter Squash, 148. *See also* Acorn Squash with Molasses
Woodward, Harry (recipe from), 230

Y

Yams. *See also* Sweet Potatoes
  Crisps, 142-43
  Dodgers, 147
  fried, *see* Yam Crisps
  Hotpot, 37
Yeast Cornbread, 199
Yeoman Supper Salad, 153
Yorkshire Pudding, *see* Batter Breads

Z

Zucchini, *see* Summer Squash